INDIAN TRANSPORT TOWARDS THE NEW MILLENNIUM

About the Author

Dr. R. Ramanathan, a Ph. D. in Industrial Management from Indian Institute of Technology Chennai, presently works as Assistant Professor at the College of Commerce and Economics, Sultan Qaboos University, Muscat, Sultanate of Oman. Previously, he has held positions of visiting professor at the Systems Analysis Laboratory, Helsinki University of Technology, Finland; Associate Professor at the Indira Gandhi Institute of Development Research, Mumbai, and Senior Research Fellow at the Faculty of Information Technology and Systems, Delft University of Technology, The Netherlands.

The author has over 50 publications to his credit. His another, titled *An Introduction to Data Envelopment Analysis* is ready for publishing. Also, he has presented over 35 papers at national and international conferences.

INDIAN TRANSPORT TOWARDS THE NEW MILLENNIUM

Performance, Analysis and Policy

R. RAMANATHAN

CONCEPT PUBLISHING COMPANY, NEW DELHI-110059

ISBN 81-8069-078-4

First Published 2004

Published and Printed by
Ashok Kumar Mittal
Concept Publishing Company
A/15-16, Commercial Block, Mohan Garden
NEW DELHI-110059 (India)

Phones: 25351460, 25351794
Fax: 091-11-25357103
Email: publishing@conceptpub.com

I DEDICATE THIS BOOK
TO
THE INDIRA GANDHI INSTITUTE OF
DEVELOPMENT RESEARCH, MUMBAI

FOREWORD

Transport plays a vital role in the economic development by providing access to jobs, education, leisure travel and other amenities essential for quality of life. Transport generates growth by facilitating trade, both nationally and internationally, and by increasing access to livelihoods, education facilities as well as local and national amenities. Value added by transport is estimated to account for 3 to 5 per cent of GDP, and transport commonly accounts for 5 to 8 per cent of total paid employment. Demand for freight and passenger transport in most developing countries is growing 1.5 to 2.0 times faster than GDP and the bulk of this increase is for road transport. Transport sector in India is not an exception to this striking trend, as is illustrated and highlighted by Dr. Ramanathan in this book.

Given such an importance of the Transport Sector, it is necessary to research to compile characteristics, trends, dynamics and transformations in this sector. This book provides the descriptions of the latest research studies carried out in the context of India. The issues of the sector are addressed holistically, encompassing the historical trends, analysis using different quantitative techniques, and policy.

I am happy to congratulate Dr. Ramanathan on his achievements. I hope that many scientists, transport planners and concerned practitioners will benefit from this unique compilation of studies.

JYOTI K. PARIKH
Senior Professor
Chairperson, Environmental Economics Research Committee, EMCaB, World Bank,
National Project Coordinator, Capacity Building Project, UNDP,
Indira Gandhi Institute of Development Research,
General Vaidya Marg, Goregaon (East), Mumbai, India 400065

PREFACE

India's transport sector has undergone structural transformations in the last few decades. The monograph is developed from the results of research studies undertaken in the late nineties for analysing the past and future performance of this sector. All these research studies have been peer-reviewed and published in reputed international and Indian journals. Some of the studies have been published in the India Development Reports, which are also peer-reviewed.

There are not many books that study the performance of India's transport sector in the last few years. On the other hand, the transport sector has grown tremendously and a detailed analysis using various tools is important to help make policy guidelines in this sector. The research studies presented in the monograph were carried out for this purpose. To this extent, the monograph is unique, and provides a unique blend of performance, analysis and policy aspects of Indian transport. Finally, it must be mentioned that the proposed monograph will not be a textbook on transport economics.

The organization of the monograph is detailed in the last section of the first chapter. Many of the research studies presented in the monograph require basic knowledge on econometrics. More sophisticated methodologies that are used in selected chapters of the monograph have been briefly explained in two appendices.

Because of the mix of basic data, research analyses and policy studies, this book is likely to be of interest to a wide variety of people interested in Indian transport. The first three chapters provide the past performance of the sector, and will be of interest to students on transport economics and others who wish to know about the performance trends in Indian transport. The next six chapters, which deal with analysis of transport issues using quantitative methods, will be of interest to researchers and students trying to understand the issues of this sector. Specifically, students on transport departments of universities and transport economics curriculum will be interested. The last three chapters, which deal mainly with policy aspects, will be of interest to researchers and policy makers engaged in transport policy.

The book will also be of interest to those involved in real world applications of different tools of analysis. The book uses modelling tools of econometrics and operations research. Those interested in applications of econometrics and operations research, such as those in the Quantitative or Systems or Operations Research departments of premier Institutions and Universities, will find the book useful. Because of the emphasis on modelling tools, Chapters 4 to 10 will be of interest to students and consultants involved in applying modelling tools to solving quantitative problems all over the world, and need not be limited to those within India.

This monograph is entirely based on the research studies carried out by the author and his colleagues when he was associated with the Indira Gandhi Institute of Development Research (IGIDR), Mumbai. The author gratefully acknowledges the infrastructure support provided by IGIDR including library, computers and secretarial assistance. Specifically, the author wishes to express his appreciation to Professor Jyoti K. Parikh, Senior Professor, and Professor Kirit S. Parikh, the then Director, IGIDR, for their constant helps and suggestions for many of the research studies used in the preparation of this monograph. They are co-authors of research studies used in the preparation of some chapters. The author acknowledges the help received from his colleague, Dr. S. Geetha, who is a co-author of one of the research papers used in the preparation of Chapter 5. The author wishes to thank all the co-authors for agreeing to include the joint research studies in some chapters of this book. The author thanks Mr. Mahesh Mohan, IGIDR, not only for his secretarial helps and computer tips, but also for his rejuvenating songs and sense of humour. The author thanks his present Institution, the Sultan Qaboos University, Muscat, Sultanate of Oman, for the assistance during the final stages of the preparation of the monograph. Finally, the author wishes to acknowledge the moral support received from his wife and children during the entire stages of preparation of this monograph.

R. RAMANATHAN

CONTENTS

PART III
POLICY

LIST OF TABLES

LIST OF FIGURES

1

TRANSPORT
An Introduction

Transport is a crucial infrastructure needed for the developmental process. This sector is capital intensive. The projects in this sector have low return and long gestation periods. This sector accounts for a major share of energy consumption in India, especially of petroleum products. The demands of this sector are likely to grow up further with economic and population growth: rapid industrialisation, urbanisation and agricultural development together increase freight and passenger transport, and higher real incomes stimulate leisure-related travel. There exists only a limited possibility for fuel switching at least in the short run of a decade or so. Hence this sector can aggravate foreign exchange burden by demanding huge oil imports.

Transport plays an important role for sustaining economic activities and creating employment opportunities. The share of this sector in the total Gross Domestic Product (GDP) in India was about 5 per cent in the nineties. Transport GDP has grown at about 4.74 per cent per year during this decade. As the share of urban areas in GDP has been increasing, the role of transport (especially urban transport) in the national economy is gaining greater significance.

Transport energy consumption has a serious effect on the economic growth of India, which is an oil-importing developing country. During 1997-98, India imported 50.5 per cent of its domestic oil demand. This formed about 24 per cent of its export earnings and about 20 per cent of total imports during the year. In absolute value, it amounted to US$ 8,227 million, which is very significant for a capital scarce country like India. The expert group on commercialisation of infrastructure projects (IIR, 1996) has projected an investment of Rs. 4,00,000 to 4,50,000 crore in infrastructure (urban development, power, telecommunication, roads, industrial parks and ports) till 2000-01. This represents a huge investment.

Transport is also one of the major polluters, especially causing air pollution in urban areas. Integrated policies are needed to tackle the pollution problems from this sector.

Hence, it is necessary to understand the complexities associated with this sector: changes in the demand patterns, modal split, performance and their trends, conservation potential, effect of fuel switching from conventional to new energy sources, and so on. This book is a collection of research efforts carried out in this direction. It aims to answer several policy oriented questions pertaining to the transport sector in India, including the following.

- What are the structural changes observed in the past, in terms of performance, energy consumption, and environmental emissions?
- How are they expected to behave in the future?
- What are the important research agenda related to this sector?
- How can important research questions pertaining to this sector be approached and tackled?
- What are the alternatives available to ensure sustainability, and how they can be implemented?

1.1 Some Economic Characteristics of Transport

The term "transport" generally means carrying people or goods from one place to another, usually in a vehicle. Non-mechanised transport, such as the carts pulled by animals and human beings (pull carts and cycle rickshaws), was popular long ago, but mechanised transport has taken over more than a century ago thanks to the industrial revolution.

There are different modes of transport, including rail, road, air and water. Rail transport mainly uses locomotives, whereas road transport is performed using cars, buses, two wheelers and other similar carriers. Pipelines are also important modes of transport for transporting mainly liquids.

Public transport includes those carriers that carry many passengers. The most prominent public transport modes are sub-urban rail and buses. They are also called mass transport modes.

Most of the demands for transport is a derived one; very few people travel for the sheer joy of travelling. Most people travel because transporting themselves to another geographical location benefits them. Transport provides the so-called *utility of place* by bridging the producer-consumer gap. If one wants to buy a product, he should transport himself to the market. If he wants a service, say the dental service, he has to transport himself to a dentist.

Transport has economic significance. It is a labour intensive large sector. In fact, Indian Railways is the largest employer of all the public sector firms in India. Automobiles are one of the fastest growing sector of the economy. As we shall see later, transport operations are responsible for about 4-5 per cent of GDP in India.

We have also seen that transport energy consumption has a serious effect on the economic growth of India. Import of oil, a major share of which consumed by the transport sector, formed about 24 per cent of its export earnings and about 20 per cent of total imports during 1997-98. Transport sector, especially the road transport, is mainly responsible for serious air pollution prevailing in many cities in India, and the associated health issues have economic impacts.

Transportation impacts land values. Land values generally increase depending upon their proximity to transportation networks. For example, if sub-urban areas are connected to the central business district of a city through an efficient transportation system, their land values improve. However, transportation does not always have positive effect on land values. The noise and air pollution accompanying transportation networks decreases adjacent land values.

Freight transport is important to the economy because it spurs economic development by giving mobility to production factors, which permits scale economies and increased efficiency. In fact, throughout the world, growth of industrial production has very close correlation with the growth of freight movement. This relationship is true for the case of India also, as will be shown in Chapter 5 using econometric models. Freight transport enlarges the area that industry and consumers can draw upon for resources and products. Goods transportation expands the area to which a given plant may distribute its products economically, and the resulting specialisation and scale economies provide a wider range for consumers at a lower cost.

Transport provides employment and enhances travel. It provides improved access to countryside through efficient networks, which will often prove handy during emergencies such as famines and flood.

1.1.1 *Transport as an Infrastructure*

Transport sector is generally considered as an infrastructure sector, just like energy, urban development, telecommunication, etc. Infrastructure sectors provide the basic engines of growth in an economy, and without them the economic development will not take place. The salient characteristics of the transport sector that make it as an infrastructure sector are the following. More details will be available in publications on transport economics, such as Button (1993).

Large Economies of Scale: Cost per unit decreases as the size of output increases. Many transport operations, especially public road transport, rail and pipelines have huge fixed costs.★ Because of the huge fixed costs, average cost per unit of transport output decreases as output increases, and hence profit increases with output resulting in economies of scale.

Long Life and Low Returns: Typically, infrastructure sectors have long lifetimes: a road once built is likely to last more than 20 years (with periodic maintenance). Returns from these sectors are often low. For example, the concept of charging users for road use is not very popular. There are also significant risks in achieving the returns due to political interference and other uncertainties associated with long payback periods.

Public Good: The provision of public good is desirable by the society. In this sense, access to roads are similar to access to clear air and water. It is difficult to exclude users from using such public goods, and charging user fees is difficult. With such infrastructure services, private point of view of costs and benefits will be different from the society's point of view. For example, when a backward region is provided with roads and other infrastructure facilities, there is likely to be industrial development leading to large revenues (*e.g.*, tax). However, if roads were to be provided by a private firm, it may not be able to get the benefits of industrial development whereas a society, or the government, can benefit in the form of increased tax revenues. Hence, a private firm will not find infrastructure provision as profitable. Again, infrastructure has typical characteristics that are not sought by private sector: infrastructure has very low internal rate of return and high payback periods, while private sector will seek high returns and low payback periods.

Private vs *Public Provision of Infrastructure:* There is another danger of exploitation if infrastructure is provided by the private sector. As infrastructure projects enjoy significant economies of scale, the business of providing infrastructure services has the characteristics of monopoly. A firm can invest heavily, achieve huge economy of scale, provide services cheaply and edge out competition. Once the competition is eliminated, he can exploit consumers. Hence private sector provision

★ See Section 1.2 for some data on the capital intensiveness of India's transport sector.

of infrastructure is often viewed with caution. Traditionally, the government has provided the infrastructure services. However, as infrastructure sectors are highly capital intensive, governments are increasingly finding it difficult to provide enough timely investments, and now-a-days, private investment is being welcomed. With private sector entry in infrastructure sector, the role of government is viewed more as a regulatory agency, that encourages competition and ensures that consumers are not exploited by the private sector.

We have seen that private sector will generally not be interested in entering the business of infrastructure provision. However, they can be attracted to this business by the government by providing some incentives. For example, a private company can be given the land adjacent to roads/rail tracks it is expected to build so that it can take advantage of the commercial potential. Government can allow tolling on the roads developed by private people. Several other fiscal incentives can also be provided by the government (*e.g.*, tax holidays). Government can provide these incentives because it gains by the new road in the form of additional revenues generated by industrial development in the long run.

1.1.2 *Negative Impacts*

Transportation imposes certain adverse side effects, although it is generally believed that the benefits provided by transportation far exceed the costs.

The most serious form of pollution due to transport is the air pollution. Internal combustion engines, mostly used in automobiles of road transport, are responsible for a majority of air pollution. For example, about 60 per cent of the total pollution load in major Indian cities were caused by road transport in 1993-94. Some basic details on environmental pollution from transport will be discussed in Section 1.5 of this Chapter, and detailed India specific information will be presented in Chapter 3.

Noise pollution is a significant problem especially in the vicinity of highways and airports.

One of the most disturbing by-products of enhanced mobility is injury and loss of life. Road accidents have overtaken major diseases in inducing human mortality. Trucks used in freight transportation are the major causes in many accidents.

1.1.2.1 *External Costs of Transport*

It is possible to classify the costs incurred in transport into a variety of categories, such as fixed costs, variable costs, etc. Some of them can be specifically attributed to units (buses, cars, etc.) while some are joint or common costs. All these costs are generally attributed to transport users. For example, the fare a passenger pays is the direct cost of his travel. Several textbooks on transport economics, such as Button (1993), provides detailed discussion of the various costs of transport. However, from the point of view of the negative impacts of transport, the so-called external costs or externalities of transport have been recently recognised as an important class of transport costs. These costs are associated with transport that are not directly borne by those generating them, *i.e.*, the travellers. Car travellers inflict pollution and vibration on those living adjacent to major roads, and ships carrying petroleum sometimes sink polluting the sea and nearby beaches. These are external costs or externalities generated by transport users and inflicted on the non-travelling public. While the travelling individuals do not consider external costs in their private costs, external costs are borne by the society. Economic theory shows that presence of externalities will result in oversupply. Thus, the presence of external costs of transport increases transportation compared to the socially optimal level. When transport users are charged for the external costs imposed by their travel, these costs are said to be internalised. Measuring the full costs of travel (including the external costs) and ensuring that the external costs are internalised are important areas of research in transport economics. Please refer to Button (1993) and Litman (1998) for more details. A variety of information resources on the efficient use of transport services are available from the publications of the Victoria Transport Policy Institute in Canada. They also provide methods for measuring the full costs of transport, *e.g.*, Litman (1998). Some of the resources can be accessed at their website at the URL: http://www.vtpi.org/.

1.2 Some Macro Economic Relationships of India's Transport Sector

The contribution of transport sector for the total Gross Domestic Product (GDP) in India has not been in tune with the plan outlays it has received. While its share in plan outlays ranged from 12-22 per cent (Table 1.1), its share in GDP has been only around 4-5 per cent (Table 1.2). This shows the capital intensiveness of this infrastructure sector.

Transport GDP has grown at about 4.74 per cent per year during the last decade. However, the growth is not uniform in the transport sub-sectors: the share of railways has shown a declining trend, from about 0.92 per cent of the total GDP in 1980-81 to about 0.84 per cent in

1990-91, while the share of other transport modes have increased from 3.01 to 4 per cent during the same period.

TABLE 1.1: Plan Allocation for the Transport Sector

(Rs. billions in current values)

Five Year Plan	*Total Plan Outlay*	*Outlay for the Transport Sector*	*% Allocation for the Transport Sector*
First (1951-56)	19.68	4.34	22.05
Second (1956-61)	46.72	11.00	23.54
Third (1961-66)	85.78	19.83	23.12
Annuals (1966-69)	66.25	10.32	15.58
Fourth (1969-74)	157.79	25.22	15.98
Fifth (1974-79)	394.26	55.43	14.06
Sixth (1980-85)	1092.92	139.62	12.78
Seventh (1985-90)	1792.77	294.57	16.44
Annuals (1990-92)	1370.33	175.87	12.84
Eighth (1992-97)	4341.00	561.42	12.91
Ninth (1997-2002)	8592.00	1213.24	14.12

Sources: Documents on the various Five Year plans published by the Planning Commission, Government of India, New Delhi.

TABLE 1.2: Contribution of the Transport Sector in Total GDP

(Values in Rs. billions at 1980-81 prices)

Year	*Railways*	*Other Transport*	*Total Transport*	*Total*
(1)	(2)	(3)	(4)	(5)
1980-81	11.24	36.80	48.04	1,224
	(0.92)	(3.01)	(3.92)	
1985-86	14.04	53.09	67.13	1,566
	(0.90)	(3.39)	(4.29)	
1989-90	16.23	75.22	91.45	1,995
	(0.81)	(3.77)	(4.58)	
1990-91	16.77	78.70	95.47	2,098
	(0.80)	(3.75)	(4.55)	
1991-92	17.78	85.03	102.81	2,123
	(0.84)	(4.00)	(4.84)	
1993-94	17.46	92.2	109.66	2,391
	(0.73)	(3.86)	(4.59)	
1994-95	17.69	99.06	116.75	2,577
	(0.69)	(3.84)	(4.53)	
1995-96	19.06	105.28	124.34	2,761
	(0.69)	(3.81)	(4.5)	
1996-97	19.64	114.07	133.71	2,968
	(0.66)	(3.84)	(4.5)	

(Contd.)

TABLE 1.2 (*Contd.*)

(1)	(2)	(3)	(4)	(5)
1997-98*	113.68 (1.12)	434.48 (4.29)	548.16 (5.41)	10,128
1998-99*	115.69 (1.07)	453.60 (4.19)	569.29 (5.26)	10,818

Note: Figures with brackets show percentages.
* Values for these two years are in 1993-94 prices.

Source: Various issues of the National Accounts Statistics published by the Government of India.

There are many reasons for such a trend. The investments in railways has not been in tune with the growth in goods and passenger transport. The Indian Railways is entirely owned by the Central Government and investment in it is controlled by the Central Government through the Planning Commission. While the railways has commanded a good share of the first three plan allocations (more than 60% of the total allocation to transport), the share has declined in the fourth and fifth plan periods (Table 1.3). This reduction would have affected the performance of the railways in the eighties. It has to be noted that there was an increase in railways' share in the investment in the seventh and in the subsequent annual plans, but in the eighth and ninth plans, there is a steady decline. The share of railways in the investment of the ninth five-year plan is about 37.5 per cent.

TABLE 1.3: Percentage Distribution of Transport Sector Allocation

Plan	*Railways*	*Roads & Road Transport*	*Ports, Light-houses, Shipping & Inland Water Transport*	*Civil Aviation*	*Other Transport Services*
First (1951-56)	50.00	33.87	10.83	5.30	0.00
Second (1956-61)	65.73	22.00	7.82	4.45	0.00
Third (1961-66)	66.87	23.55	7.11	2.47	0.00
Annuals (1966-69)	52.97	32.73	8.36	5.94	0.00
Fourth (1969-74)	37.03	39.25	16.69	7.02	0.00
Fifth (1974-79)	37.22	39.76	17.72	5.30	0.00
Sixth (1980-85)	47.45	36.61	9.05	6.89	0.00
Seventh (1985-90)	56.18	28.81	8.24	6.61	0.16
Annuals (1990-92)	58.10	26.40	9.48	5.34	0.68
Eighth (1992-97)	48.45	30.39	13.55	7.31	0.30

Source: Documents on different five year plans, Planning Commission, Government of India, New Delhi.

In the next chapter, the structural changes in the performance of Indian transport sector will be explored in more detail.

1.3 Measuring Transport Performance

Normally, we need to transport two different kinds—passengers and freight. Two basic measures are commonly employed in transport—those of quantity and movement. For passenger movement, the number of passengers transported represents the quantity. For freight movement, the quantity measure is the tonnes of materials transported. These quantity measures do not adequately describe the transport effort involved, because the effort depends not only upon the quantity but also on the distance through which the quantity is moved. This necessitates the need for composite measures for measuring transport performance, that measure both the quantity and extent of movement. The composite measure for measuring passenger transport is Passenger-kilometres (PKM) (or passenger-miles): if a passenger is moved by one kilometres, then a total of 1 PKM is said to have been effected. Similarly, the performance of freight transport is often measured by the composite measure, Tonne-kilometres (TKM) (or Tonne-miles): if a freight of 10 Tonne is transported through 10 kilometres, then 100 TKM is effected. In freight transport, sometimes the term Net Tonne-Kilometres (NTKM) is used when the weight of the rolling stock is excluded.*

Interpretation of these composite measures is important. Suppose that the freight performance by Indian Railways increased from 200 billion TKM to 250 billion TKM during a certain period. This could be due to a 25 per cent increase in average journey length (usually called as the *average lead*) of the materials with the quantity of freight remaining constant, or due to an increase of 25 per cent in the freight quantity with the average lead remaining the same, or a combination of increasing freight quantity and distance travelled.

1.4 Share of Different Modes of Transport: Modal Split

The term "modal split" or "mode split" is used to denote the share of different modes of transport in the entire passenger or freight market. It represents the ratio in which the total transport performance is shared by different transport modes. As will be highlighted in the next chapter, passenger and freight modal splits in India has moved towards road

---

* Please see CMIE (1999) for a definition of some important concepts and terms pertaining to the transport sector.

transport, the shift being more prominent in passenger segment. Historically, the different modes of transport were dominant at different periods. Horses and other animals dominated travel long back (prior to industrial revolution), then rail transport has dominated in early decades of the twentieth century, and presently road dominates travel. The modal share of air transport is growing. When the modal shares are plotted against time, the approximate pattern shown in Fig. 1.1 evolves. Note that the patterns are S-shaped and can be approximated by the so-called logistic curves. The long run evolution of transport structures in various countries of the world and verification of the logistic relationships have been analysed by many researchers, including Grubler and Nakicenovic (1991). This pattern has been verified for the case of India, and details of the logistic analysis will be presented in Chapter 4.

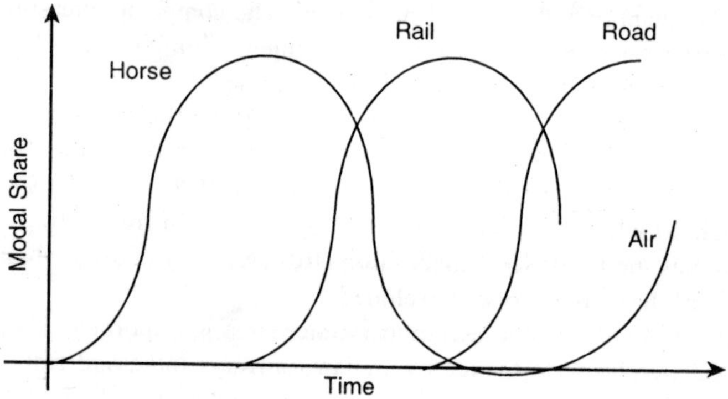

FIG. 1.1: Composition among Different Modes of Transport in the long run

1.5 Some Basics of Estimating Energy and Environmental Implications of Transport

Later chapters of this book deal with the direct fuel consumption in transport modes and pollutant emissions due to the energy consumption. Hence, it is important to understand how the energy contents of different fuels can be compared, and pollutant emissions can be estimated.

As a standard, the energy contents of fuels are expressed in terms of calorific values. Calorific value is the amount of heat released by the combustion of a specified mass of fuel. Calorific values are expressed in terms of energy units. There are different units of energy. The joule (denoted as J) is the *Système International d'Unités* or the International System (SI) derived unit of energy. A joule is the energy required to heat 1 cc of water by about a quarter (0.239) of a degree Celsius.

Calories, kilocalories, British thermal units, etc. are some other units of energy. It is possible to convert the energy expressed in one unit (say in Joules) to another (say calories) using suitable conversion factors. For example, one calorie is equal to 4.184 J.

In the metric system of units, 10^3 is normally denoted as Kilo (k), 10^6 as Mega (M), 10^9 as Giga (G), 10^{12} as Tera (T), 10^{15} as Peta (P) and 10^{18} as Exa (E). Thus, 1000 J = 1 kJ, and 10^{18} J = 1 EJ = 10^9 GJ.

The calorific values of some common fuels, obtained from Indian Petroleum and Natural Gas Statistics, are given in Table 1.4.

TABLE 1.4: Calorific Values of Fuels in MJ/kg

Coal	20.92
Lignite	9.67
Firewood	19.87
Charcoal	28.87
Motor Gasoline	46.59
Kerosene	44.51
Jet fuel	49.33
Diesel oil	45.15
Fuel oil	43.68
Natural gas (in MJ/m^3)	35.56
Electricity (in MJ/kWh)	3.60

Source: Petroleum and Natural Gas Statistics 1990-91, Government of India.

Transport operations result in emission of certain gases that pollute the atmosphere. Some pollutants are called local pollutants because their effects are limited to some geographic region around the place where they are emitted. Some prominent local air pollutants include the following.

1. Carbon monoxide (CO)
2. Sulphur oxides (SO_2 and SO_3)
3. Nitrogen oxides — Nitric oxide (NO), nitrogen dioxide (NO_2) and nitrous oxide (N_2O). Sometimes, NO and NO_2 are collectively denoted as NO_x.
4. Volatile organic compounds (VOC), that include methane (CH_4), benzene (C_6H_6), formaldehyde (CH_2O), chloroflurocarbons, etc.
5. Suspended particulate matter (SPM) — solid particles such as dust, soot, pollen, asbestos, lead, arsenic, cadmium, etc. and liquid droplets of sulphuric acid, oil, pesticides, etc.
6. Photochemical oxidants — Ozone (O_3), hydrogen peroxide

(H_2O_2), formaldehyde (CH_2O), etc., formed in the atmosphere by the reaction of oxygen, nitrogen oxides and VOCs under the influence of sunlight.

7. Radioactive substances—Radon 222, Plutonium 239, etc.

Most of these pollutants have different impacts on human health. Please consult textbooks on environmental science (*e.g.*, Miller, 1993) for more details on different air pollutants and their impacts. The pollutant emissions from vehicles in Indian conditions have been estimated by the Indian Institute of Petroleum, Dehradun, by conducting laboratory experiments. They have provided emission factors that can be used for estimating pollutant emissions from Indian vehicles (IIP, 1985). Some representative emission factors are given in Table 1.5, but those interested are advised to refer to the above publication for a more detailed information on estimating emission of local pollutants from Indian vehicles.

TABLE 1.5: Emission Factors for Estimating Emission of Local Pollutants for Indian Urban Driving Conditions

	Unit: g/km			
	CO	*CH*	*NOx*	*Particulates*
Gasoline vehicles				
2 Wheelers	8.3	5.18	—	—
3 Wheelers	12.2	57.65	—	—
Cars	24.03	3.57	1.57	—
Jeeps	24.03	3.57	1.57	—
Taxis	24.03	3.57	1.57	—
Diesel Vehicles (in g/g of fuel)	0.0228	0.00883	0.0431	0.00143

Source: IIP (1985).

Some air pollutants are called global pollutants because their adverse impacts are the same irrespective of the place they are emitted. The greenhouse gases, that include Carbon dioxide (CO_2), Methane (CH_4), Nitrous oxide (N_2O), Hydrofluorocarbons (HFCs), Perfluorocarbons (PFCs) and Sulphur hexafluoride (SF_6), are global pollutants. The greenhouse effect caused by them will be the same irrespective of whether they are emitted in India or the US or Japan. In recent years, the greenhouse effect, and its results on global warming have come to the centre stage of much of energy related research. Of the major greenhouse gases, CO_2 has received the most attention as it is projected to contribute between 67 and 96 per cent of the future enhanced global warming (Mac Kenzie, 1994). CO_2 is the one that is directly related to energy consumption, and the transport sector is one of the most important emitter of CO_2 (Parikh and Gokarn, 1993; Michelis and Davidson, 1966). Hence, direct CO_2 emissions arising out of the energy used in transport sector will be analysed in Chapter 3 of this book.

CO_2 emissions are normally computed based on energy consumption data using appropriate emission factors (OECD, 1991; Parikh and Gokarn, 1993). The emission factors are presented in Table 1.6. Thus, about 0.546 tonnes of carbon equivalent (tC)* will be emitted for every tonne of solid fuels burnt.

TABLE 1.6: Carbon Dioxide Emission Coefficient of Different Fuels

Fuels	*Unit*	*Value*
Solid Fuels	tC/t	0.546
Liquid Fuels	tC/t	0.88
Gaseous Fuels	tC/1000 m^3	0.678

Source: OECD (1991).

1.6 Organisation of this Book

For ease of exposition, the book is divided into three different parts, which are inter-related.

Performance trends will be analysed in the first part. It comprises Chapters 2 and 3. The performance of different transport sub-sectors will be analysed in detail in the next chapter. The associated energy and environmental implications will be analysed in Chapter 3.

Several research studies on Indian transport sector will be presented in Part II, which comprises the next six chapters (Chapters 4-9). These research studies draw heavily from the discussion on performance trends discussed in Part I. An analysis of modal split will be presented in Chapter 4. It has been shown in this chapter that, like in most countries of the world, the modal split in India also follows the logistic rule discussed in Section 1.4. Two different econometric models for exploring the relationship between gasoline consumption and other macro-economic variables will be presented in Chapter 5. Another econometric modelling exercise to capture the long-term relationships between performance of

* Carbon emissions are normally expressed in terms of two different units: in CO_2 units and in carbon equivalents. From their respective molecular or atomic weights, 12 g of carbon is equal to 44 g of CO_2. Thus 0.546 tonnes of carbon equivalent is equal to about 2 tonnes of CO_2.

passenger and freight transport, and other macro-economic variables will be presented in Chapter 6. A crucial link between the trends in population and number of vehicles in Indian cities is presented in Chapter 7 using a logistic regression model. Chapters 8 and 9 have been devoted in identifying performance efficiencies in Indian transport sector. Relative energy efficiencies of rail and road transport over the last few years will be assessed in Chapter 8 while productivity of selected state transport undertakings will be assessed in Chapter 9.

Policy aspects of Indian transport sector will be discussed in Part III. This part has three chapters (10-12). Once again, the chapters in this part draw heavily on the results of the analyses presented in chapters of Part II. A scenario analysis will be presented in Chapter 10 to explore the sustainability impacts if the past trends of the Indian transport sector are allowed to continue in the future. Alternative ways to contain the negative impacts are studied in this chapter in the form of different scenarios. Important problem areas pertaining to different transport sub-sectors will be identified, recent developments carried out to overcome the bottlenecks will be studied and future directions of further actions will be explored in Chapter 11. The last chapter, Chapter 12, will be devoted to the policy issues of urban transport in India. Trends in urbanisation, the process by which number of vehicles in Indian cities follows urban population, and the associated problems and urban policy issues will be explored in this chapter.

This book is based on several publications of the author over the last eight years in reputed international journals, Indian journals and in the India Development Reports. Each chapter is based on one or more publications, which will be mentioned as a footnote at the beginning of the respective chapters. Most of the studies have been carried out in the later part of the nineteen nineties, using data up to the early nineties. Wherever feasible, efforts have been made to update the data in this book till the late nineties. However, the research studies, which involve complicated analyses, are not updated.

Because of the mix of basic data, research analyses and policy studies, this book is likely to be of interest to a wide variety of people interested in Indian transport. The first two chapters provide the past performance of the sector, and will be of interest to students and others who wish to know about the performance trends in Indian transport. The research studies presented in Part II will be of interest to researchers and students trying to understand the issues of this sector. Part III will be of interest to researchers and policy-makers.

PART I

PERFORMANCE

This part comprises two chapters. Chapter 2 describes the physical performance of different modes of Indian transport sector, while Chapter 3 describes the energy and environmental aspects of the performance.

level of people, allowing them to invest more in personalised travel. Also, increased economic activities demand a larger mobility of passenger and freight, and larger additions to transport infrastructure and equipment. However, growth of vehicles tends to reduce beyond another critical level. This can happen when infrastructural bottlenecks tend to limit the economic activities and insufficient road infrastructure discourages personalised travel in large mega cities. However, when additional infrastructure for transport are provided in these large cities, economic activities and hence vehicular growth will continue to increase at a higher rate. For example, Table 2.6 shows slow growth in the number of vehicles in Mumbai in the nineties, which may reverse as several flyovers and elevated driveways are proposed to be completed by the end of the year 1999.

There can be another reason for the saturation levels found in larger mega cities. Vehicular growth in these cities can get shifted to city fringes and regions adjacent to the city as people working in the city tend to reside on the cheaper city fringes. People may also prefer to register their vehicles outside the city-limits to avoid the high cost of vehicle registration.

Urban form tends to affect the growth of vehicles in cities. Linear cities, such as Mumbai, cannot expand on all sides. With its main activities focussed on the small island area, Mumbai has expanded linearly. People in these cities stay in the faraway suburban areas, and commute a long distance daily. In contrast, a circular city will have more efficient urban form, as people can stay in all directions of the main city centre. Thus the urban form can be an important factor in determining the growth of vehicles.

Prices can also influence vehicular growth. In principle, vehicular growth can be checked using appropriate pricing policies. However, available evidence seems to indicate that price may not substantially influence the vehicular growth. For example, the econometric models presented in Chapters 5 and 6 show that prices have a very small (though significant) influence on gasoline consumption and transport performance in India.

The S-shaped pattern can also be altered by other policy formulations. For example, if a city is developed to encourage walking and cycling by providing all the facilities in a smaller geographical area, the growth of motorised vehicles may be reduced. Many cities expand because people settle in the cheaper periphery regions of the city, and prefer travel for work. This will reduce the population density in cities. This can happen so long as travel is relatively inexpensive compared with land. However,

2

TRENDS IN TRANSPORT PERFORMANCE

The most important structural trends of the Indian transport sector will be discussed in this chapter. The data for the analysis have been compiled from various governmental and non-governmental data sources. The sources include various issues of the Monthly Abstract of Statistics published by the Central Statistical Organisation, Indian Railway yearbooks, Motor Transport Statistics, and various issues of the Basic Statistics of the Indian Economy published by the Centre for Monitoring Indian Economy, Mumbai.

The total passenger kilometres (PKM) effected in India by rail, road and air transport in 1993-94 was about 1811 billions. During the year, about 607 TKM was effected. During the period 1956-94, PKM grew at a rate of 8.12 per cent per annum, while TKM grew at 5.89 per cent per annum. A gradual transformation from rail-dominated transport to road-dominated transport has been witnessed in the last few decades. As can be seen in Table 2.1, the share of railways has decreased from 36.9 per cent of the total PKM in 1980-81 to 16.4 per cent in 1993-94. During the same period, the share of railways in freight transport (TKM) declined from 61.9 per cent to 42.3 per cent. Road transport grew at a tremendous

TABLE 2.1: Trends in Modal Split (%) in India

		Rail	*Road*	*Air (domestic)*
1993-94	PKM	16.43	83.20	0.38*
	TKM	42.34	57.64	0.02*
1980-81	PKM	36.90	62.32	0.79
	TKM	61.85	38.12	0.03

Note: * This data pertains only to public carriers, and does not include information on private operators.

Note: This chapter is partly based on Ramanathan (1996) and Parikh, J. and Ramanathan (1997).

rate during this period. The data in the table shows that the share of air transport has reduced from 1980-81 to 1993-94. However, this may not be a realistic picture as the data on air transport for the year 1993-94 does not include the performance of domestic private airlines.* The table could not be updated as there are no data on PKM and TKM performed by road beyond 1993-94.

2.1 Railways

The Indian railway system is the second largest in the world under a single management. It is a multi-gauge system operating on three gauges—the broad, the metre and the narrow. Of the 62,495 route kilometres at the end of March 1998, about 69 per cent was on the broad gauge, 25 per cent was on the metre gauge, while the narrow gauge covered the remaining 6 per cent. Electrified route length constituted about 21.6 per cent of the total route length. The Indian railways have a fleet consisting of 7,206 locomotives, 34,728 coaches and 2,63,981 wagons.

2.1.1 *Passenger Traffic*

Passenger traffic on the Railways has two main components, namely suburban and non-suburban.

The total passenger kilometres performed by the non-suburban passenger rail traffic were 301 billions during 1997-98. It has grown at an average rate of 4.2 per cent per year during 1970-98. Fig. 2.1 shows that this increase is mainly due to the increase in the average distance travelled by passengers, which grew at about 3 per cent per year during the period.

Suburban passenger traffic has grown at a faster rate than the non-suburban segment. Suburban traffic in India at present includes only traffic moving on EMU services in the metropolitan cities of Mumbai, Kolkata, Chennai and Delhi. These suburban railway traffic accounts for about 15 to 20 per cent of the total passenger traffic in these cities. In spite of this, it forms an important part of the total rail passenger traffic system on the railways. The growth in suburban passenger kilometres is shown in Fig. 2.2. The PKM during 1997-98 was about 79 billions, and has grown at the rate of about 4.5 per cent per year during the period

* Section 2.3 discusses the performance of air transport in more detail, including that of private operators.

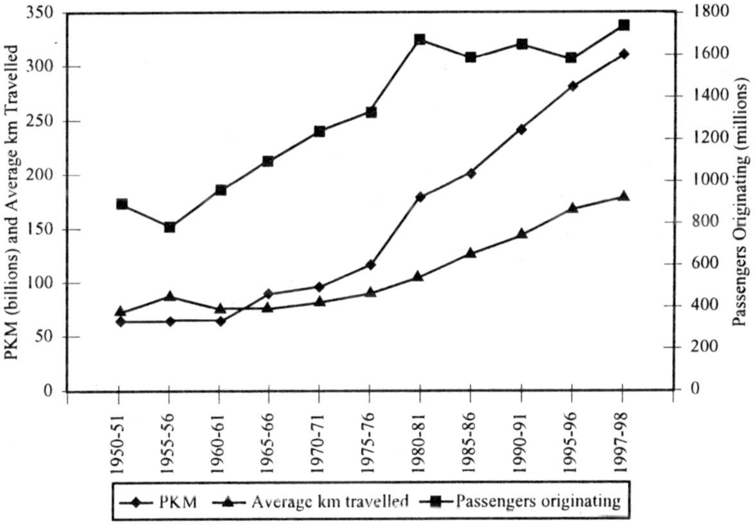

FIG. 2.1: Growth of Non-suburban Passenger Traffic in Indian Railways

Source: Various issues of Indian Railway year books, Railway Budgets of the Government of India and CMIE (1999).

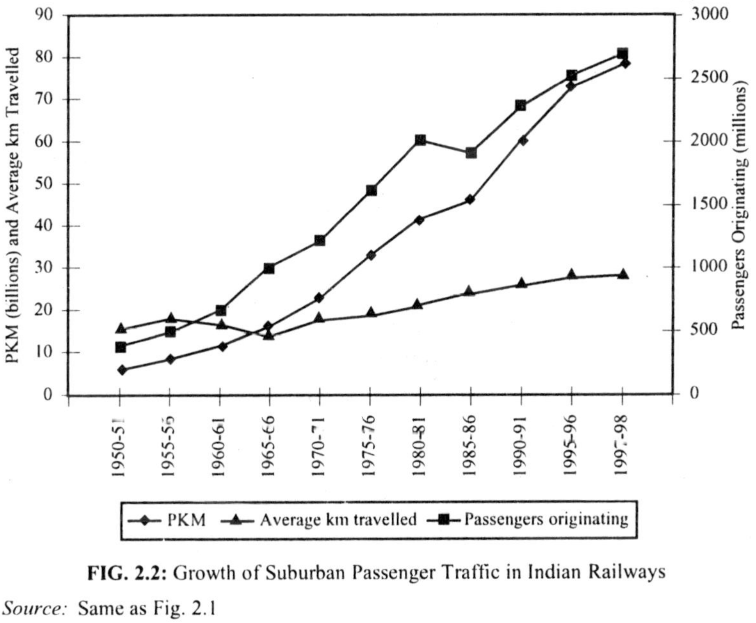

FIG. 2.2: Growth of Suburban Passenger Traffic in Indian Railways

Source: Same as Fig. 2.1

1970-98. The number of passengers using the suburban services increased, and the average distance travelled by a suburban passenger nearly doubled during this period.

A notable feature is that the growth rate in rail passenger transport in the eighties and nineties (around 3% per year) has been much lower than the growth rate that existed during the seventies (more than 5% per year). As mentioned earlier, a main cause for this is the reduced budgetary support to railways in the late seventies, which has resulted in capital shortages for investment.

There has been a steady decline in the share of steam traction in the total passenger traffic over the years. It occupied about 98.16 per cent of the total passenger traffic in 1955-56. Fig. 2.3 shows more recent changes. The share of this traction was about 49 per cent in 1980-81 (in terms of train kilometres), which reduced to about 22 per cent in 1990-91, and further reduced to just 0.2 per cent in 1997-98. The rate of reduction of steam train kilometres was much higher in the nineties (–45% per year during 1990-98) compared to the eighties (–5%). This traction is on the way out as they have low efficiency, and demand higher operating expenses. For example, in 1991-92, they accounted for 31 per cent of the total operating expenses (RITES, 1993). The share of diesel and

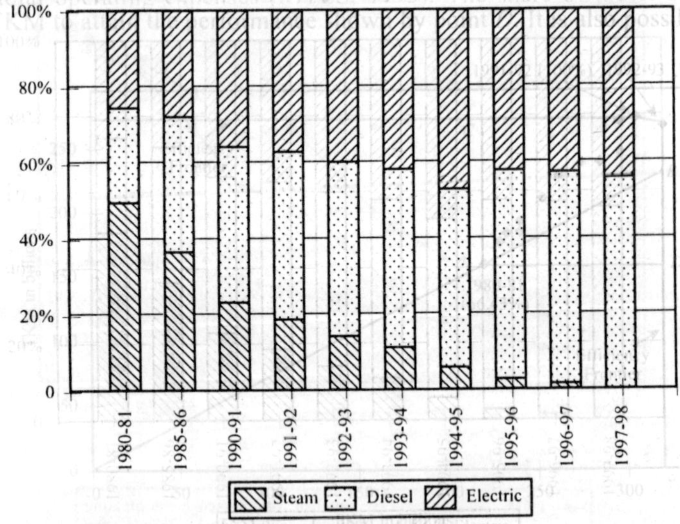

FIG. 2.3: Share of Different Tractions in Rail Passenger Transport in India (in terms of train kilometres)

Source: CMIE (1999).

electric traction have increased, with the former registering faster growth. Again, the two traction increased their train kilometres at a faster rate in the eighties compared to the nineties.

2.1.2 *Freight Traffic*

Revenue freight traffic on the railways has two main components, namely bulk commodities and others. Bulk commodities comprise coal, fertilisers, iron and steel, iron ore and other ores, cement, mineral oil, foodgrains, limestone and dolomite, and stones other than marbles. They constitute a majority (about 85-90%) of the total revenue originating tonnage in railways. The proportion of bulk commodities has been steadily increasing over the years.

Fig. 2.4 shows that coal has been the single major commodity accounting for more than one-third of the total originating freight traffic. Its share has increased from 40 per cent in 1980-81 to 46 per cent in 1998-99. While no major change occurred in the share of many of the other bulk commodities, cement has increased its share from 7 per cent to 9 per cent during the period. Share of other goods reduced from 14 per cent to 9 per cent during this period.

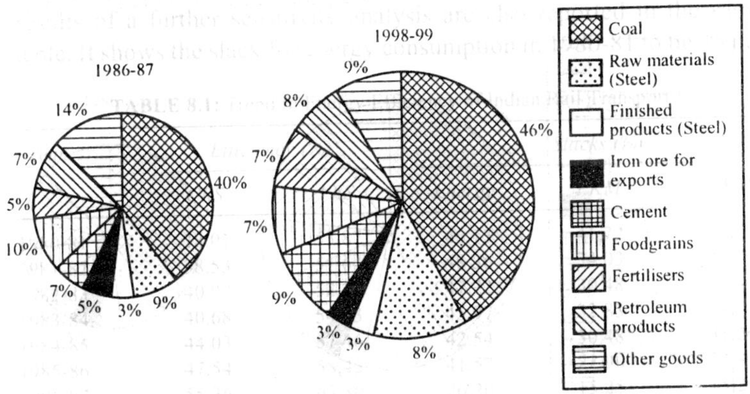

FIG. 2.4: Composition of Originating Traffic (Million Tonnes)

Source: CMIE, 1999.

During 1998-99, railways effected 281.5 billion tonne-kilometres of goods traffic, moving about 421 million tonnes of freight at an average lead of 669 kilometres. The overall performance of the rail freight traffic is sketched in Fig. 2.5. Originating tonnage showed a moderate growth in the first half of the seventies, then there was a slump till 1980, then it sharply increased in the eighties, but the growth has slowed somewhat in the nineties. Consequently, the growth rate in TKM has shown a sudden jump in the eighties. The growth rate was 2.65 per cent per year in the seventies, which increased to 4.33 per cent in the eighties, but reduced to just 1.92 per cent per year in the nineties. There has been a steady decrease in the average lead of freight carried since the late seventies. This is due to the reduction in the average lead of coal and fertiliser. The average lead for other commodities did not show much variation. Fig. 2.6 shows the variations for many of the major commodities.

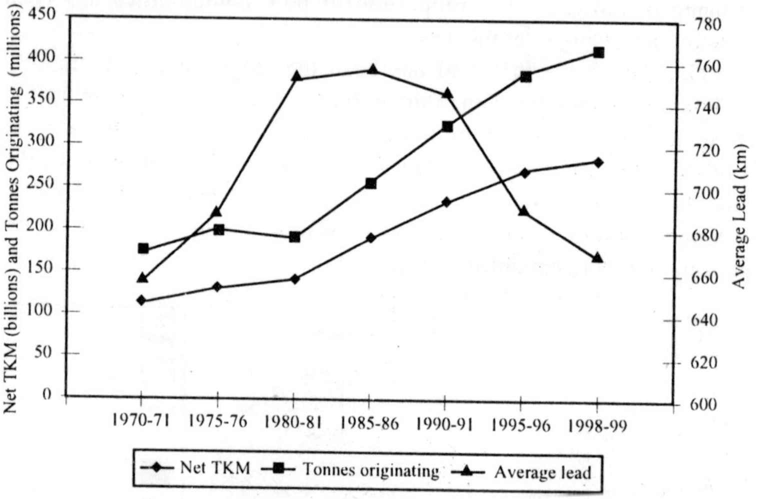

FIG. 2.5: Growth of Freight Traffic in Indian Railways

Sources: Various issues of Indian Railway year books, Railway Budgets of the Government of India and CMIE (1999).

The contribution of steam traction in rail freight train kilometres was about 15 per cent in 1980-81. It reduced to just 1.3 per cent in 1990-91, and has been almost phased out by 1997-98 (Fig. 2.7). Diesel train kilometres has increased in the eighties but reduced in the nineties. During the period, the contribution of electric traction has increased very much. Diesel traction formed about 62 per cent of the total freight train kilometres in 1990-91, but reduced to 45 per cent in 1997-98. The increased emphasis on electrification of the main traffic routes has resulted in reducing share of diesel traction.

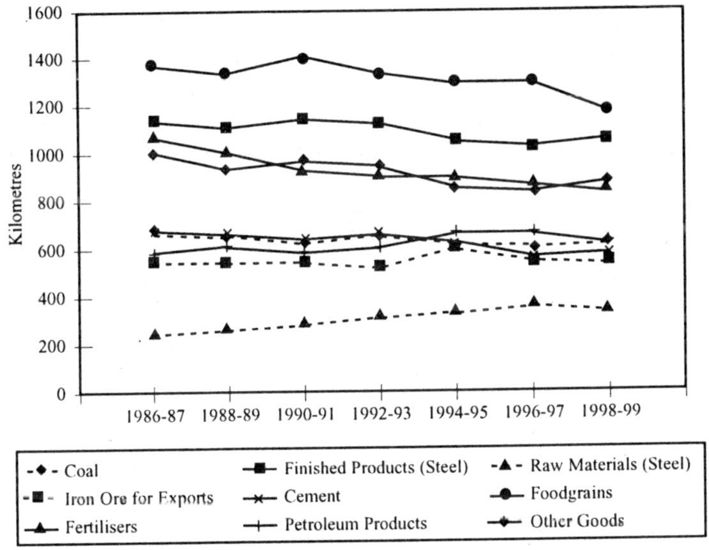

FIG. 2.6: Average Lead of Important Commodities in Rail Freight Traffic in India

Sources: Various issues of Indian Railway year books, Railway Budgets of the Government of India and CMIE (1999).

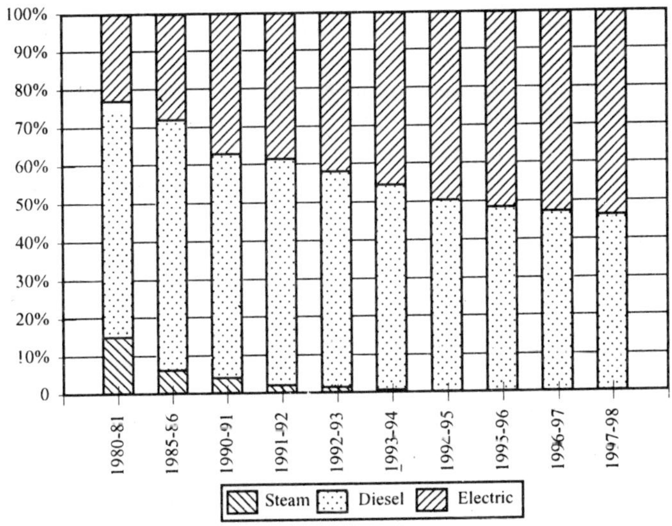

FIG. 2.7: Share of Different Tractions in Rail Freight Transport in India (in terms of train kilometres)

Source: CMIE (1999).

An important issue about the performance of the railways is its reducing share in the total transportation. As we have seen above, even though there is an increase in the absolute values of PKM and TKM by the railways, its share is decreasing. The growth rate in rail passenger transport during 1980-94 has reduced to nearly half of the growth rate of 1970-80, whereas the rate has increased considerably for freight traffic. However, rail transport has been proved to be more energy efficient and much cheaper compared to road transport, and hence a number of studies have recommended a more dominant role for railways in future (NTPC, 1980; IR, 1985; MEDEE, 1991). There has not been enough investment in railway infrastructure to encourage growth. For example, the growth of total route kilometres has been very marginal during the last two decades, and the rate has been much lower in the last decade compared to the seventies. This implies that further growth of railway performance cannot be achieved by capacity utilisation alone but requires significant investment in infrastructure. This means that it is necessary to increase investment in railways for augmenting the capacity. The policy issues related to Indian Railways will be discussed in Chapter 11.

2.2 Roadways

Road caters to all types of traffic—long distance, inter- and intra-district, and even to remote villages. Road transport is of great importance both for movement of passengers and goods. It is ideally suited for short and medium distances because of its inherent advantages such as easy availability and flexibility of operation, adaptability to individual needs, door to door service and reliability. It is also the main mechanised means of transport in hilly and rural areas not served by railways.

One of the major limitations for the analysis of the progress of road transportation in India is the non-availability of consistent set of data. At least four data sources that provide information on the performance of road transport can be identified:

(a) The basic statistics on the Indian Economy, published by the Centre for Monitoring Indian Economy (CMIE, 1994),
(b) A report submitted to the Government of India (GOI, 1987) as available from TEDDY (1990-91),
(c) Reports periodically prepared for the Government of India, for example the MEDEE-S report (MEDEE, 1991), and
(d) Data available in books such as Saxena (1992).

Unfortunately, they are not in agreement with each other. For example, the total road PKM in the year 1980 is estimated in these sources as 353 (for 1980-81), 471.8, 543 and 421 billions respectively. Another data limitation for analysis is that except GOI (1987), the other two do not give any break down of the PKM in terms of cars, two wheelers, buses, etc. In the following analysis, we have used the CMIE data source (CMIE, 1994) as it happens to be the source for many other data used in this study. Further information on inconsistencies between road transport data is discussed in Ramanathan (1997).

2.2.1 *Passenger Traffic*

Unlike the railways which showed a relatively even growth in PKM both in the seventies and eighties, road transport has recorded very high growth in recent years, especially since the mid-eighties. Road transport contributed to 905 billion PKM in 1988-89, which is more than 2.5 times the PKM effected in 1980-81. According to IIR (1996), roadways have accounted for 1500 billion PKM during 1993-94. Such a sharp growth can be contrasted with the very gentle growth during the sixties and seventies as shown in Fig. 2.8*. The growth rate was 6.93 per cent

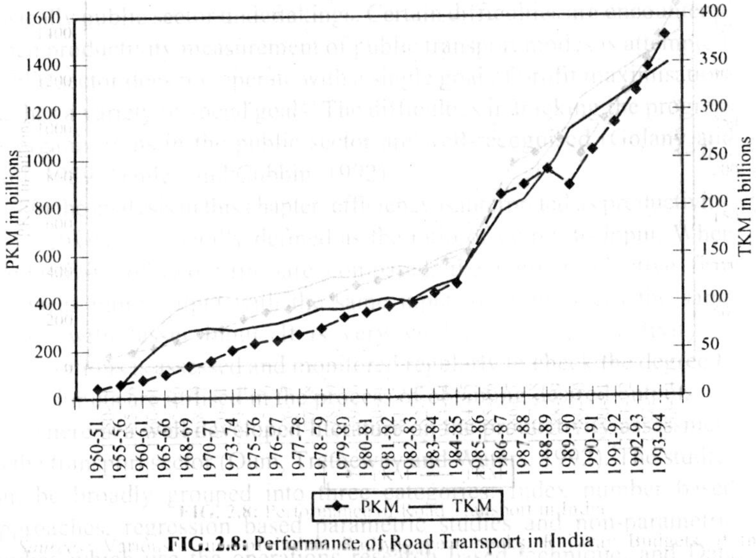

FIG. 2.8: Performance of Road Transport in India

Sources: Various issues of Indian Railway year books, Railway Budgets of the Government of India and CMIE (1999).

* Please note that a regular time series data on road transport performance was available only till the year 1988-89. After this year, the only data available is for the year 1993-94 from IIR (1996). In the figure, the data points for the years 1989-93 have been interpolated.

per year for the period 1970-81, but shot up to above 11 per cent per year during 1980-89. Using the data available in IIR (1996), the growth rate during 1988-94 was about 8.8 per cent per year.

Thus road transport in India in recent years is characterised by a dramatic rise in its performance, which is similar to the trends observed in many parts of the world (Schafer, 1998). There are many reasons for this. The door-to-door service offered by this mode is not possible in other modes of transport. The investment in capacity augmentation in this transport mode is shared by many—by the government for laying roads and by the individual owners of vehicles. However, such a huge increase in performance also involves huge opportunity costs. Road transport is relatively costlier, more energy intensive and more polluting (compared to railways and waterways, wherever applicable)*. Hence, it will be in the national interests if efforts are made to check the growth of this mode of transport, and substitute by railways and waterways by suitably diverting the investments.

The tremendous growth in road transport is due to an equally rapid growth in the population of vehicles. Table 2.2 gives the trend of the registered vehicles over the past years. The number of all the vehicles have registered a higher compound growth rate during the last decade. While the rate was 9.3 per cent per year during the seventies, eighties have recorded a rate of 14 per cent. Of these vehicles, perhaps the most significant increase in the growth rate (compared to that of seventies) occurred for Two wheelers, and Cars, Jeeps and Taxis. Buses also recorded a higher growth rate during the last decade.

Two wheelers constituted a major portion, occupying 66.53 per cent of total vehicles in 1991-92. While the total number of passenger buses is estimated to have more than doubled during the last decade, the share of public sector buses in the country as a whole has declined by 26.66 per cent, from about 45.5 per cent in 1980-81 to 32.7 per cent in 1989-90.

Only limited data are available for analysis of the performance of the passenger road transport. The most structured data are available on the performance of the State Transport Undertakings (STU). The details are shown in Table 2.3 for selected years. The average distance travelled by a single passenger was about 19 km. Specific diesel consumption showed a healthy trend, reducing from 4.53 tonnes per million PKM in 1991-92 to 4.44 in 1996-97. There is, on an average, a steady increase in

* A comparison of energy consumption and pollution emission intensities of various modes of transport is available in the next section (see Table 3.4).

TABLE 2.2: Registered Motor Vehicles in India (Numbers)

Year	Two Wheelers	Cars, Jeeps and Taxies	Trucks	Buses			Other Vehicles	All Vehicles
				Private	Public	Total		
1970-71	5,76,000	6,82,000	3,43,000	56,927	37,073	94,000	1,70,000	18,65,000
1975-76	10,45,000	7,79,000	3,51,000	58,650	56,350	1,15,000	3,79,000	26,69,000
1980-81	26,18,000	11,60,000	5,54,000	92,000	70,000	1,62,000	8,97,000	53,91,000
1981-82	30,65,000	12,43,000	6,13,000	91,000	74,000	1,65,000	9,61,000	60,47,000
1982-83	36,54,000	13,85,000	6,75,000	1,00,000	76,000	1,76,000	10,74,000	69,64,000
1983-84	43,51,000	14,55,000	7,42,000	1,19,000	77,000	1,96,000	12,02,000	79,46,000
1984-85	51,79,000	16,07,000	8,22,000	1,31,000	80,000	2,11,000	13,39,000	91,58,000
1985-86	62,45,000	17,80,000	8,63,000	1,43,000	84,000	2,27,000	14,62,000	1,05,77,000
1986-87	77,39,000	20,07,000	9,84,000	1,52,000	89,000	2,41,000	16,43,000	1,26,14,000
1987-88	93,00,000	22,95,000	11,14,000	1,70,000	95,000	2,65,000	18,40,000	1,48,14,000
1988-89	1,09,65,000	24,86,000	11,79,000	1,79,000	99,000	2,78,000	20,12,000	1,69,20,000
1989-90	1,26,10,000	26,94,000	12,38,000	2,03,000	1,02,000	3,05,000	23,11,000	1,91,58,000
1990-91	1,42,00,000	29,54,000	13,56,000	2,25,000	1,06,000	3,31,000	25,33,000	2,13,74,000
1991-92	1,56,61,000	32,05,000	15,14,000	2,51,000	1,07,000	3,58,000	27,69,000	2,35,07,000
1992-93	1,70,60,000	33,44,000	15,92,000	2,71,000	1,10,000	3,81,000	29,70,000	2,53,47,000
1993-94	1,83,38,000	36,17,000	16,50,000	2,82,000	1,10,000	3,92,000	32,03,000	2,72,00,000
1994-95	2,08,31,000	38,41,000	17,94,000	3,15,000	1,10,000	4,25,000	34,06,000	3,02,97,000
1995-96	2,32,52,000	42,04,000	20,31,000	3,38,000	1,11,000	4,49,000	38,47,000	1,28,56,200
1996-97	2,56,93,000	46,62,000	22,60,000	3,77,000	1,11,000	4,88,000	41,28,000	3,72,31,000
CARG* 1970-81	14.76%	4.95%	4.45%	4.46%	5.95%	5.07%	16.32%	10.13%
CARG 1980-91	16.62%	8.87%	8.48%	8.47%	3.84%	6.71%	9.90%	13.34%
CARG 1990-97	8.84%	6.74%	7.57%	7.65%	0.66%	5.70%	7.23%	8.25%
Share 1996-97	69.01%	12.52%	6.07%	1.01%	0.30%	1.31%	11.09%	100.00%
Share 1970-71	30.88%	36.57%	18.39%	0.00%	1.99%	5.04%	9.12%	100.00%

Note: * CARG = Cumulative Annual Rate of Growth.

Sources: Motor Transport Statistics, plan documents, and various publications of the Government of India.

the volume of PKM effected by these buses indicating their more efficient utilisation. While the private bus operators are expected to have recorded better performance as they operate only on profitable routes (Chand, 1994), structured data on their performance are not available.

TABLE 2.3: Performance of State Road Transport Undertakings

Details	*1979-80*	*1991-92*	*1993-94*	*1995-96*	*1996-97*
Average no. of buses held	66,476	99,093	95,375	1,08,423	1,08,830
Fleet utilisation (%)	na	87	88	87.7	88
Passenger kilometres (billion)	211.7	4376.48	381.70	457.02	453.06
Average distance travelled by a passenger (km)	na	18.40	18.37	19.44	19.12
Tonnes of Diesel per million PKM	na	4.53	4.49	4.41	4.44
PKM per bus (million)	3.19	3.80	4.00	4.22	4.16

Source: Various issues of Performance review of STUs, published by the Central Institute of Road Transport, Pune.

Non-motorised vehicles such as cycle-rickshaws and bicycles constitute an appreciable part of the PKM. They are energy efficient, and are more suited for very short distance traffic. If properly promoted and encouraged, bicycles can be efficient alternatives to the problems of growing automobile use (Gardner, 1998). However, they did not receive sufficient encouragement in the past. Their share in the total PKM is estimated to be steadily declining from about 8.85 per cent in 1961 to 7.08 per cent in 1985 (GOI, 1987). The production of bicycles in India has increased from 5.4 millions in 1983-84 to 13.7 millions in 1999-2000, which represents an average growth rate of 5.65 per cent per year. Table 2.4 shows that this growth is very small compared to the growth rates in the production of motorised vehicles such as passenger cars and two wheelers.

TABLE 2.4: Trends in Production of Transport Equipment in India (1983-2000)

Equipment	*Cumulative Annual Growth Rate (%)*
Bicycles	5.65
Passenger Cars	13.36
Two Wheelers	13.55

Source: Documents on Trends in Industrial Production published by Centre for Monitoring Indian Economy, Mumbai.

Thus we see that the role of non-mechanised travel is reducing. However, its role in promoting sustainable development should be appreciated, as otherwise motorised transport using fossil fuels will be employed in its place. Hence, non-mechanised travel such as bicycles should be encouraged wherever possible (*e.g.* for short distance travel).

2.2.2 *Freight Traffic*

During 1988-89, the volume of road freight traffic was 275 billion TKM, which is more than 2.8 times the performance in 1980-81 (see Fig. 2.8). According to IIR (1996), roadways have accounted for 350 billion TKM during 1993-94. Similar to the case with PKM, the freight transport performance (TKM) by road also has recorded high growth rates in the eighties. The growth rate was merely 3.52 per cent per year for the period 1970-81, but shot up to above 12 per cent per year during 1980-89. Using the data available in IIR (1996), the growth rate during 1988-94 was moderate at about 4.1 per cent per year.

Obviously, the main reason behind such a steep rise in TKM is the tremendous increase in the number of trucks (Table 2.2). While the number grew at an average rate of about 4.5 per cent per year in 1970-81, the growth during 1980-91 was nearly twice this rate, at about 8.5 per cent per year. The rate has slightly slowed in the nineties, but is still high at 7.6 per cent per year (during 1990-97).

More than 99.5 per cent of the trucks are privately owned, and no structured information is available about their performance in more detail. A study has indicated that the average load of trucks grew from 4.12 tonnes in 1951 to about 7.25 tonnes in 1985 (GOI, 1987).

Non-motorised vehicles such as animal drawn carts have constituted about 1.4 per cent of the total TKM in 1985. This has decreased from the share of 8.73 per cent in 1961. Agricultural tractors constituted about 0.54 per cent of the total TKM in 1985 (GOI, 1987).

2.2.3 *Road Infrastructure*

During 1950-92, road length in India grew at a rate of about 4.2 per cent per annum. India had about 2.47 million kilometres of road length at the end of 1996-97, nearly 50 per cent of which were not surfaced. The long distance traffic is served by the national highways and state highways, which accounted for about 1.7 per cent and 6.1 per cent respectively of the total road length. Only about 45.8 per cent of the total villages have been connected by all-weather roads.

Road density, measured as road length per one thousand square kilometre of geographical area has been increasing in India. It was just

122 km in 1950-51, increased to about 279 km in 1970-71, to 452 km in 1980-81, and to 609 km in 1990-91. Road density was about 750 km per thousand square km in 1996-97, which represented a cumulative annual growth rate of about 4 per cent during the period 1950-1997.

As we have seen in the last sub-section, the road transport in India in recent years is characterised by a dramatic rise in its performance. However, there has not been equivalent investment in road infrastructure to match the tremendous growth of road vehicles and road usage. The total road length in India grew at the rate of 2.9 per cent per annum during the last decade, which is extremely small compared to the growth rates of PKM, TKM or the growth of vehicles. Further, the growth rate of road length in the eighties has reduced to nearly half the growth rate that existed during the seventies. Capacity additions to the National Highways, which form about 1-2 per cent of the total road length but account for about 40 per cent of the road traffic in India, has been extremely low. The growth rate of National Highways during the seventies was a mere 2.88 per cent per annum, which further reduced to a paltry 0.56 per cent per annum during 1980-94.

The slow growth of road infrastructure and high growth of transport performance and number of vehicles imply that Indian roads are reaching a saturation point in utilising the existing capacities. If the tremendous growth of the road performance is to continue in future, significant investments are necessary. For example, a recent expert study has estimated a resource requirement of Rs. 410 billion for the creation of sufficient road infrastructure for the period 1996-2001 (IIR, 1996). A whole range of strategies are required to raise funds of this magnitude, including levying special taxes, private sector participation and specialised institutional mechanisms. These policy aspects of Indian transport will be discussed in Chapter 11.

2.3 Air Transport

There are two main functional divisions in civil aviation sector, *viz.*, operational and infrastructural. The former deals with airline capacities (domestic and international) while the latter pertains to airport and allied facility development. The third segment, namely, the regulatory and developmental functions are carried out by the Ministry of Civil Aviation and the offices of the Directorate General of Civil Aviation (DGCA).

Indian Airlines Limited and private operators [scheduled private airlines and air taxi operators (ATOs)] provide domestic air services in India. Air India Limited is mainly responsible for international air services even though Indian Airlines Limited also serves flights to some neighbouring countries. Pawan Hans Limited provides helicopter support services. In 1994, Indian Airlines and Air India have been restructured as public limited companies.

Infrastructural facilities are provided by the Airports Authority of India (AAI). The two authorities, *viz.* International Airport Authority of India (IAAI) and the National Airports Authority (NAA) have been merged with effect from 1st April, 1995 to form AAI.

Air transport primarily caters to passenger traffic, but its share of the total passenger traffic in the country is only one per cent. It has a distinct advantage over surface transport due to its superiority in speed and substantial time saving over long distances.

Fig. 2.9 describes the performance of air transport during the last decade. Air traffic (both domestic and international) accounted for 23,909 million PKM and 548 million TKM (freight and mail) during 1998-99. Two trends can be observed from the figure. There is an upward trend in PKM and TKM till 1989-90, and since then the performance is fluctuating. The growth rate during 1981-91 was moderate at 2.79 per cent and 3.68 per cent per annum for PKM and TKM respectively. Beyond 1990-91, there seems to be a fall in the performance. A main reason for this is the emergence of private air taxi operators (ATO) in the Indian air transport scene. Information on the operations

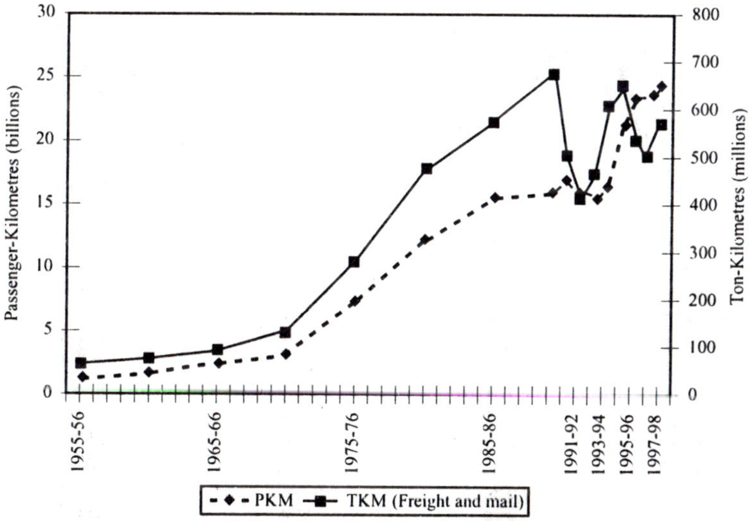

FIG. 2.9: Performance of Air Transport in India (Domestic and International)

Source: CMIE (1999).

of private scheduled operators are included only after 1995-96. These operators carried 2.85 million passengers during 1995-96, which increased to about 5.7 million in 1997-98.

2.4 Water

Waterways of transport is an important mode of transport for both passenger and cargo traffic in India. They include Shipping, Ports and Inland Water Transport.

2.4.1 *Shipping*

Almost 98 per cent of India's overseas trade, in terms of volume, is moved by sea. A relatively small volume of domestic traffic is also carried by coastal shipping. The number of Indian ships has increased from 368 to 484 during 1985-98, which is an increase by 25 per cent. The Gross Registered Tonnage (GRT) has increased from 6 million tonnes to 6.79 million tonnes during the period. Table 2.5 shows the aggregate performance of shipping sector in India.

In 1996-97, Indian vessels handled 51.3 million tonnes of cargo, which formed just below 30 per cent of the country's overseas trade. This share is a significant improvement, as the share of Indian ships has been declining consistently since 1991-92. However, in 1987-88, Indian ships had accounted for over 40 per cent of overseas cargo.

TABLE 2.5: Performance of Indian Shipping Industry and Ports

	Shipping Tonnage—Coastal and Overseas		*Total Cargo Handled at Major Ports (million tonnes)*
	Number of Ships	*Gross Registered Tonnage ('000)*	
1985-86	368	5,950	119.6
1986-87	359	5,479	124.4
1987-88	362	5,469	134.6
1988-89	378	5,593	147.1
1989-90	405	5,922	147.6
1990-91	418	6,027	151.7
1991-92	415	5,939	157.6
1992-93	441	6,288	166.6
1993-94	443	6,267	179.3
1994-95	437	6,346	197.2
1995-96	470	7,002	215.3
1996-97	484	7,052	227.3
1997-98	476	6,878	251.7
1998-99	484	6,785	251.7

Sources: Annual reports of the Ministry of Surface Transport, Government of India, and CMIE (1999).

2.4.2 *Ports*

India has eleven major ports—six on the west coast and five on the east coast and 163 minor and intermediate ports along the nearly 6,000 km long Indian coastline. The major ports are under the executive responsibility of the Central Government. Total capacity of major ports has been estimated at 239.5 million tonnes as on 31st March, 1999. During 1998-99, the total cargo handled at these ports was 251.7 million tonnes (see Table 2.5), which constituted about 87 per cent of the total cargo traffic handled at all the ports in the country.

A break-up of the cargo handled in major Indian ports is shown in Fig. 2.10. Petroleum products constitute the bulk of the cargo. Coal has registered an impressive growth.

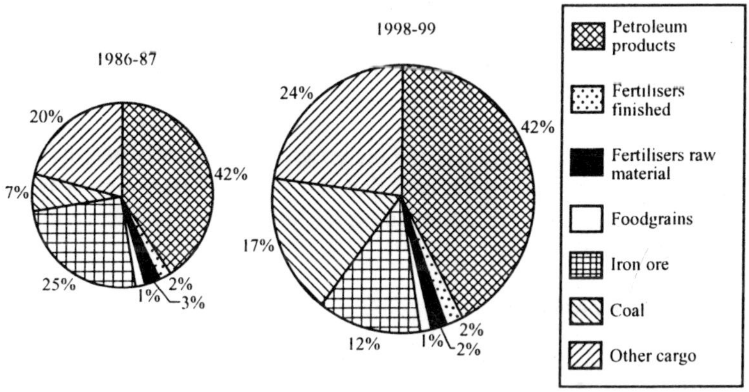

FIG. 2.10: Cargo Handled at Major Indian Ports (Million Tonnes)

Source: CMIE (1999).

2.4.3 *Inland Water Transport*

Inland water transport is also an important means of transport in India. There are a variety of navigable waterways comprising river systems, canals, creeks and tidal inlets in India, which can be fruitfully exploited. Where viable, waterways can be the cheapest modes of transport, pollution free, and energy efficient. The Ministry of Surface Transport is responsible for coordinated development of inland water transport in general and for declaration and development of National Waterways in particular.

The Inland Waterways Authority of India was set up in 1986 for the development, maintenance and regulation of National Waterways in the country. At present, there are three National Waterways in the country (Annual Report, 1995). They are:

(a) National Waterway No. 1: Allahabad-Haldia stretch of the Ganga-Bhagirathi-Hooghly river system (1620 km). Cargo transportation in the stretch Haldia-Farakka-Patna are being carried out by the Central Inland Water Transport Corporation (CIWTC) Limited, and recently by Goa Barge Owners Association.
(b) National Waterway No. 2: Sadiya-Dhubri stretch of the Brahmaputra river (891 km). The CIWTC is operating cargo services between Calcutta and Guwahati.
(c) National Waterway No. 3: The West Coast Canal from Kottapuram to Kollam along with Udyogmandal and Champakara canals (205 km). Kerala Shipping and Inland Navigation Corporation, ABC & Sons, and Hindustan Petroleum Corporation Limited operate cargo services in this waterway.

Presently, no concrete data are available about the progress of inland water transport modes, and the progress is generally perceived to be slow. Recent articles indicate that this mode of transport is being developed especially in Mumbai as an alternative to the saturated suburban train services.

2.4.4 *Urban Transport*

Urban road transport is an important element of road transportation studies. Over the years, many of the Indian cities have become more and more congested (Patankar, 1989). Air pollution due to transport in cities is becoming a cause for major concern. A brief discussion on urbanisation and trends in urban transport is provided below. These issues will be elaborated in later chapters.

2.4.4.1 *Urbanisation*

India has witnessed a tremendous growth in urbanisation since independence. Urban population has increased from 62.4 million in 1951 to 217.2 million in 1991, nearly 3.5 times. In 1991, urban population accounted for 25.7 per cent of total population. Urban population has approximately doubled in two decades (say 1961-1981 or 1971-1991). There were 296 Class I cities (forming just 8.2% of the total towns of all classes) accommodated 65.2 per cent of the urban population in 1991.

Just 23 metropolitan cities (having a population of one million and above) had more than 50 per cent of the population of Class I cities.

Many small metropolitan cities have been registering higher population growth, *e.g.* the population of Bhopal in 1991 was more than 10 ten times its population in 1951.

As per the 1991 Census, India had 93 cities with population above 0.2 million and 73 cities with population above 0.3 million. According to a study made by the Government of India, there will be 83 cities in India by 2001 with a population of 0.25 million. Travel demand in these cities will be 443 billion PKM. Nearly 80 per cent of this demand is expected to be met by road based transport systems (MoUD, 1987).

2.4.4.2 *Patterns of Urban Transport Growth in India*

Urban transport patterns in general, and growth of private modes of transport in particular, closely follow urban population. In the affluent societies of the developed countries, increased urbanisation has increased the number of cars, while the cities of developing countries are witnessing a tremendous growth of two and three wheeler vehicles as the city size increases. India is no exception to this trend.

Table 2.6 provides details on growth of registered motor vehicles in various metropolitan cities of India. Metropolitan cities account for about one-third of total vehicles in India. The table shows that the growth rate of all registered vehicles was more than 10 per cent per year in the big cities of Ahmedabad, Bangalore, Delhi, Hyderabad, Lucknow, Chennai, Nagpur and Pune in the eighties, which dropped to about 9 per cent per year or less for the period 1991-97. However, the growth rate has been quite high (about 10% or more per year during 1991-97) for the next level cities of Bhopal, Cochin, Coimbatore, Madurai, Surat and Vadodara (which are recognised as metropolitan cities according to the 1991 Census). In fact Cochin has recorded a very high growth rate of about 41 per cent per year during the period 1991-97. These trends indicate that the growth rate of vehicles could increase with city size.

The importance of urban transport can be gauged by the sheer magnitude of the annual loss inflicted by the poor traffic and transportation in urban India, which is estimated to be of the order of Rs. 200 billion. The rapid urbanisation and urban transport growth have several energy implications, including problems due to transport, energy consumption, pollution, congestion, waste generation and slums (Linden, 1996; CSE, 1998). Some of these issues will be discussed in more detail in Chapter 7 and Chapter 12 of this book.

TABLE 2.6: Registered Motor Vehicles in Metropolitan Cities in India (Year on 31st March)*

(in '000)

City	*1981*	*1991*	*1997*	*Annual Growth Rate*	
				1981-91	*1991-97*
Ahmedabad	103	374	631.00	13.76%	9.11%
Bangalore	175	577	972.37	12.67%	9.09%
Bhopal	—	130	241.77	—	10.89%
Chennai	120	544	889.82	16.32%	8.55%
Cochin	—	29	226.18	—	40.82%
Coimbatore	—	66	255.74	—	25.33%
Delhi	536	1,813	2,847.70	12.96%	7.82%
Hyderabad	89	443	769.40	17.41%	9.64%
Indore	—	214	360.55	—	9.08%
Jaipur	48	266	448.62	18.68%	9.10%
Kanpur	56	169	—	11.68%	—
Kolkata	—	475	587.58	—	3.61%
Lucknow	53	216	330.75	15.08%	7.36%
Ludhiana	—	202	359.23	—	10.07%
Madurai	—	38	122.16	—	21.49%
Mumbai	307	629	796.91	7.44%	4.02%
Nagpur	45	167	238.58	14.01%	6.13%
Patna	—	180	—	—	—
Pune	107	280	476.37	10.10%	9.26%
Surat	—	197	361.89	—	10.67%
Vadodara	—	162	332.07	—	12.71%
Varanasi	—	112	183.92	—	8.62%
Visakhapatnam	—	142	206.83	—	6.47%
Total for the Metropolitan Cities*	1,639	7,425	11,639.41	6.31%	7.78%
Total for India	5,391	21,374	37,231.00	14.77%	9.69%
Share of Metropolitan cities (%)	30.4	34.7	31.2	—	—

* Columns 2 and 5 in the last three rows pertain only to the 11 cities for which data is available for 1981.

Source: Motor Transport Statistics of India, 1991-94, by Ministry of Surface Transport, 1995, and CMIE (2000).

2.5 Summary

Performance of the Indian transport sector over the past decade has been reviewed in this chapter. The most prominent trend was the dramatically sharp rise in the road transportation, and declining modal share of railways. This trend has serious energy and environmental implications. Important trends in energy consumption and environmental emissions from India's transport sector will be analysed in the next chapter.

3

TRENDS IN ENERGY CONSUMPTION AND ENVIRONMENTAL EMISSIONS

Increased transport performance demands increased fuel consumption, and has energy and environmental implications. The trends in energy consumption and environmental emissions in the context of the operations of the Indian transportation sector will be described in this chapter.

The last few decades have seen a substantial growth in transport energy use and emissions. Energy consumed in transport has a close link with the main spheres of energy policy: economic development, environmental protection and national security. The transport sector is responsible for a growing share of final consumption, energy-related CO_2 emissions and the market for oil on which it is almost exclusively dependent.

Transport sector in India, just like most of the other countries of the world, has shown certain key trends. There is a near total dependence of transport on oil. In the last few years, the share of petroleum products is about 95 per cent, which increased from about 38 per cent in 1970-71. The share of transport in the consumption for petroleum products continues to grow from about 30 per cent in the seventies, to about 35 per cent in the nineties. CO_2 emissions from the transport sector is growing at a high rate.

The effect of growing transport energy consumption has a serious effect on the economic growth of India, which is an oil-importing developing country. We have already seen that, during 1997-98, oil imported by India formed about 24 per cent of its export earnings and about 20 per cent of total imports during the year. We have also seen earlier that transport is the main user of petroleum products, and petroleum products constitute a very high percentage of total energy consumed in transport. Hence, it is very important to study the efficiencies of energy

Note: This chapter is mainly based on Ramanathan (1996).

utilisation in transport in order to formulate policies to promote efficient energy use.

3.1 Energy Consumption: Transport *vs.* Other Sectors

Transport sector was the largest consumer of energy during fifties and sixties. However, its share has gradually come down from about 46 per cent in 1953-54 to about 25 per cent in 1980-81. The share was about 24 per cent in 1997-98 (Fig. 3.1). The reduction in the share of coal traction of railways is mainly responsible for this transformation. Coal traction is highly energy inefficient. As mentioned in Chapter 2, this traction has almost been phased out by Indian Railways (see Figs. 2.3 and 2.7).

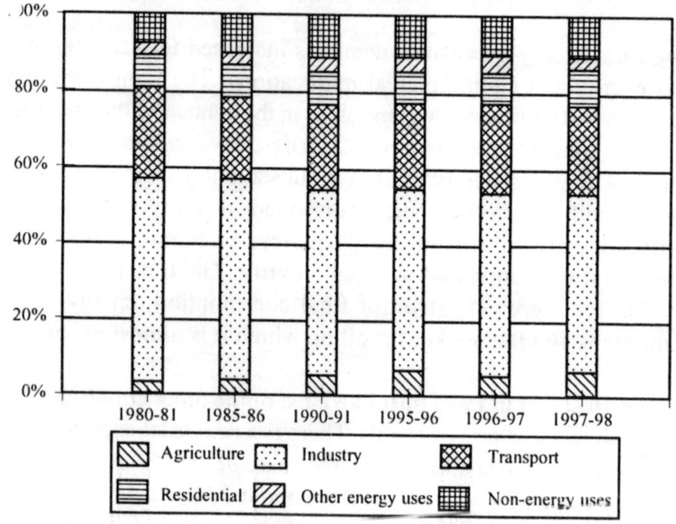

FIG. 3.1: Share of Different Sectors in Commercial Energy Consumption

Source: CMIE (2000).

The share of petroleum products in the total energy consumption of Indian transport sector has increased tremendously. In 1970-71, petroleum products constituted just 38 per cent of the total energy consumption in this sector. This increased to about 90 per cent in 1990-91, and further increased to more than 98.5 per cent in 1996-97. As stated earlier, the excellent growth of road transport, the growth of air transport, and the phasing out of energy inefficient coal traction in railways are the main causes behind such an increase.

In the following sections, the energy consumption in Indian transport will be further analysed in more detail.

3.2 Energy Consumption Trends

During the year 1996-97, Indian transport sector (including shipping) consumed just 0.1 million tonnes (mt) of coal (about 0.12% of total transport energy consumption in that year), 6,599 million kWh of electricity (1.36%), 5 mt of gasoline (13%), 2.16 mt of aviation turbine fuel (ATF) (6%), 30 mt of High Speed Diesel (HSD) (78%), 0.66 mt of Light Diesel Oil (LDO) (0.17%) and 0.35 mt of Fuel Oil (0.88%). Table 3.1 provides the details for rail, road and air for the last few years.

TABLE 3.1: Energy Consumption for Transport in India

(Units for liquid fuels: '000 Tonnes)

Year	*1989-90*	*1990-91*	*1993-94*	*1996-97*
I. *Road and Other Transport (Incl. Agri. Retail Trade)*				
Gasoline	3,491	3,545	3,840	4,955
HSD	16,691	17,156	21,402	28,613
LDO	16	14	14	17
Fuel Oil	88	121	94	87
II. *Railways*				
Coal (MT)	5.73	5.01	1.93	0.1
Electricity (million kWh)	4,070.00	4,112.00	5,538.00	6,599.38
HSD	1,455	1,453	1,441	1,498
LDO	5	4	2	2
Fuel Oil	24	22	16	12
III. *Aviation*				
HSD	11	11	17	6
LDO	1	1	1	1
Fuel Oil	3	4	3	3
ATF	1,775	1,677	1,740	2,158
IV. *Shipping*				
HSD	184	193	199	240
LDO	76	67	65	46
Fuel Oil	346	300	292	249
V. *LSHS*	8	13	12	n.a.
Total Energy Consumption (PJ)	1,237.65	1,240.79	1,387.97	1,751.94
Share of:				
Petroleum fuels	89.10%	90.31%	95.62%	98.52%
Road and other transport	74.39%	76.21%	82.84%	87.17%
Rail transport	16.28%	15.02%	9.09%	7.60%
Air transport	7.13%	6.72%	6.25%	8.64%
Shipping	2.17%	2.00%	1.78%	1.92%

Source: Energy, Centre for Monitoring Indian Economy, Mumbai (March, 2000), and various issues of *Petroleum and Natural Gas Statistics*, Government of India.

During the period 1990-97, coal consumption has reduced very significantly (by about – 43% per year). Consumption of all other fuels have increased, with diesel and electricity registering the highest increase at the rate of about 7 per cent per annum.

The last decade has witnessed a change in the structure of the total transport energy consumption. Railways have accounted the highest transport energy consumption in the early years, while road transport is responsible for the bulk of the energy consumption in recent years. Fig. 3.2 shows the details for the last decade. The total energy consumption by railways has shown a decrease of about 9.6 per cent per year during 1990-97, while that of roadways increased at the rate of 7 per cent per year. As stated earlier, this change is due to two factors: railways has reduced the use of coal traction, which is very energy inefficient, and, the growth of rail transport has been slower than that of road transport. Fuel consumption by air transport registered a growth rate of 2.7 per cent per annum. The share of water transport is not shown in Fig. 3.2 and has been less than 1.5 per cent during the last decade (UN, 1988, 1994).

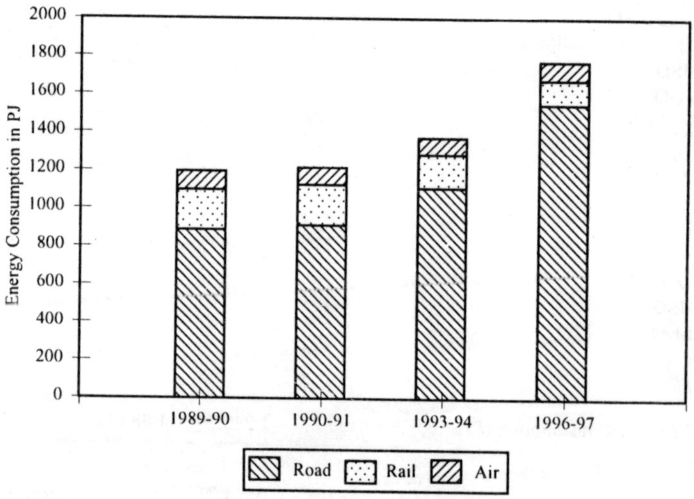

FIG. 3.2: Share of Different Modes in Transport Energy Consumption

Sources: Table 3.1 and CMIE (2000).

As expected, there is a change in the share of different fuels consumed in the transport sector. The shift is from coal to petroleum products (Fig. 3.3). For example, coal constituted about 30 per cent of the total fuel consumption in 1980-81, which decreased to 9 per cent in 1989-90, and further reduced to a mere 0.12 per cent in 1996-97. Electricity formed about 1 per cent in 1980-81, which increased to 1.2 per cent in 1989-90, and further to 1.4 per cent in 1996-97 indicating the increased emphasis put on railway electrification. The share of gasoline in total fuel consumption has increased from about 9 per cent in 1980-81 to above 13 per cent in 1996-97. During the period, the share of diesel increased from 53 per cent to 78 per cent.

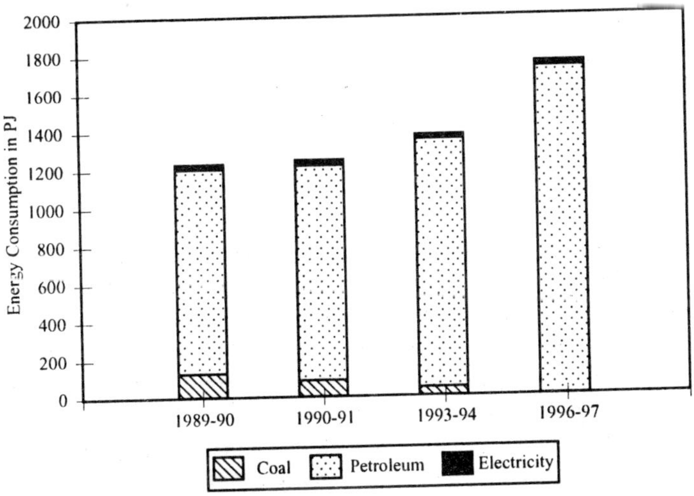

FIG. 3.3: Share of Different Fuels in Transport Energy Consumption

Sources: Table 3.1 and CMIE (2000).

3.2.1 *Railways*

The energy consumption pattern of the railways highlights the drift from coal traction, and a move towards diesel and electric traction. The shift towards electric traction is much more pronounced compared to diesel. For example, during 1990-97, the consumption of electricity grew at the rate of 7 per cent per year, compared to the growth in diesel consumption in railways, which was about 0.44 per cent per year.

Diesel and electric traction have shown efficiency improvements (Table 3.2). For broad gauge, diesel consumption for passenger traffic has reduced from 5.16 litres per thousand gross tonne-kilometres to 5.05 litres. The efficiency improvements have been more striking in the case of electricity consumption. The reason is that electrification is given priority for high traffic routes.

TABLE 3.2: Energy Consumption per 1000 Gross Tonne-Kilometres (Broad Gauge)

Year	*Passenger Traffic*		*Freight Traffic*	
	Diesel (Litres)	*Electricity (kWh)*	*Diesel (Litres)*	*Electricity (kWh)*
1980-81	5.16	22.3	3.45	13.40
1981-82	5.23	21.3	3.50	12.10
1985-86	5.15	20.7	3.43	11.10
1986-87	5.25	20.8	3.32	10.90
1990-91	5.24	20.7	3.32	8.96
1991-92	5.05	20.5	3.26	9.00

Source: RITES (1993).

3.2.2 *Roadways*

Table 3.1 shows that the energy consumption in road transport has increased in general, while the growth in the consumption has been dramatic in the later half of the past decade. This is in line with the observations on the performance of this sector in the past decade.

Fuel efficiencies in buses of state transport undertakings have registered general improvements (see Table 2.3).

Very few direct data are available for assessing the efficiencies of utilisation of road transport. From the available data, it appears that efficiencies of road transportation have reduced. Table 3.3 shows that the growth of energy consumption by road transport (7% per year) is less than the growth of PKM (11%) and TKM (7.5%), indicating roughly an increase in energy efficiency. A similar observation can show an increase in energy efficiency in rail transport as well. However, it is not possible to compare the improvement in the efficiencies of the two modes because of the different levels of changes in energy consumption and performance. Also, such a simplistic analysis cannot yield the pattern of efficiency changes over time. More sophisticated methodologies are required to track the progress of energy efficiency of the transport modes. Such a methodology, called the Data Envelopment Analysis, can be used for the purpose. This will be described in Chapter 8 of this book.

3.2.3 *Airways*

Nearly 50 per cent increase in energy efficiency in air travel is reported in literature (Dunkerley *et al.*, 1987) in the last decade. In spite of this, air transport is still the costliest, and the most energy intensive of all the modes of transport.

TABLE 3.3: Physical Performance and Energy Consumption in Road and Rail Transport in India

Year	*Railways*			*Roadways*		
	Energy in TJ	*PKM in billions*	*TKM in billions*	*Energy in TJ*	*PKM in billions*	*TKM in billions*
1980-81	2,76,547	209.0	159.0	4,42,590	353	98
1981-82	2,88,503	221.0	174.0	4,59,360	377	103
1982-83	2,84,951	227.0	178.0	4,98,588	408	106
1983-84	2,75,747	223.0	178.0	5,30,511	448	116
1984-85	2,59,278	227.0	182.0	5,73,339	486	124
1985-86	2,54,974	241.0	206.0	6,27,644	850	193
1986-87	2,33,496	257.0	223.0	6,83,686	893	210
1987-88	2,23,517	269.0	231.0	7,55,410	980	238
1988-89	2,07,529	264.0	230.0	8,29,482	905	275
1989-90	1,96,795	280.8	236.9	9,16,163	N.A.	N.A.
1990-91	1,83,191	295.6	242.7	9,39,671	N.A.	N.A.
1991-92	1,74,779	314.6	256.9	10,06,974	N.A.	N.A.
1992-93	1,51,194	300.1	258.1	10,76,886	N.A.	N.A.
1993-94	1,44,332	296.2	257.1	11,53,121	1,500	350
CARG* 80-94(%)	-4.54	2.52	3.49	7.08	10.89	9.52

Note: *CARG = Cumulative Annual Rate of Growth.
Source: Compiled from various publications of Government of India, and Tables in Chapters 2 and 3.

Consumption of the Aviation Turbine Fuel (ATF) has been fluctuating from 1990-91 (Table 3.1). During the period 1990-1997, consumption of ATF has grown at the rate of about 3.67 per cent per year, while the total tonne-km (including passenger, freight and mail) by domestic and international scheduled operations increased by about 3.48 per cent per annum. This indicates that the energy efficiency in air transport remained approximately constant during this period.

3.2.4 *Shipping*

The share of water transport in total energy consumption was 1.45 per cent in 1983-84, which did not show much variations during the decade, and remained at 1.69 per cent in 1991-92 (UN, 1988, 1994). The ratio of the total energy consumption in shipping to the gross registered tonnage, and the ratio of the total energy consumption in shipping to cargo handled at major ports have been decreasing with some fluctuations, indicating an increasing trend in energy efficiency in Indian shipping industry.

3.2.5 *Specific Energy Consumption of Transport Modes*

Specific direct energy consumption, in MJ/PKM, have been estimated for different passenger and freight transport modes. These represent average values computed using actual data for the first few years of the nineties, as there has not been much change in the values over the last few years. The estimates are given in Table 3.4. For example, diesel traction of railways consumed, on an average, about 0.24 MJ for every PKM it has performed, and 0.23 MJ for every TKM it has performed. The estimates in the table provide interesting insights. With the exception of the coal traction, which is on the way out, railways have consumed the least direct fuel energy per PKM or TKM. They are also one of the least emitters of carbon dioxide per PKM or TKM. Hence, development of railways is desirable for a sustainable transport future for India. Energy consumption per PKM by personalised vehicles has been more than twice the corresponding values for public transport modes. The energy consumption per TKM by trucks has been nearly five times more than the corresponding values for rail transport. Finally, data in Table 3.4 show that air transport has been the least energy efficient mode for both passenger and freight transport.

3.3 Environmental Implications

Transport sector is mainly responsible for the severe air pollution existing in the towns and cities, where most of the world's population live. Pollution from petroleum burning engines, whether in cars, trains, ships or planes, also has regional and global significance. Sulphur in diesel fuel contributes to acid rain. Unburnt hydrocarbons, nitrogen oxides and carbon monoxide contribute to regional pollution. The final waste product of petroleum consumption, namely the carbon dioxide, is the most important gas contributing to global warming.

Air pollution due to road transport is of high significance in terms of the quantity of pollutants emitted. In India, it is estimated that vehicular emissions alone account for about 60 per cent of the total pollution from all sources (Patankar, 1991). An international study has indicated that the emission of selected local air pollutants (such as the carbon monoxide, nitrogen dioxide, etc.) in the megacities of India is above the WHO guidelines (Grubler, 1993).

TABLE 3.4: Specific Energy Consumption and CO_2 Emissions from Different Transport Modes in India

	Energy Consumption[a]	*CO_2 Emission*[b]
Passenger		
Rail-Coal	1.39	36.98
Rail-Diesel	0.24	4.70
Rail-Electricity	0.12	6.69
Road-Personalised	0.53	10.05
Road-Public	0.21	4.19
Air	3.34	59.49
Freight		
Rail-Coal	1.62	42.18
Rail-Diesel	10.2	34.48
Rail-Electricity	0.11	6.38
Road	1.63	31.66
Air	39.04	696.43

[a] in MJ per PKM or TKM.

[b] in grams of carbon equivalent per PKM or TKM.

Source: Ramanathan and Parikh (1996, 1999).

3.3.1 *Emissions of Local Pollutants*

In terms of air pollution, the impact due to road transport is much more serious than that of railways as estimated by a study conducted for the German Railways (Table 3.5). Hence, the focus in this section will be on the road transport.

TABLE 3.5: Toxicity of Pollution in Road and Rail Transport (CO equivalents in kg, weighted according to toxicity)

Passenger Transport (kg/PKM)		*Freight Transport (kg/TKM)*	
Road	Rail	Road	Rail
1.9	0.1	1.45	0.1

Source: Peterson and von Weizsacker (1993).

The emissions of local pollutants due to road transport have been calculated using the emission factors estimated by the Indian Institute of Petroleum (IIP, 1985) for Indian vehicles (see Table 1.5). The emissions have been computed using the procedures outlined in the same report. In 1993-94, fuel consumption in the transport sector accounted for the emission of about 1.8 million tonnes of carbon monoxide (CO), 0.6 million tonnes of hydrocarbons (HC), 1 million tonnes of nitrogen oxides (NOx), and 33 kilo tonnes of particulate matter. A detailed break-down in terms of different vehicles is shown in Table 3.6. While gasoline vehicles account for a large part of CO and HC emissions, diesel vehicles account for a majority of NOx, and all the particulate emissions.

TABLE 3.6: Emission of Local Pollutants due to Road Transport in India (KT per Year) in 1993-94

Vehicle Category	*CO*	*HC*	*NOx*	*Particulates*
Gasoline vehicles				
—2 Wheelers	427	266	0	—
—3 Wheelers	119	74	0	—
—Cars, Jeeps and Taxis	697	104	46	—
Diesel Vehicles	526	204	994	33
Total	1,769	648	1,039	33

Source: Ramanathan and Parikh (1999).

Air pollution due to road transport vehicles is particularly responsible for increasing the ambient concentration of local pollutants in urban areas. Concentrations of selected local environmental pollutants for the four megacities of India are shown in Table 3.7. Note that Kolkata recorded a very high concentration of NO_2 during 1985. Chennai recorded the least variability in concentrations.

TABLE 3.7: Annual Mean Concentration of Some Local Air Pollutants in Four Megacities of India (μg/m^3)

Year	*Mumbai*			*Delhi*			*Kolkata*			*Chennai*		
	SPM	SO_2	NO_2	SPM	SO_2	NO_2	SPM	SO_2	NO_2	SPM	SO_2	NO_2
1980	190	30	20	440	38	38	405	38	20	150	14	14
1985	205	22	78	350	60	42	320	50	140	120	8	10
1990	200	40	28	480	30	52	330	50	40	120	12	23
1991	230	28	26	540	34	46	390	62	40	110	8	13
1992	330	18	28	520	22	32	405	38	30	90	10	12
1993	280	24	28	440	16	28	550	46	44	80	8	8

Source: Based on graphs in the Annual Report of the National Environmental Engineering Research Institute, Nagpur, India for the year 1992-93.

3.3.2 *Emissions of Global Pollutants*

CO_2 emissions have been computed using the past energy consumption data presented in previous sections, and emission factors listed in

Table 1.6. The emissions corresponding to electricity consumption are obtained as the emissions of equivalent coal after assuming 30 per cent electricity generation efficiency in coal based thermal power plants. Two-thirds of the total electricity generation in India is assumed to be from coal based thermal power plants, while the remaining is assumed to be from non-CO_2 emitting technologies, namely hydro and nuclear power plants.

Table 3.8 shows the estimates for direct (*i.e.*, fuel related) CO_2 emissions due to transport in India for a few years in the nineties. The direct CO_2 emissions in 1996-97 due to the fuel consumption in transport sector works out to be about 34.77 million tonnes of carbon equivalent (mtC). Road and other transport (including agricultural retail trade) is responsible for more than 85 per cent of the emissions, followed by rail (8%) and air (5.5%). This value may be compared with the estimates of direct CO_2 emissions computed in Parikh and Gokarn (1993). The value was 7.3 mtC for the year 1983-84. These are only direct CO_2 emissions due to transport, and the emissions will be higher when both direct and indirect emissions are considered as has been done using Input-Output analysis by Parikh and Gokarn (1993) and Parikh, Panda and Murthy (1994).

TABLE 3.8: CO_2 Emission by Different Transport Modes (mtC)

Year	*Road and Other*	*Rail*	*Air*	*Shipping*	*Total*
1989-90	17.85	5.28	1.58	0.53	25.24
1990-91	18.34	5.00	1.49	0.49	25.32
1993-94	22.31	3.53	1.55	0.49	27.88
1996-97	29.63	2.76	1.91	0.47	34.77

Source: Ramanathan (1996) and updated by the author.

Emissions due to the transport operations of four megacities of India are shown in Table 3.9 for the year 1993-94. These values have been estimated based upon the share of each of the cities in the registered number of vehicles. For example, gasoline consumption of Mumbai in a year is estimated from the All India data for gasoline consumption assuming the same proportion as the number of gasoline vehicles. Electricity consumption in Mumbai's suburban operation is estimated as follows. From the annual report of Indian Railways, the average share of electricity consumption for suburban operations (which includes the operations in all the four megacities) in total electricity consumption of all electric traction has been estimated. Once this value is available, the share of Mumbai is estimated as proportional to the share of PKM of Mumbai's suburban operations in the total suburban PKM. Electricity consumption due to the rail freight operations originating from each of these cities could not be estimated owing to lack of data, and the CO_2 emissions of Table 3.9 do not include these rail freight operations. Similarly, the estimates of this table do not consider air and shipping operations.

TABLE 3.9: CO_2 Emissions due to Urban Transport in Four Megacities in India (1993-94)

	Mumbai	*Delhi*	*Kolkata*	*Chennai*	*Total*
CO_2 emissions (mtC)	1.70	1.40	1.94	1.34	6.38
Share in All India Emissions	6.11%	5.03%	6.98%	4.81%	22.92%

Source: Ramanathan and Parikh (1997).

Thus, it can be seen that transport operations in Mumbai are responsible for about 1.7 mtC of CO_2 in 1993-94, which forms about 6.1 per cent of the all India transport emissions in that year. The four megacities accounted for about 23 per cent of the total direct CO_2 emissions due to transport operations. Note that this share has been increasing over the years. For example, in 1990-91, urban transport in Mumbai was responsible for about 1.38 mtC, which was about 5.5 per cent of the total CO_2 emissions in that year.

Specific direct CO_2 emissions (arising from the fuel use), in grams of carbon equivalent, have been estimated for different passenger and freight transport modes, and the values are listed in Table 3.4. For example, CO_2 emitted from the fuel consumed by the diesel traction of railways, on an average, was about 6.69 grams of carbon equivalent for every PKM it has performed, and 6.38 grams of carbon equivalent for every TKM it has performed.

A number of policy alternatives are available for curbing the rate of CO_2 emissions: efficiency improvements, intermodal substitution of high CO_2 modes by lower CO_2 modes, use of alternative vehicles which operate on CO_2 friendly and renewable technologies are some of them (Grubler, Nakicenovic and Schafer, 1993). These will be explored in greater detail in Chapter 10.

3.4 Summary

In this chapter, the most important trends in energy consumption and environmental emissions due to fuel consumption from transport sector were analysed. Petroleum fuels provided more than 90 per cent of fuel input to this sector, and road and other transport (other than rail, air and shipping) accounted for more than 80 per cent of the fuel consumption during 1993-94. Energy consumption and environmental emissions due to the energy consumption from Indian transport sector have been increasing at a high rate in the last decade.

As there has been dramatic structural changes in physical performance, energy consumption and associated environmental emissions due to the operations of Indian transport sector, it is important to study this sector in more details. Some of the research efforts to understand the complexities of the transport sector will be presented in the next few chapters. Specifically, the patterns by which the modal shares of different transport modes have been changing over the last few decades will be studied using a logistical model in the next chapter.

PART II

ANALYSIS

Several research and modelling studies on Indian transport sector is presented in this part, which comprises six chapters. The patterns of modal split have been explored using a logistic substitution model in the next chapter. Econometric models of gasoline consumption and transport performance are presented in Chapters 5 and 6 respectively. A logistic relationship between number of vehicles and population in Indian cities is identified and empirically tested using a logistic regression model in Chapter 7. Relative energy efficiency of rail and road transport modes is explored using a linear programming based Data Envelopment Analysis model in Chapter 8. The last chapter of this part assesses the performance of selected State Transport Undertakings in India using Data Envelopment Analysis.

Knowledge on some modelling tools will be required to understand these six chapters. Specifically, Chapters 5 and 6 require basic understanding of econometric modelling, and the more recent technique of cointegration modelling. Chapters 8 and 9 require knowledge on linear programming, and an advanced tool based on linear programming, called the Data Envelopment Analysis. Cointegration modelling and Data Envelopment Analysis are presented briefly in Appendices 1 and 2 respectively.

PART II

4

AN ANALYSIS OF MODAL SPLIT IN INDIAN TRANSPORT

In general, once an investment is made, the possibilities of fuel switching is minimal for at least about a decade in the transport sector. Hence, investments must be made after due understanding of the likely changes in modal split. An understanding of the patterns of modal split can enable policy makers to formulate policies for ensuring sustainable transport development.

There exist a few studies in the literature, which examine the patterns of modal split in the transport sector using the logistic competition approach. While there has been studies on the modal splits with examples from developed countries (Marchetti, 1987; Grubler and Nakicenovic, 1991), similar studies are not available for developing countries in general and for India in particular. In this chapter, a similar analysis is described in the context of the Indian passenger transport. Specifically, the prevailing pattern of competition among major passenger transport modes is studied using the logistic competition approach (Nakicenovic, 1979).

4.1 The Logistical Substitution Model

When two technologies exist for satisfying the same need, the substitution of the older by the newer is found to follow a logistic pattern (Nakicenovic, 1979). This finding stems from the binary technological substitution model formulated by Fisher and Pry (1971). The basic assumption postulated by them is that once substitution of the new for the old has progressed as far as a few per cent, it will proceed to completion along a logistic substitution curve defined by the following equation.

Note: This chapter is partly based on Ramanathan (1998a).

$$f/(1-f) = \exp(\alpha t + \beta) \quad ...(4.1)$$

where t is the independent variable representing time, α and β are constants, and f is the fractional market share of the new technology. The logistic curves shown in Fig. 4.1 can be captured using Equation 4.1, where the Y-axis is the modal split f.

Note that Equation 4.1 can be linearized by taking logarithms on both the sides.

$$\log[f/(1-f)] = \alpha t + \beta$$

Thus when $\log[f/(1-f)]$ is plotted against time, a linear pattern will confirm the logistic relationship. Instead of plotting $\log[f/(1-f)]$, one can also plot $f/(1-f)$ on a logarithmic scale.

When there are more than two competing technologies, logistical substitution cannot be preserved in all cases of substitution. Of the three phases of technological change, namely growth, saturation and decline, growth and decline are found to follow logistical pattern, while saturation is not. At any given period, there exists competition between saturating technology and all other technologies.

Such a logistical model has already been validated for the energy and transport systems of several countries. Marchetti (1987) showed that the substitution of horses by cars at the beginning of this century in US followed the logistical pattern. A similar analysis was carried out by Grubler and Nakecenovic (1991) for competition among different modes (cars, bus, rail, air and boat) in the USA, (former) USSR and France for intercity and/or intracity passenger traffic. A similar analysis on the Indian transport performance is presented in this chapter.

4.2 Analysis of Modal Split in Indian Transport

Fig. 4.1 shows the result of the logistic analysis on the aggregate performance of passenger transport. First of all, it validates the logistic pattern of development in Indian transportation sector, as the graph, which plots the ratio $f/(1-f)$ on a logarithmic scale, shows approximately linear relationships for all the three competing modes of passenger travel in India, *viz.*, rail, road and air. The graph shows that rail transport is on the decline, which is rapidly getting substituted by road. Road transport is in its growth phase.

Similarly, Fig. 4.2 gives a similar relationship for substitution among rail, road and air for freight transport in India.

However, the result of this logistical competition analysis is disturbing for the development of sustainable transport in India. The graph shows that railways are losing their share in the modal split in India. The shares of road and air are steadily increasing, with road occupying a major share. According to the logistic regression equations, the modal split in passenger traffic in the year 2010-11 is expected to be about 8.9 per cent, 89.6 per cent and 1.5 per cent for rail, road and air respectively.

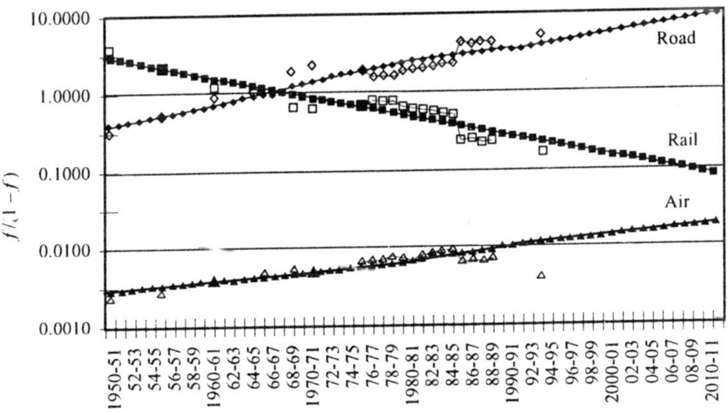

FIG. 4.1: Logistical Competition among Major Modes of Passenger Transport in India

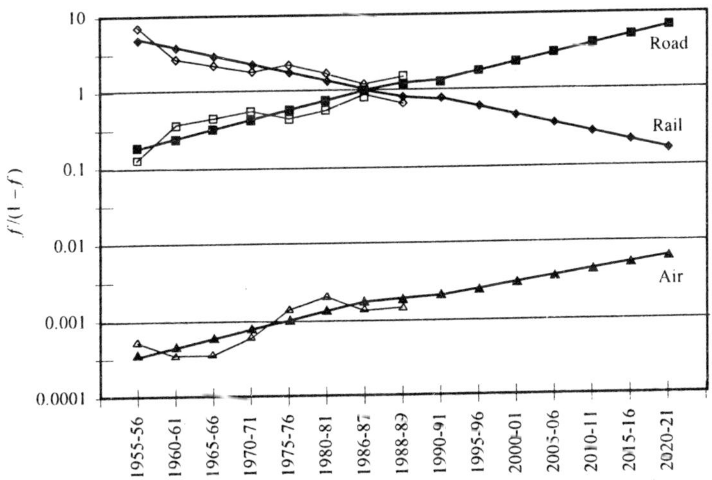

FIG. 4.2: Logistical Competition among Major Modes of Freight Transport in India

We have already seen in the previous chapter that rail transport consumes the least energy per PKM or TKM and results in the least direct emissions per PKM or TKM. Hence, it is necessary to reverse this trend of reducing modal split of railways. The basic assumption of logistical substitution, which states that substitution of the new for the old will proceed till completion, holds good only in the absence of any external control. However, controls on the extent of substitution by devising suitable policies can check the growth of road transport and improve the modal split in favour of rail transport. These policies will be discussed in Chapter 11 of this book.

4.3 Summary

It has been shown in this chapter that the growth of different passenger transport modes in India follow the logistic pattern, with rail transport on the decline and road transport in its growth phase.

5

ECONOMETRIC MODELS FOR GASOLINE CONSUMPTION IN INDIA

The Indian economy is poised for accelerated economic growth in the liberalised scenario. Industrial activities are expected to increase resulting in higher GDP, reduction in unemployment and improvement in basic infrastructure. Petroleum industry is vital for the economic development. As a consequence of liberalisation, there will be a huge demand for the petroleum products in the coming years. It is well known that there is a huge demand-supply gap of petroleum products in India.

Gasoline is one of the important petroleum products for which the demand has been increasing over the years. For example, the average annual growth rate of gasoline demand was about 5 per cent during 1990-97 (see Table 3.1). It has registered the third highest growth in transport fuel consumption in India during the period, after electricity and diesel. The growth rate is expected to increase to more than 12 per cent per annum in the next fifteen years (Rao and Parikh, 1996). Such a sharp growth is expected to continue in the near future because of the increased economic activities caused by economic reforms. The production of road vehicles is likely to increase because of several tie-ups resulting in India after the economic reforms, and this increase in the number of vehicles is likely to sharpen further the growth of gasoline demand. Hence, it is necessary to study the patterns in gasoline demand in India.

There are several studies estimating the demand for gasoline in the industrialised countries. For example, the relationship between gasoline

---

Notes: 1. This chapter requires understanding of the basics of econometric modelling. Please consult appropriate materials such as Koutsoyiannis (1977). Section 5.2 requires knowledge on advanced cointegrating econometrics, which is briefly described in Appendix 1.

2. This chapter is based on two different econometric studies. The studies will be indicated in appropriate sections.

consumption and vehicle stock in Switzerland has been analysed by Wasserfallen and Guntensperger (1988). Baltagi and Griffin (1983) have studied the gasoline demand in the OECD countries. McRae (1994) has used a similar approach to study gasoline demand in several developing Asian countries. Blum, Foos and Gaudry (1988) have studied the relationship for the case of West Germany. A review and analysis of recent studies on aggregate time series gasoline demand models is also available in this article. Dahl and Sterner (1990) have provided another survey of the gasoline demand models. Some studies such as Garbacz (1989) for a specific country, Taiwan and some such as Dunkerley and Hoch (1987) for a collection of developing countries address the issue of estimating the gasoline demand in the case of developing countries. Particularly, McRae (1994) used econometric models to estimate the gasoline demand in the case of developing Asian countries, including India. All his estimates were based on data from 1973 to 1987. In the changed liberalised scenario of India with structural adjustment in the nineties, it becomes imperative to look at the demand pattern for gasoline with enhanced data set including the nineties.

In this chapter, two different econometric models for estimating gasoline consumption in India, will be discussed. One is a relatively simple multi-variate regression model and the other is a relatively sophisticated regression model that makes use of cointegrating relationships between variables representing transport performance and other macroeconomic variables.

5.1 A Simple Econometric Model*

5.1.1 *Econometric Model and Database*

The simple econometric models for estimating the gasoline demand are generally drawn from the ones discussed by McRae (1994). In addition to the price of the gasoline and the stock of motor vehicles in the economy, the demand for gasoline depends on the general levels of income of the people. Therefore, the relevant variables for the purpose of modelling are the actual gasoline consumption, the real GDP of the economy, the price of gasoline, the actual stock of motor vehicles and the total/urban population during the year over the period under consideration.

Generally, the econometric modelling of gasoline consumption begins with the following identity (Baltagi and Griffin, 1983).

*This section is based on Ramanathan and Geetha (1998).

gasoline demand = [distance/vehicle] . (number of vehicles) . [1/efficiency]

where efficiency is defined as the distance travelled per unit of gasoline. Obviously, appropriate normalisation has to be done. For example, gasoline demand has to be normalised on a per vehicle or per capita basis. Using appropriate proxy variables to capture the effects of the terms in the right hand side of the identity and with relevant normalisation, one arrives at the log-log or double log form of econometric model to estimate the gasoline demand. In the log-log form the coefficients represent the elasticities of the respective variables. In this chapter, the basic econometric models used for estimating the gasoline demand are

$$\ln [G/N]_t = \alpha_0 + \alpha_1 \ln [Y/N]_t + \alpha_2 \ln [P]_t + \alpha_3 \ln [V/N]_t + u_t \qquad t = 1, 2, ... T \qquad (5.1)$$

$$\ln [G/NU]_t = \beta_0 + \beta_1 \ln [Y/N]_t + \beta_2 \ln [P]_t + \beta_3 \ln [V/NU]_t + v_t \qquad t = 1, 2, ... T \qquad (5.2)$$

$$\ln [G/V]_t = \gamma_0 + \gamma_1 \ln [Y/N]_t + \gamma_2 \ln [P]_t + \gamma_3 \ln [V/NU]_t + w_t \qquad t = 1, 2, ... T \qquad (5.3)$$

where

G — the gasoline consumption in tonnes
N — total population in millions
NU — the urban population in millions
Y — the real GDP in million rupees in 1980-81 prices
P — the gasoline price index with 1980-81 as the base year
V — the stock of gasoline vehicles in thousand units
t — the time period
u_t, v_t, w_t — error terms

The variable G/N represents the gasoline demand normalised on a per capita basis. This dependent variable is considered widely in the literature while estimating the gasoline demand (see for example Eltony and Al-Mutairi, 1995). The variable Y/N gives the real per capita income. The stock of gasoline vehicles, V includes the passenger cars, two and three wheelers in the country. The number of vehicles per capita is represented by V/N. In Equation (5.2), NU replaces N giving the gasoline demand and number of vehicles normalised on the basis of per capita urban population. This normalisation is justified as urban population consumes a larger part of gasoline. In the left-hand side of Equation (5.3) the gasoline demand is normalised on a per vehicle basis. The Equations (5.1) to (5.3) represent the basic models

In addition to the variables listed above, several other variables were attempted to arrive at robust models capturing the gasoline demand for the Indian economy. One possible adjustment can be based on average gasoline consumption per vehicle by vehicle type. But as the data on gasoline consumption by different vehicle types are not available, this adjustment could not be used. Therefore, the following was attempted. In place of stock of vehicles, V, an equivalence of V incorporating the efficiency of the gasoline driven vehicles was introduced. Gasoline is used for two, three wheelers and passenger cars in the Indian context. V is the total stock of these vehicles in India. The efficiency of the various types of gasoline driven vehicles are generally different. One measure of efficiency can be in terms of the gasoline consumed for covering one km distance by various types of vehicles, that is in terms of the mileage given by different vehicles. We replaced V by V_{EQ} where V_{EQ} is defined as follows.

$$V_{EQ} = \text{No. of cars} + 0.5\,(\text{No. of 3-wheelers}) + 0.33\,(\text{No. of 2-wheelers}) \tag{a}$$

$$V_{EQ} = \text{No. of cars} + 0.5\,(\text{No. of 3-wheelers}) + (15/45)\,(\text{No. of 2-wheelers}) \tag{b}$$

$$V_{EQ} = \text{No. of cars} + 0.5\,(\text{No. of 3-wheelers}) + (12.5/40)\,(\text{No. of 2-wheelers}) \tag{c}$$

The mileage in kilometres per litre assumed in the case of (a), (b) and (c) are 10 for cars, 20 for 3-wheelers, 30 for 2-wheelers; 15 for cars, 30 for 3-wheelers, 50 for 2-wheelers; 12.5 for cars, 25 for 3-wheelers, 40 for 2-wheelers respectively. The models using V and V_{EQ} gave more or less similar results.

Further, an equivalence of the variable *NU* was also attempted. The purpose of using the variable *NU* is basically to normalise the gasoline consumption and the stock of vehicles with appropriate population that uses gasoline. The Indian economy is about 25 percentage urbanised as per the 1990-91 data. There is also a good percentage of people consuming gasoline in the rural sector of India. Ideally, it would have been better to consider the percentage of people above a certain income level as potential consumers of gasoline. But, generally, the income data at the household level are not available. So it was felt that it would be better to decide the percentage of population using gasoline as a function of the basic subsistence level, defined as *poverty line*. In India, the survey on consumer expenditure is conducted periodically by National Sample

Survey Organisation. These surveys provide the vital information on the frequency distribution of households according to the consumption expenditure classes defined in terms of Indian rupees. Considering a basic consumption basket of commodities, the poverty line is estimated. This is updated every year adjusting for fluctuations in the prices of the commodities. The percentage of people above two and three times the poverty line was used as potential consumers of gasoline in the place of *NU* and the gasoline demand models were estimated. But they turned out to be poor fits. Models incorporating time trends were also attempted.

The data used for estimation cover the period 1970-71 to 1993-94. Data for the year 1971-72 could not be included, as the data for all the variables under consideration are not available for that year. Data have been obtained from various sources including CMIE (1996), the various issues of the basic statistics on the Indian economy published by the Centre for Monitoring Indian Economy, Mumbai, various issues of the National Accounts statistics, Petroleum and Natural Gas statistics published by the Government of India, the India Database (Chandok, 1990), and various issues of TEDDY published by the Tata Energy Research Institute(latest name is The Energy and Resources Institute), New Delhi.

5.1.2 *Empirical Results*

Over the period under consideration, the gasoline demand for the Indian economy ranged between 1,453 and 3,840 thousand tonnes with an average of 2,184.4 thousand tonnes whereas the stock of gasoline driven vehicles ranged between 1,258 to 21,955 thousand units (see Table 5.1).* Between 1970-71 and 1993-94 the GDP increased by more than 2.6 times in real terms with 2,360.64 billions reported for the year 1993-94. The population of India ranged between 541 and 888 millions with the range of urban population being 107.66 and 231.28 millions.

The behaviour of the dependent and independent variables over the time period under consideration is plotted in Fig. 5.1. Note that population data are plotted against the right Y-axis. The figure reveals existence of correlation between the independent and the dependent variables.

* It is interesting to note the large variation in gasoline consumption per vehicle per year in 1970-71 and 1993-94. There are at least two reasons for such a large variation. The variation can be explained mainly by the very different vehicular mix in the two years. The share of two-wheelers in total gasoline consuming vehicles rose tremendously from about 45 per cent in 1970-71 to more than 83 per cent in 1993-94. This change in vehicular mix, coupled with the increase in vehicular efficiencies, can explain the variations in the gasoline consumption per vehicle in the two years.

TABLE 5.1: Basic Statistics of the Variables

	N in Millions	*P*	*NU in Millions*	*G in Tonnes*	*V in '000 Units*	*Y in Millions*
Average	712.22	130.93	167.21	21,84,391	7,728	14,70,417
Max	888.00	324.14	231.28	38,40,000	21,955	23,60,640
Min	541.00	23.22	107.66	14,53,000	1,258	9,04,260
SD	105.36	84.92	37.72	9,05,160	6,577	4,63,549

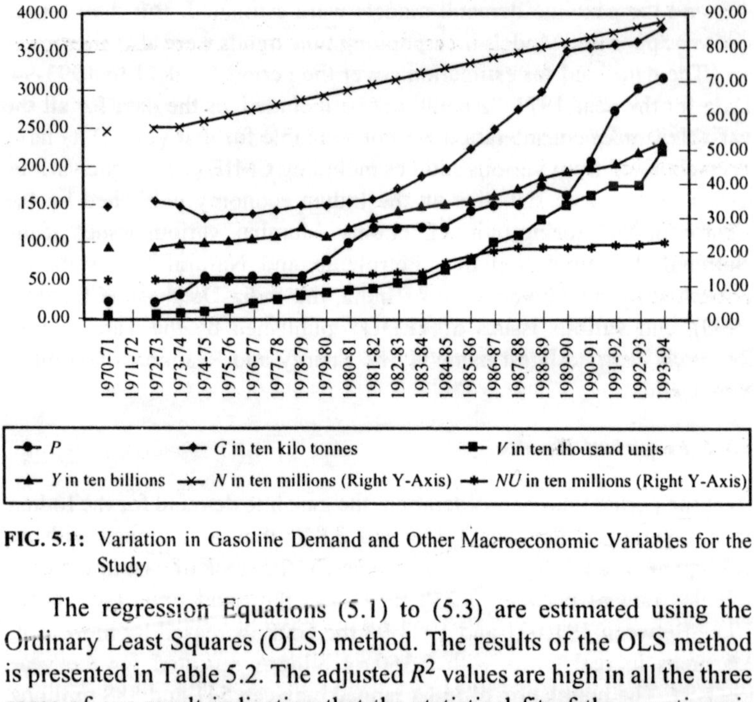

FIG. 5.1: Variation in Gasoline Demand and Other Macroeconomic Variables for the Study

The regression Equations (5.1) to (5.3) are estimated using the Ordinary Least Squares (OLS) method. The results of the OLS method is presented in Table 5.2. The adjusted R^2 values are high in all the three cases of our result indicating that the statistical fit of the equations is good. But, the Durbin-Watson test for autocorrelation revealed the existence of correlation between the error terms. Note that in the case of OLS estimates of the parameters have the expected signs in Equations (5.1) and (5.2). In the case of Equation (5.3), the signs turned out to be inappropriate in addition to the presence of autocorrelation.

Based on these results, an attempt has been made to correct for autocorrelation. The failure of Durbin-Watson test can be due to the presence of autocorrelation or due to the omission of some dependent variables. We checked for omission of some relevant lagged variable

TABLE 5.2: Results based on OLS Method

Dependent Variable	*Independent Variables*					*Adj.* R^2	*D-W Stat.*
	Intercept	ln *(Y/N)*	ln *(P)*	ln *(V/N)*	ln *(V/NU)*		
ln *(G/N)*	−1.69***	1.43**	−0.42*	0.35***	—	0.92	0.88
	(−0.53)	(3.23)	(−5.85)	(2.97)			
ln *(G/NU)*	−0.60***	1.46***	−0.46*	—	0.32**	0.86	0.80
	(−0.53)	(2.91)	(−6.40)		(2.25)		
ln *(G/V)*	−1.72***	1.44**	−0.42*	−0.65*	—	0.98	0.89
	(−0.53)	(3.23)	(−5.78)	(5.49)			

Note: Value of the *t*-ratio is given in the parenthesis below each estimated coefficient.
D-W is the Durbin-Watson autocorrelation test statistic.
*, **, *** indicate the 1 per cent, 5 per cent, 10 per cent level of significance of the estimated coefficients.

like Y_{t-1}, but it did not result in any improvement of the results. Finally, we corrected for autocorrelation and the second order correlations led to better fits.* The results of the econometric models with autoregression representing the gasoline demand for the Indian economy are given in Table 5.3.

TABLE 5.3: Results based on Autoregression Procedure

Dependent Variable	*Independent Variables*				
	Intercept	ln *(Y/N)*	ln *(P)*	ln *(V/N)*	ln *(V/NU)*
ln *(G/N)*	5.98*	0.34***	−0.35*	0.51*	—
	(4.27)	(1.83)	(−4.58)	(6.00)	
ln *(G/NU)*	6.88*	0.34**	−0.35*	—	0.46*
	(6.40)	(2.25)	(−5.30)		(5.90)
ln *(G/V)*	6.13*	0.32***	−0.35*	−0.49*	—
	(4.35)	(1.71)	(−4.50)	(−5.69)	

Note: Value of the *t*-ratio is given in the parenthesis below each estimated coefficient.
*, **, *** indicate the 1 per cent, 5 per cent, 10 per cent level of significance of the estimated coefficients.

In the models (5.1) and (5.2) the signs of the coefficients are correct and significant. In the case of model (5.3), the sign of the coefficient of the variable representing the per capita stock of vehicles is incorrect; further, the effect of per capita GDP on the gasoline demand turns out to be insignificant. So, the models (5.1) and (5.2) corrected for

* Procedure "*Autoreg*" of the econometric package SAS was used in this case.

autocorrelation turn out to be better fits for estimating the gasoline demand for the Indian economy. As has been pointed out the coefficients of the regression models represent the elasticities of the respective variables. The GDP per capita elasticity (hereafter referred as *income elasticity*) and the price elasticity are 0.34 and 0.35 respectively for both the models. The vehicle per capita elasticity (hereafter referred as *vehicle elasticity*) is 0.51 and 0.46 respectively for models (5.1) and (5.2). Knowledge about these elasticities is useful in making policy decisions. For example, the income elasticity for gasoline in India is shown in this chapter to be around 0.35, which means that if the GDP per capita increases by one per cent, then there is likely to be an increase in per capita gasoline consumption by 0.35 per cent. Thus, future gasoline consumption can be estimated if the future trends in GDP are known.

The results of this simple econometric study can be compared with those of McRae (1994). Table 5.4 provides the details of comparison. Before making the comparison, it is important to note that the Indian data used by McRae (1994) pertains to fifteen years (1973-1987) prior to the initiation of the liberalisation process in India, whereas our data pertains to 23 years (1970-1994) which includes some years after liberalisation. Hence the results of the two studies are not perfectly comparable. The results of McRae (1994) for India has indicated auto-correlation (DW reported is 2.88), but no remedial measures were reported. In our study, the correction for autocorrelation is done while obtaining the robust econometric model representing the gasoline demand. Note that the price elasticities reported by the present study compare well with those reported in McRae (1994). Income elasticity reported in McRae (1994) compares well with the OLS estimates reported in Table 5.2, but it has reduced drastically (indicating relative inelasticity) when adjustments are carried out to correct for autocorrelation. McRae (1994) has reported a negative vehicle elasticity, but the present study has reported positive vehicle elasticity, which is more appropriate.

TABLE 5.4: Comparison of Results

Study	*Method of Estimation*	*Income Elasticity*	*Price Elasticity*	*Vehicle Elasticity*
McRae (1994)				
(Estimates for India)	OLS	1.384	–0.321	–0.358
Model 5.1	OLS	1.43	–0.42	0.35
Model 5.2	Autoregression	0.34	–0.35	0.51

Thus, the best fitted autoregression econometric model of this section has indicated an income elasticity of 0.34, vehicle elasticity of 0.51 and a price elasticity of –0.35 for India. This model may be considered as a first step in obtaining better robust econometric models for estimating gasoline demand for the Indian economy. In the next section, a more sophisticated econometric modelling methodology, namely cointegrated model, is employed for the same set of data. It can be seen later that this newer methodology provides much more insight to the analysis of gasoline demand, including short-term and long-term elasticities.

5.2 Cointegration Econometric Analysis*

In this section, the relationship between gasoline demand, national income and price of gasoline in India is empirically examined using cointegration and error correction techniques. These are some of the widely researched techniques in the econometric literature.

Studies confirming the existence of cointegrating long-run relationship between gasoline demand and other macro-economic variables have been reported. For example, Bentzen (1994) and Eltony and Al-Mutairi (1995) have studied the behaviour of gasoline consumption in Denmark and Kuwait respectively using cointegration. Samimi (1995) has identified cointegrating relationship between road transport energy demand and other macro-economic variables in Australia. Cointegration has also been used to identify long-run relationships between industrial energy demand in G-7 countries (Jones, 1997), and electricity demand in Turkey (Karbuz *et al.*, 1997) and in Taiwan (Chen, 1997). Masih and Masih (1997a) have reported cointegrating relationship among energy consumption, real income and prices in energy dependent newly industrializing Asian countries. In this section, the long-run and short-run behaviour of gasoline demand in India is analysed using cointegration analysis.

The method of cointegration econometric analysis has been briefly described in Appendix 1. For more details, readers should consult the references mentioned in the appendix.

5.2.1 *Basic Model and Database*

The econometric models considered in this section is based on the results of the simple econometric model presented in the previous section. In general, several studies have reported income and price to be the

* This section is based on Ramanathan (1999c), and requires knowledge on cointegration econometric analysis (described briefly in Appendix 1).

main parameters in determining gasoline demand. Specifically, the following model will be used for study in this section.*

$$G_t = \alpha_0 + \alpha_1 Y_t + \alpha_2 P_t + V_t \qquad t = 1, 2, ... T \qquad (5.4)$$

where

G — the per capita gasoline consumption in tonnes
Y — the real per capita GDP in million rupees in 1980-81 prices
P — the gasoline price index with 1980-81 as the base year
V — residual.

As before, data used for estimation cover the period 1972-73 to 1993-94.

5.2.2 *Empirical Results*

The first step in the cointegration analysis is to check for the stationarity of all the variables (both dependent and independent). Note that all series have been converted to natural logarithms for the purpose of cointegration analysis. The stationarity tests and all other regression analysis presented in this chapter have been conducted using the econometric software package, Microfit for Windows, Version 4.0. It has been found that all the variables are non-stationary $I(1)$ variables. Details are presented in Table 5.5.

TABLE 5.5: Tests for Stationarity of the Variables

Variables	*Levels*	*First Differences*
G	–0.334(1)[a]	–2.693[b]
Y	0.667(1)	–5.983[c]
P	–0.548(1)	–3.371[b]

a Figures in parentheses represent the number of lags used in the ADF Test.
b significant at 5 per cent level;
c significant at 1 per cent level; Critical values have been obtained from Charemza and Deadman (1992), Table 3, pp. 325-330 ($n = 20$, $m = 0$).

The second step is to estimate cointegrating relationships shown in Model (5.4). The residual V has been found to be stationary $I(0)$, indicating the existence of the above cointegrating relationships among the variables. Details are given in Table 5.6. Thus the long-run income

* Note that this model (5.4) is different from the simple models presented in the previous section (models 5.1 and 5.2). Model 5.4 has not incorporated the per capita vehicle as an independent variable. As will be explained later, this term did not show any evidence of cointegration with per capita gasoline consumption.

elasticity of gasoline has been found in this chapter to be quite high, at 2.682, indicating that a significant increase in gasoline demand can be expected as GDP in India increases. The long-run price elasticity is -0.319, indicating relative inelasticity.

The final step is the construction of ECM. As explained in Equation (A1.3), the first difference of dependent variable have been regressed with the first differences of the independent variables (with appropriate lags), the residual of cointegrating regression (model A1.2 or 5.4) with a unit lag and lag terms of the first difference of the dependent variable. Specifically, the following regression has been performed.

$$\Delta G_t = \beta_0\, \Delta Y_t + \beta_1\, \Delta P_t + \beta_2 U_{t-1} + \beta_3\, \Delta G_{t-1} + U_t \qquad (5.5)$$

TABLE 5.6: Results of Cointegrating Regressions

Dependent Variable	*G*
Constant	–10.923
	(–5.249)[a]
Y	2.682
	(8.359)
P	–0.319
	(–3.890)
Adjusted R-squared	0.902
D-W Statistic	1.156
t-statistic of residual in the unit-root test (without intercept)	–3.331[b]

[a] Figures within parentheses show *t*-statistic.
[b] significant at 5 per cent level; Critical values have been obtained from Charemza and Deadman (1992), Table 2, pp. 319-324 ($n = 20$, $m = 2$).

The results of the regression are detailed in Table 5.7. The ECM shows very good fit. All the coefficients are significant, and have the expected signs. The coefficient of the residual has been found to be significant, confirming the cointegrating relationships presented earlier. Also, there is no evidence of residual autocorrelation in these regressions. The coefficient of error correction term indicates that the gasoline consumption adjusts towards its long-run equilibrium levels at a relatively slow rate, with about 28 per cent of the adjustment occurring within the first year.

The short-run and long-run elasticities are presented in Table 5.8 for comparison. The short-run elasticities are smaller than their long-run counterparts. This is not unusual in the case of large systems, whose long-term responses are more perceptible than the short-term responses.

The smaller short-run elasticities can also be explained by the slow adjustment pattern of use of automobiles by households.

TABLE 5.7: Results of the Error Correction Model

Coefficient	*Value*
ΔY_t	1.178
	(5.178)[a]
ΔP_t	–0.209
	(–3.577)
$U_{(t-1)}$	–0.284
	(–2.205)
ΔG_{t-1}	0.422
	(3.375)
Adjusted R-squared	0.707
DW Statistic	2.075

[a] Figures within parentheses show *t*-statistic.

TABLE 5.8: Comparison of Results

Study	*Method of Estimation*	*Income Elasticity*	*Price Elasticity*
Present section (Long-run elasticities)	Cointegration	2.682	–0.319
Present section (Short-run elasticities)	Error Correction	1.178	–0.209
McRae (1994) (Estimates for India)	OLS	1.384	–0.321
Previous section (Simple model)	OLS	1.43	–0.42

The results of our study can be compared with the results reported in earlier studies. For comparison, the studies by McRae (1994) and the results of the simple model reported in the previous section have been used. The details of comparison are also provided in Table 5.8. Before making the comparison, it is important to note the following basic differences among the models. The Indian data used by McRae (1994) pertains to fifteen years (1973-1987) prior to the initiation of the liberalisation process in India, whereas the data used in this chapter (previous and this section) pertain to 22 years (1972-73 to 1993-94) which includes some years after liberalisation. McRae (1994) considers gasoline demand per vehicle as the dependent variable. Both the models of this chapter consider per capita gasoline consumption as the dependent variable, but the former has considered the number of vehicles per capita as another variable in their model. Such an additional variable could not be considered in this section as the relationship showed no evidence of cointegration. Note that the long-run income elasticity reported by the present study is higher than those reported in the two previous studies, while the long-run price elasticity is smaller. The short-run elasticities are smaller than those reported in the two previous studies.

The elasticities obtained in the study provide valuable policy level information. The higher long-run income elasticity compared to the short-run income elasticity means that the response of gasoline demand to income will be larger in the long-term than in the short-term. High levels of long-run income elasticity indicates that gasoline demand in India is likely to increase quite sharply as the GDP increases. Even the short-run elasticity is more than unity, indicating a faster increase in gasoline demand as GDP in India increases. The results show that gasoline demand is likely to be inelastic to gasoline price changes, both in the long-run and in the short-run.

Increasing the prices of gasoline is considered as one policy option to discourage the use of personalized transport modes in favour of more efficient mass transport modes. However, the empirical results of this chapter indicate a low price elasticity even in the long-run. This means that over-pricing of gasoline as a policy instrument is not likely to be very influential on future gasoline demand in India. Hence other policy options, such as emphasis on conservation, promotion of alternative fuels, etc., will be needed. These will be further discussed in Chapter 11.

6

AN ANALYSIS OF LONG-TERM TRANSPORT PERFORMANCE IN INDIA

In Chapter 2, it has been highlighted that the Indian transport sector has witnessed a very sharp growth in performance in the last few decades, and that this exponential growth has resulted in an equally sharp increase in energy consumption and pollutant emissions. Hence it is necessary to carefully plan the growth of this sector. The performance of this sector has to be properly estimated and future growth has to be accurately predicted, to ensure that adequate infrastructure is made available ahead of the transport demand with due consideration to least cost options. An accurate model which can predict the long-run behaviour of PKM and TKM is thus a prerequisite for an efficient transport planning. In this chapter, an analysis of the long-run relationships between variables representing transport performance and other macro-economic variables in India using the concepts of cointegration and error correction is presented.

The technique of cointegration econometric analysis has been discussed in Appendix 1 and its application described in the previous chapter for the analysis of gasoline consumption. Cointegration based econometric studies have been reported (*e.g.*, Bentzen, 1994) for tackling the issues pertaining to the transport sector. However, most of them have considered estimating fuel consumption in this sector. These studies have been mentioned in the previous chapter. Though the application areas of cointegration have become very extensive, from purchasing-power-parity (Baharumshah and Ariff, 1997) to family-planning (Masih and Masih, 1997b) and interest rates (Mustafa and Rahman, 1995), cointegration studies on analysing the performance levels (such as PKM or TKM in the case of transport sector) are almost non-existent. In the

---

Note: This chapter requires knowledge of cointegration econometric analysis (described briefly in Appendix 1) and is based on Ramanathan (2001).

context of the transport sector, there are only very few simple econometric models for studying the behaviour of PKM and/or TKM (*e.g.*, Parikh, 1980). This chapter describes the application of cointegration to predicting the behaviour of performance levels (PKM and TKM) for the transport sector in India.

6.1 Basic Model and Database

In this chapter, the presence of two cointegrating relationships, one each with PKM and TKM as the dependent variables, is explored. PKM has close relationship with population. As most of vehicles in India are concentrated in urban India, urban population rather than total population is a more relevant variable. In this study, we use the ratio of urban population to total population (denoted as POPRATIO) as it has shown the required cointegration properties to be described later. Several cointegration studies (Bentzen, 1994; Eltony and Al-Mutairi, 1995), as also the previous chapter, have found that gross domestic product and price of gasoline have long-term relationship with gasoline demand. Gasoline is mainly used for passenger transport. Hence, gross domestic product or GDP is chosen as the income variable influencing PKM in this study. As passenger transport uses more than one fuel, a comprehensive mineral oil price index (denoted as PRICE) is used to represent the price variable. Earlier studies (J. Parikh, 1980; see also the previous chapter) have found that industrial operations (measured in terms of the Index of Industrial Production and denoted as IIP) influences freight transport more than the income variable. Hence, for the cointegration analysis of TKM, IIP and PRICE have been chosen as the independent variables.

Data have been obtained from several official documents, including various issues of the monthly abstract of statistics and national accounts statistics published by the Government of India, basic statistics relating to the Indian economy published by the Centre for Monitoring Indian Economy, Mumbai, India.

6.2 Empirical Results

The first step in the cointegration analysis is to check for the stationarity of all the variables (both dependent and independent). Note that all series have been converted to natural logarithms for the purpose of cointegration analysis. The stationarity tests and all other regression analysis presented in this chapter have been conducted using the econometric software package, Microfit for Windows, Version 4.0. It has been found that all the variables are non-stationary $I(1)$ variables. Details are presented in Table 6.1.

TABLE 6.1: Tests for Stationarity of the Variables

Variables	*Levels*	*First Differences*
PKM	0.190	–5.51[a]
TKM	–0.520(1)	–3.69[c]
GDP	0.603(1)	–9.89[a]
IIP	0.205(1)	–4.02[b]
POPRATIO	1.190	–4.85[b]
PRICE	0.142(1)	–4.00[b]

Note: Figures in parentheses represent the number of lags used in the ADF Test; Critical values have been obtained from Charemza and Deadman (1992), Table 3, pp. 325-330.

[a] Significant at 1 per cent level; [b] significant at 5 per cent level; [c] significant at 10 per cent level.

The second step is to estimate cointegrating relationships. The following two relationships have been attempted for each of the dependent variables, PKM and TKM.

$$PKM_t = \alpha_0 + \alpha_1 GDP_t + \alpha_2 POPRATIO_t + \alpha_3 PRICE_t + V_{PKMt} \quad (6.1)$$

$$TKM_t = \beta_0 + \beta_1 IIP_t + \beta_2 PRICE_t + V_{TKMt} \quad (6.2)$$

The residuals V_{PKMt} and V_{TKMt} have been found to be stationary $I(0)$, indicating the existence of the above cointegrating relationships among the variables. Details are given in Table 6.2. Thus the long-run income and price elasticities of PKM are 1.147 and –0.209. The long-run elasticity of PKM with respect to the ratio of urban to total population is 4.414.

Comparing the results of this study with others is difficult because the only available study (Parikh, J., 1980) pertains to a much older time period, and has considered the performances in various modes of transport separately. For example, Parikh (1980) has considered air and land transports separately, and has differentiated rail and road while analysing the road transport.

The final step is the construction of ECM. As explained in Appendix 1 (Equation A1.3), the first differences of dependent variables have been regressed with the first differences of the independent variables (with appropriate lags), lag terms of the first difference of the dependent variable and the residuals of cointegrating relationships (Equation 6.1 or

6.2) with a unit lag. Specifically, the following regressions have been performed.

TABLE 6.2: Results of Cointegrating Regressions

Dependent Variable	*PKM*	*TKM*
Constant	0.684 (0.114)	1.241 (10.147)
GDP	1.147 (4.105)	
POPRATIO	4.414 (2.606)	
PRICE	−0.209 (−1.381)	−0.188 (−4.160)
IIP		1.183 (15.687)
Adjusted R-squared	0.980	0.978
D-W Statistic	1.307	0.622
t-statistic of residual in the unit-root test	−3.98[a]	−3.447[a]

Note: Critical values have been obtained from Charemza and Deadman (1992), Table 3, pp. 325-330 ($m = 3$ for PKM regression and $m = 2$ for TKM regression).

[a] significant at 5 per cent level.

$$\Delta PKM_t = \gamma_0 + \gamma_1\,\Delta GDP_t + \gamma_2\,\Delta POPRATIO_t + \gamma_3\,\Delta PRICE_t + \gamma_4\,V_{PKM(t-1)} + \gamma_5\,\Delta PKM_{t-1} + U_{PKM(t)} \qquad (6.3)$$

$$\Delta TKM_t = \delta_0 + \delta_1\,\Delta IIP_t + \delta_2\,\Delta PRICE_t + \delta_3\,V_{TKM(t-1)} + \delta_4\,\Delta TKM_{t-1} + \delta_5\,\Delta TKM_{t-2} + U_{TKM(t)} \qquad (6.4)$$

The results of the regression are detailed in Table 6.3. Note that the coefficients representing elasticities of the dependent variable with respect to the independent variables have not been found significant. In fact, the variable PRICE does not have the expected sign in the TKM regression. However, in all these regressions, the coefficient of the residual have been found to be significant, confirming the cointegrating relationships presented earlier. Also, there is no evidence of residual autocorrelation in these regressions.

The short-run and long run elasticities estimated by the present study are summarised in Table 6.4. Note that all the short-run elasticities are much smaller than their long-run counterparts, indicating a relative inelasticity in the short-run. As discussed in the previous chapter, this is not unusual in the case of large systems, whose long-term responses are more perceptible than the short-term responses. Being an infrastructural sector, transportation sector requires huge capital input and long gestation periods, which make short-run adjustments quite difficult. The smaller short-run elasticities can also be explained by the slow adjustment pattern of use of automobiles by the consumers, especially the households.

TABLE 6.3: Error Correction Models for PKM and TKM

	PKM	*TKM*
Constant	0.060 (2.024)	−0.044 (−1.679)
ΔGDP_t	0.122 (0.663)	
$\Delta POPRATIO_t$	0.464 (0.288)	
$\Delta PRICE_t$	−0.010 (−0.090)	0.072 (0.907)
ΔIIP_t		0.994 (3.174)
$V_{PKM(t-1)}$	−0.345 (−2.460)	
ΔPKM_{t-1}	0.098 (0.482)	
$V_{TKM(t-1)}$		−0.400 (−2.006)
ΔTKM_{t-1}		0.331 (1.614)
ΔTKM_{t-2}		0.295 (1.558)
Adjusted R-squared	0.047	0.285
DW Statistic	2.073	2.132

TABLE 6.4: Short-run and Long-run Elasticities

Period	*Income*	*Price*	*Ratio of Urban Population to Total Population*
PKM			
Short-Run	0.122[a]	−0.010	0.464
Long-Run	1.147[a]	−0.209	4.414
TKM			
Short-Run	0.072[b]	0.994	—
Long-Run	1.183[b]	−0.188	—

Note: [a] Elasticity with respect to GDP; [b] Elasticity with respect to IIP.

As discussed earlier, the elasticities of the residuals V_{PKMt} and V_{TKMt} show the speed of adjustment towards the long-run equilibrium. The results shown in Table 6.3 show that both passenger and tonne kilometres adjust to their respective long-run equilibrium at a moderate rate, with about 35 per cent of adjustment in passenger kilometres and 40 per cent of adjustment in tonne kilometres occurring in the first year.

6.3 Policy Implications

The elasticities tabulated in Table 6.4 have important policy implications on the future of Indian transportation trends. The long-run income elasticity of PKM has been found in this chapter to be 1.147 indicating that a significant increase in PKM can be expected as GDP in India increases. The long-run price elasticity of PKM is –0.209, while that of TKM is –0.188. Thus, TKM is slightly less sensitive to price variations than PKM. The long-run elasticity of TKM with respect to industrial output in India (*i.e.*, IIP) is 1.183, which shows that significant increase in TKM can be expected as the level of industrial activity in India increases. The long-run elasticity of PKM with respect to the ratio of urban to total population is 4.768, indicating that a huge increase in PKM is expected as urbanization in India progresses.

In a policy perspective, the present study has identified that urban population growth to be the most important variable for controlling the PKM growth. If the ratio of urban population to total population is reduced by 1 per cent, PKM increase can be reduced by as much as 4.4 per cent. The results of this study shows that, as the GDP and IIP for India increase by 1 per cent in future, in the long-run, PKM and TKM respectively will increase by more than 1 per cent. Finally, the low price elasticities identified in this study signify that adjusting the price of mineral oils may not be an effective policy option in controlling future PKM and TKM growth, and that other policy options, such as conservation, alternative fuels, etc. are necessary. The use of these options will be explored in more detail in Chapter 10.

6.3.1 *Forecasting Future Transport Performance*

As cointegration analysis identifies long-run relationships, the above models can be employed for providing long-term forecasts of PKM and TKM in India. The forecasts have been obtained by running a series of ordinary least squares regressions using the models (6.1) and (6.3) for PKM and models (6.2) and (6.4) for TKM, as explained in Engle and Yoo (1987). The results are tabulated in Table 6.5. Note that the growth rates forecasted using the cointegration analysis are higher than the forecasts obtained using simple econometric models (*i.e.*, using model 6.1 alone for PKM and using model 6.2 alone for TKM). Obviously such a sharp growth has a number of significant implications, both in terms of transport investment needs, and energy and environmental concerns. Some of these concerns will be explored in the scenario analysis presented in Chapter 10.

TABLE 6.5: Growth Rates (% per annum) of Forecasts using Regression Analysis

Period	*Model(s) used for Forecasting*	*PKM*	*TKM*
1950-1989	Actuals	8.00	6.22
1970-1989	Actuals	8.58	5.53
1990-2006	Simple Models (Model 4 for PKM and Model 5 for TKM)	7.17	7.74
1990-2006	Cointegration Models	7.85	8.10

6.4 Summary

The long-run behaviour of transport performance in India, expressed in terms of passenger kilometres and tonne kilometres for the passenger transport and freight transport performance respectively, has been analysed in this chapter using cointegrating and error correction analyses. The long-run income and price elasticities of passenger kilometres has been found to be 1.147 and –0.209 respectively. Further its elasticity with respect to the ratio of urban to total population has been found to be quite large, at 4.414. The long-run price elasticity of tonne kilometres in India is also quite low, at –0.188, while its elasticity with respect to industrial output is 1.183. The short run elasticities have been found to be much smaller, but they are insignificant though a strong cointegration is identified among the variables. Their speed of adjustment towards long-run equilibrium is moderate, with about 35 per cent of adjustment in passenger kilometres and 40 per cent of adjustment in tonne kilometres occurring in the first year. The future transport requirements projected using cointegration model has shown that both passenger and freight transport are likely to increase at a high rate in future, at about 8 per cent per annum. As the low price elasticities indicate the ineffectiveness of price control as a policy options, it is necessary to consider other policy options to arrest such a rapid growth.

7

A CRUCIAL LINK BETWEEN POPULATION AND NUMBER OF VEHICLES IN INDIAN CITIES

As mentioned in Chapters 1 and 2, India is undergoing rapid urbanisation. This means not only that more people than ever before will be living and working in cities, but also that more people and more goods will be making more trips in urban areas, often over longer distances. Transport is a crucial infrastructure for development and hence vehicular growth closely follows the trend of urbanisation. This has been highlighted using data on vehicular population of some Indian cities in Chapter 2. In this chapter, a crucial link between population and the number of vehicles observed in Indian cities, that is likely to have far reaching consequences for urban planning, will be highlighted. Specifically, it will be shown that the number of vehicles in Indian cities could increase along an S-shaped pattern with population.

7.1 Patterns of Growth of Urban Transport in India

In Chapter 2, an analysis of the growth of registered motor vehicles in various metropolitan cities of India has been presented (See Table 2.6). It was highlighted in that chapter that the trends shown by the data of the table indicate that the growth rate of vehicles could increase with city size.

This observation is graphically depicted in Fig. 7.1* where the trend of vehicular population is plotted with respect to city size (measured in

Note: This chapter is based on Ramanathan (2000a).

* Vehicular population represents the population as on 31st March 2001. Note that the graph for the year 1996 is slightly different from those of the previous years. The reason is the non-availability of data for some cities such as Hyderabad, Kolkata, etc. Data pertaining to Delhi has been excluded, as the number of vehicles in Delhi is much higher as compared to the number in other cities and hence is considered as an outlier.

terms of population) for different years. The figure indicates that the number of vehicles in a city is likely to grow approximately along an S-shaped pattern as the city size increases. The figure also shows the fitted S-curves for two different time periods—the eighties and the nineties. Some statistical details regarding the fitted curves are given in Table 7.1. The F-test indicates a significant fit for the two time periods. Note that the trend is more pronounced in the nineties than in the eighties.

TABLE 7.1: Statistical Details of the Fitted S-Curves

Period	*R-squared*	*F-value**
1990s	0.71	242.70
1980s	0.64	48.25

* Indicates a highly significant fit for both the time periods.

A similar pattern of growth is observed for individual cities also. The growth pattern of the city of Mumbai is plotted in Figure 7.2, which approximately confirms to the S-shaped pattern. The fitted S-curve, also shown in the figure, shows a significant fit, with $R^2 = 0.94$, *F*-value at 90, revealing a very significant fit.

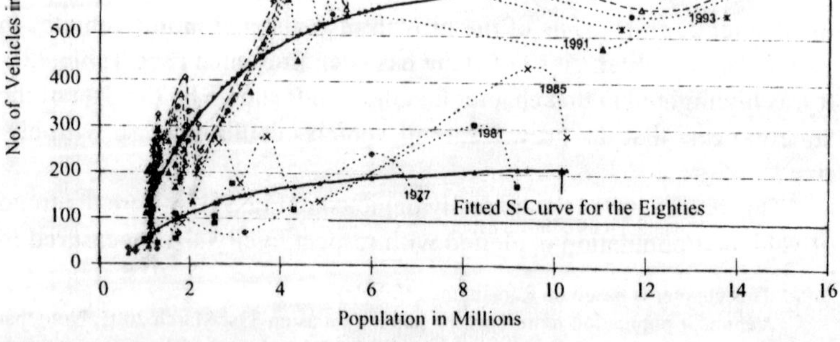

FIG. 7.1: Variation of Number of Vehicles with Population in Indian Cities (excluding Delhi data)

Sources: Various issues of Motor Transport Statistics and Census documents, published by the Government of India.

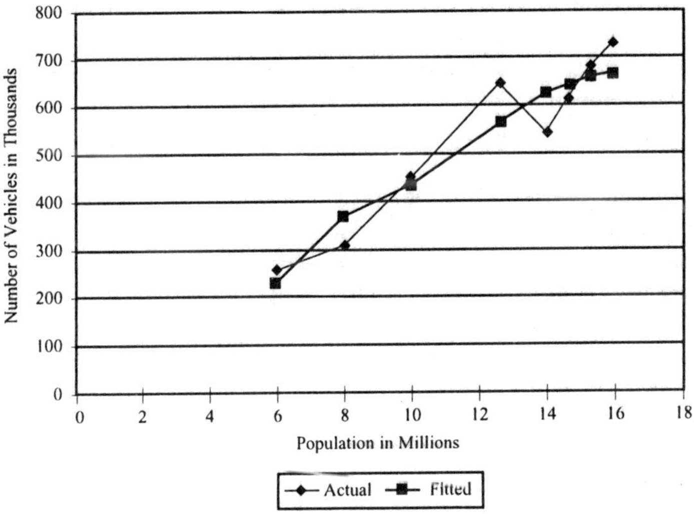

FIG. 7.2: Variation of Number of Vehicles with Population in Mumbai

Source: Same as for Fig. 7.1.

This study seems to be the first one to identify such S-shaped logistic relationship between the number of vehicles and population of different cities. It is hoped that similar patterns will be identified if similar plots for different cities in the world are attempted.

7.2 Some Factors contributing the S-shaped Growth Pattern

It is important to study the determinants of S-shaped growth pattern. Economic growth is a main factor determining the demand for vehicles. The S-shaped pattern can be argued using the following hypothesis involving income levels and availability of transport infrastructure.

Smaller cities obviously have smaller number of vehicles. But, as the city size increases, the number of vehicles tends to grow slowly until the city reaches a certain critical size. This happens when the existing transport network and transport vehicles are enough to meet the demands of the economic activities in these cities. The general income levels of people in these cities also are not high enough in investing more on personalised transport. Once the critical size is reached, the city enters a rapid phase and there is a sudden and rapid rise in the number of vehicles. This rapid growth may be attributed to the level of economic activity in the city. The increased economic activities rise the income level of people, allowing them to invest more in personalised travel. Also, increased economic activities demand a larger mobility of passenger and freight, and larger additions to transport infrastructure and equipment. However, growth of vehicles tends to reduce beyond another critical level. This can happen when infrastructural bottlenecks tend to limit the economic activities and insufficient road infrastructure discourages personalised travel in large mega cities. However, when additional infrastructure for transport are provided in these large cities, economic activities and hence vehicular growth will continue to increase at a higher rate. For example, Table 2.6 shows slow growth in the number of vehicles in Mumbai in the nineties, which may reverse as several flyovers and elevated driveways are proposed to be completed by the end of the year 1999.

There can be another reason for the saturation levels found in larger mega cities. Vehicular growth in these cities can get shifted to city fringes and regions adjacent to the city as people working in the city tend to reside on the cheaper city fringes. People may also prefer to register their vehicles outside the city-limits to avoid the high cost of vehicle registration.

Urban form tends to affect the growth of vehicles in cities. Linear cities, such as Mumbai, cannot expand on all sides. With its main activities focussed on the small island area, Mumbai has expanded linearly. People in these cities stay in the faraway suburban areas, and commute a long distance daily. In contrast, a circular city will have more efficient urban form, as people can stay in all directions of the main city centre. Thus the urban form can be an important factor in determining the growth of vehicles.

Prices can also influence vehicular growth. In principle, vehicular growth can be checked using appropriate pricing policies. However, available evidence seems to indicate that price may not substantially influence the vehicular growth. For example, the econometric models presented in Chapters 5 and 6 show that prices have a very small (though significant) influence on gasoline consumption and transport performance in India.

The S-shaped pattern can also be altered by other policy formulations. For example, if a city is developed to encourage walking and cycling by providing all the facilities in a smaller geographical area, the growth of motorised vehicles may be reduced. Many cities expand because people settle in the cheaper periphery regions of the city, and prefer travel for work. This will reduce the population density in cities. This can happen so long as travel is relatively inexpensive compared with land. However, if travel is made more expensive, the horizontal growth of cities will be arrested and consequently there will be lesser travel.

7.3 Implications

This S-shaped logistic pattern of growth of vehicles in urban India has important implications for formulating proper policies for urban transport. These implications can be discussed in terms of two trends: the rapid urbanisation of India and the domination of private modes of transport in the growth of road transport vehicles. These and other policy analysis pertaining to urban transport sector in India will be discussed in Chapter 12.

7.4 Summary

The crucial link between the growth in the number of vehicles in cities and population has been studied in this chapter by fitting regression models. It has been established using data from Indian cities that the number of vehicles in towns could follow a logistic pattern as the town population increases; the number of vehicles will rise slowly when population is small, but will grow rapidly as population increases, and reach a saturation phase as the population reaches larger levels.

8

AN ANALYSIS OF TRENDS IN EFFICIENCY OF RAIL AND ROAD TRANSPORTS IN INDIA

In Chapter 3, it has been pointed out that mass transport modes—rail transport and public bus transport in road—provide the cheapest and the most environmental friendly travel. Hence, it is important to carry out efficiency analysis of these two modes. Such an analysis will be carried out in the next two chapters. Specifically the comparative efficiencies of rail and road transport in India is focussed in this chapter, while the performance of public bus operators in India will be focussed in the next chapter.

It has further been shown in Chapter 3 that estimating the efficiency of rail and road transport is relatively difficult. Using the time series data presented in Table 3.3, some broad conclusions could be drawn, but it was not possible to make more quantitative efficiency estimates, especially over time. It was also highlighted that sophisticated methodologies could help make more quantitative analyses. This will be attempted in this chapter.

Performance of rail and road transport in terms of PKM and TKM has been listed in Table 3.3 for various years. Rail and road transport require several inputs, such as infrastructure, labour and energy, in order to produce output performance in terms of PKM and TKM. Normally, these inputs are used for both passenger and freight transport. For example, trucks and buses use the same road. It is difficult to disaggregate the consumption of these inputs in terms of their use for passenger or freight transport.

In this chapter, one of the most important input to transport, namely energy is considered for analysis. Normally, energy consumption figures

Note: This chapter and the next one will be better appreciated with a basic understanding on linear programming (see Taha, 1997) and this chapter is based on Ramanathan (2000b).

for transport do not clearly distinguish whether the energy is spent for passenger transport or freight transport. This is because the same locomotive or vehicle can be potentially used for either carrying passengers or materials, and it may not be possible to disaggregate the total energy consumption in terms of exclusive use for passenger or freight transport. Though it is possible to estimate the energy efficiencies of both the forms of transport by apportioning energy consumption on the basis of some norms, the accuracy of these estimates depends upon that of the norms. Instead, assessment of 'true' efficiency is possible if a holistic methodology, which considers both the passenger and freight performance, is used. This can help to get rid of the effects of norms in making decisions on energy policy. Such a holistic methodology, called the Data Envelopment Analysis (DEA) (Ramanathan, 2003), has been used in this chapter to estimate the relative energy efficiencies of transport in India and trace the pattern of change in these efficiencies over the years.

8.1 Energy Efficiency of Road and Rail Transport—A DEA Analysis

In this chapter, DEA is employed to study the patterns of efficiency changes in rail and road transport modes. DEA is an interesting methodology based on operations research principles. The analysis uses the data on PKM, TKM and energy consumption given in Table 3.3. The analysis has been carried using the software package from the University of Warwick (Windows version 1.03).

8.2 Frontier Analysis: Basic Concepts of DEA

Data Envelopment Analysis (DEA) has been successfully employed for assessing the relative performance of a set of firms, usually called as the Decision-Making Units (DMU), which use a variety of identical inputs to produce a variety of identical outputs. The concept of Frontier Analysis suggested by Farrel (1957) forms the basis of DEA, but the recent series of discussions started with the article by Charnes, Cooper and Rhodes (1978).

For an intuitive understanding of the principle behind Frontier Analysis, let us consider only two outputs (PKM and TKM) (no inputs) for railways and describe how the efficiency scores are calculated in DEA. The performance of Indian railways for different years in terms of PKM and TKM is graphically depicted in Fig. 8.1. Note that the performance on the years 1991-92 and 1992-93 lie at the extreme end of the graph (at the upper right side) and are the best performances recorded.

It is not possible to say the performance of 1991-92 is superior to that in 1992-93 or *vice versa* as more PKM was achieved in 1991-92, while more TKM was achieved in 1992-93. In DEA terminology, these two years are said to be the most efficient of all the years *under consideration*, and are said to have formed a frontier of best-*achieved* performance. The frontier is formed by the line joining 1991-92 and 1992-93 together with horizontal and vertical lines to the axes, and envelops the remaining years in such a manner that any point on the frontier performs better than any point within the frontier. For example, take the case of the year 1980-81. By increasing the performance of this year in the same proportion, we move along the extension of *OA* until the frontier is touched at *B*. As there is no evidence that the PKM can be increased beyond the current best (*i.e.*, 314.6 billions achieved for the year 1991-92), point *B* represents the best possible performance that could have been achieved in 1980-81. Hence, we can measure the relative efficiency of performance of Indian Railways in the year 1980-81 in achieving the two outputs as the ratio *OA*/*OB*, which is equal to 66.43 per cent. Thus, the frontier provides a benchmark against which the performance in 1980-81 is evaluated. It is possible to compute the targets for inefficient performances using the frontier. For example, the performance in 1980-81 will be considered 100 per cent efficient if it increases only its PKM to attain the performance shown by the point *C*, or if it increases only its TKM to attain the performance shown by point *D*. It is also possible to

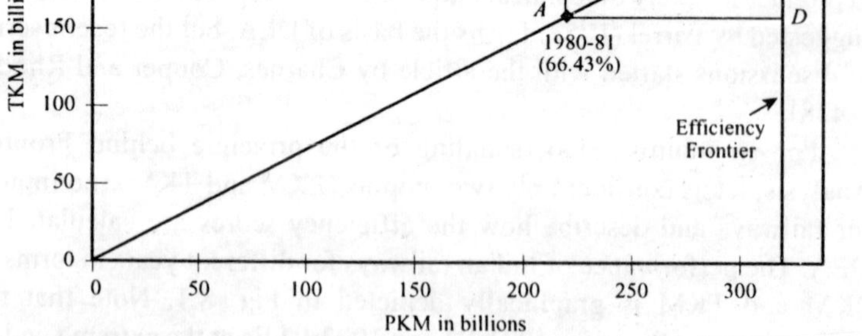

FIG. 8.1: Illustration of Frontier Analysis used in DEA. Various Points represent the Performance of Indian Railways in Different Years

raise performance in both, PKM and TKM, to reach 100 per cent efficiency at the point *B*, but normally DEA models consider performance in only one parameter at a time.

In our actual analysis, two outputs (PKM and TKM) and one input (energy consumption) have to be considered for performance assessment. In this case, however, it is not possible to take the help of graphical analysis presented above, and one has to depend totally on a mathematical model to capture the efficiency relationships to higher dimensional cases. Data Envelopment Analysis (DEA) provides such a mathematical tool. The mathematical programming details of DEA are briefly presented in Appendix 2.

8.3 Efficiency of Rail Transport over Time

Table 8.1 shows the efficiency scores for different years. As expected, rail transport in India has shown an increasing trend in energy efficiency. Results for both the CRS and VRS assumptions are reported, though VRS is likely to be applicable for a monopoly service such as the railways. Under the VRS assumption, Indian Railways in 1980-81 was only 54 per cent efficient as compared to the performance in 1993-94. As we have discussed earlier, a main reason for this pattern is the continuous decline in the use of energy intensive coal traction. The results of a further sensitivity analysis are also reported in the same table. It shows the slack for energy consumption in 1980-81 to be 46 per

TABLE 8.1: Trend in Energy Efficiency of Indian Rail Transport

Year	*Efficiency (%)*		*Slacks (%)*		
	CRS	*VRS*	*Energy*	*PKM*	*TKM*
1980-81	38.01	53.87	46.13	41.72	61.70
1981-82	38.53	51.64	48.36	34.03	47.76
1982-83	40.07	52.28	47.72	30.48	44.44
1983-84	40.68	54.03	45.97	32.83	44.44
1984-85	44.03	57.46	42.54	30.48	41.26
1985-86	47.54	58.43	41.57	22.90	24.81
1986-87	55.36	63.80	36.20	15.25	15.29
1987-88	60.53	66.65	33.35	10.11	11.30
1988-89	64.22	71.79	28.21	12.20	11.78
1989-90	71.77	75.70	24.30	5.48	8.53
1990-91	81.16	81.32	18.68	0.20	5.93
1991-92	90.53	100	0.00	0.00	0.00
1992-93	99.83	100	0.00	0.00	0.00
1993-94	100	100	0.00	0.00	0.00

cent. This means that, had the Indian Railways achieved the same performance in PKM and TKM with a 46 per cent reduction in energy consumption in 1980-81, then it would have been as energy efficient as the Indian Railways in 1993-94. The table also shows the slacks for PKM and TKM to be 42 per cent and 62 per cent respectively. They mean that, if the Indian Railways in 1980-81 were to be as energy efficient as it was in 1993-94, then in 1980-81, it should have registered 42 per cent higher PKM for the same energy consumption and TKM performance, or it should have registered 62 per cent higher TKM for the same energy consumption and PKM performance. Note that there is a gradual reduction in the slacks over the years.

8.4 Efficiency of Road Transport over Time

Table 8.2 shows the efficiency scores of the road transport over the last decade under both the CRS and VRS assumptions. Because any increase in road transport performance is due mainly to increase in private vehicles, CRS assumption seems to be more appropriate. The results with the CRS assumption show that the road transport in India was more energy efficient during late eighties than in the nineties. The sensitivity analysis presented in the same table shows interesting information. It shows that the input (energy consumption) was the most important factor in increasing the efficiency of the road transport. For example, to be 100 per cent efficient (relative to the performance at the other years), energy consumption in 1980-81 in the road transport ought to have reduced by 32 per cent for the level of performance in PKM and TKM reported for that year.

TABLE 8.2: Trend in Energy Efficiency of Indian Road Transport

Year	*Efficiency (%)*		*Slacks (%)*		
	CRS	*VRS*	*Energy*	*PKM*	*TKM*
1980-81	68.10	100.00	31.90	0	0
1981-82	69.21	98.47	30.79	0	0
1982-83	66.39	92.88	33.61	0	0
1983-84	68.34	90.09	31.66	0	0
1984-85	67.83	86.03	32.17	0	0
1985-86	100.00	100.00	0.00	0	0
1986-87	98.62	98.71	1.38	0	0
1987-88	100.00	100.00	0.00	0	0
1988-89	100.00	100.00	0.00	0	0
1993-94	97.73	100.00	2.27	0	0

8.5 Comparison of Efficiencies of Rail and Road Transport

Table 8.3 shows the efficiency scores when both the rail and road transport are considered. Results of only the CRS assumption are shown here, as this assumption seems to be more appropriate for road transport, which dominates rail in both PKM and TKM performance. The results show the performance of the rail transport in the year 1993-94 to be the relative best in terms of energy efficiency. The energy efficiency of rail transport in the year 1980-81 was only 37 per cent of its efficiency in

TABLE 8.3: Trend in Energy Efficiency of Indian Transport (Rail and Road)

Year	*Efficiency* %	*Slack (%)*		
		Energy	*PKM*	*TKM*
Rail				
1980-81	36.83	63.17	0.00	14.09
1981-82	37.33	62.67	0.00	10.23
1982-83	38.82	61.18	0.00	10.67
1983-84	39.41	60.59	0.00	8.76
1984-85	42.66	57.34	0.00	8.24
1985-86	46.06	53.94	0.00	1.55
1986-87	53.63	46.37	0.00	0.04
1987-88	58.64	41.36	0.00	1.08
1988-89	62.22	37.78	0.38	0.00
1989-90	69.53	30.47	0.00	2.87
1990-91	78.63	21.37	0.00	5.73
1991-92	87.71	12.29	0.00	6.31
1992-93	96.72	3.28	0.00	0.93
1993-94	100.00	0.00	0.00	0.00
Road				
1980-81	38.86	61.14	0.00	212.65
1981-82	39.99	60.01	0.00	217.67
1982-83	39.87	60.13	0.00	234.06
1983-84	41.15	58.85	0.00	235.26
1984-85	41.30	58.70	0.00	240.16
1985-86	65.99	34.01	0.00	282.28
1986-87	63.65	36.35	0.00	269.10
1987-88	63.21	36.79	0.00	257.39
1988-89	53.16	46.84	0.00	185.64
1993-94	63.39	36.61	0.00	272.00

1993-94, while the energy efficiency of road in 1993-94 was only 63 compared to the relative best efficiency. The results of the sensitivity analysis, shown in the same table, shows that to be as energy efficient as the railways in 1993-94, railways in 1980-81 ought to have reduced its consumption by 63 per cent for the same levels of PKM and TKM performance, or it could have increased its TKM performance by 14 per cent. Note that, to achieve the relative best efficiency, road transport in 1993-94 should have consumed about 36 per cent less energy, or it should have almost tripled its freight performance.

8.6 Summary

The trends in energy efficiencies of Indian road and rail transport over the years have been assessed in this chapter using the Data Envelopment Analysis (DEA). The advantage of DEA is that it does not involve any assumption on the disaggregation of energy consumed in terms of passenger or freight transport performance. The analysis has shown that the energy efficiency of rail transport has been increasing. Of all the years considered, the performance of rail transport was relatively the best in the year 1993-94 (which is the latest year considered in the analysis), while the performance of road transport in the year 1993-94 was only 63 per cent compared to the relative best. Thus, the DEA analysis highlights huge savings in energy consumption if rail transport is made to capture future transport requirements.

9

PRODUCTIVITY OF THE STATE TRANSPORT UNDERTAKINGS IN INDIA

An Assessment using Data Envelopment Analysis

In this chapter, DEA is employed for assessing the performance efficiency of selected State Transport Undertakings in India. These STUs are basically public sector undertakings. Certain difficulties are encountered when productivity measurement of public transport modes is attempted. Public sector does not operate with a single goal of profit maximisation, but has a variety of social goals. The difficulties in tracking the progress of organisations in the public sector are well-recognised (Golany and Roll, 1989; Ganley and Cubbin, 1992).

In the analysis in this chapter, efficiency is interpreted as productivity. Productivity is generally defined as the ratio of output to input. When productivity of two firms are compared, the more productive firm produces more output with the same input, or it produces the same output with lesser input. It is very vital that the productivity of organisations is assessed and monitored regularly to check the degree to which inputs are utilised in the process of obtaining desired outputs.

There is a well developed literature on the productivity assessment in the transport sector (Oum, Tretheway and Waters, 1992). The studies can be broadly grouped into three categories: Index number based approaches, regression based parametric studies and non-parametric studies which use the operations research based technique, and Data Envelopment Analysis (DEA). There is an extensive literature on transport productivity measurement using index number based and/or regression based techniques, especially for bus transport (Hensher, 1992; Hensher and Daniels, 1995). Studies on transport productivity assessment using

Note: This chapter is based on Ramanathan (1999b).

DEA are relatively few. Hjalmarsson and Odeck (1996) have assessed the performance of trucks in road construction and maintenance using DEA. Adoplhson *et al.* (1989) have used DEA for railroad property valuation. However, a survey of the literature shows that the use of DEA for bus transport operations has been very few. Viton (1997) has used DEA for assessing the efficiency of multi-mode bus transit. In this chapter, the performance of public bus transport operators (called the State Transport Undertakings—STUs) in India is studied using DEA.

9.1 Data

In this chapter, productivity of STUs in India are assessed using DEA. DEA is an interesting methodology based on operations research principles. The basic concepts behind DEA have been intuitively explained in the previous chapter. The technique is briefly described in Appendix 2.

All the data used in this chapter have been obtained from the information published regularly by the Association of State Road Transport Undertakings (*e.g.*, CIRT, 1995). The published information do include several partial productivity indicators such as fleet utilisation (share of buses on road to total buses), vehicle productivity (kilometres per bus held per day), staff productivity (kilometres per worker per day), kilometres operated per litre of fuel, and cost per kilometre. However, a holistic approach, such as using DEA, for comparing the productivity is not available.

Performance of the STUs during the year 1993-94 are assessed in this chapter. Though, there are nearly 50 public bus operators, only 29 operators are considered. The choice of operators is influenced by two factors: size and data availability. We have tried not to exclude big operators. Some of the data for all the variables under consideration are not available for the all firms. Firms for which important data are not available had to be omitted. The public bus operators considered for analysis in this chapter are listed in Table 9.1 along with other geographical information.

9.1.1 *Inputs*

Three inputs have been considered in this chapter as most important in producing the output. Fleet size is a representative of the capital input, total number of staff is a representative of the labour input, and diesel consumption, which represents a dominant material input. Table 9.2 lists the inputs.

TABLE 9.1: Names and Geographical Information about the STUs

Acronym	*Name*	*Nature of Service*	*State of Operation*	*Nature of the Organization*
AMTS	Ahmedabad Municipal Transport Service	Urban	Ahmedabad City	Municipal Undertaking
APSRTC	Andhra Pradesh State Road Transport Corporation	Mofussil	Andhra Pradesh	Corporation
ASTC	Annai Satya Transport Corporation Limited	Mofussil	Tamil Nadu	Company
BEST	Bombay Electric Supply & Transport Undertaking	Urban	Mumbai City	Municipal Undertaking
CRC	Cholan Roadways Corporation Limited	Mofussil	Tamil Nadu	Company
CTC	Cheran Transport Corporation Limited	Mofussil	Tamil Nadu	Company
DTC	Delhi Transport Corporation	Urban	Delhi	Corporation
GSRTC	Gujarat State Road Transport Corporation	Mofussil	Gujarat	Corporation
HRTC	Himachal Road Transport Corporation	Hilly	Himachal Pradesh	Corporation
KMTU	Kohlapur Municipal Transport Undertaking	Urban	Kohlapur City	Municipal Undertaking
KnSRTC	Karnataka State Road Transport Corporation	Mofussil	Karnataka	Corporation
MGRTC	Puratchi Thalaivar MGR Transport Corporation Limited	Mofussil	Tamil Nadu	Company
MPTC	Maruchu Pandiyar Transport Corporation Limited	Mofussil	Tamil Nadu	Company
MSRTC	Maharashtra State Road Transport Corporation	Mofussil	Maharashtra	Corporation
NBSTC	North Bengal State Transport Corporation	Mofussil	West Bengal	Corporation
NGST	Nagaland State Transport	Hilly	Nagaland	Government Department
NTC	Nesamony Transport Corporation Limited	Mofussil	Tamil Nadu	Company
OSRTC	Orissa State Road Transport Corporation	Mofussil	Orissa	Corporation
PATC	Pattukkottai Azhagiri Transport Corporation Limited	Mofussil	Tamil Nadu	Company
PRC	Pandiyan Roadways Corporation Limited	Mofussil	Tamil Nadu	Company
PTC	Pallavan Transport Corporation Limited	Urban	Chennai City	Company
RMTC	Rani Mangammal Transport Corporation Limited	Mofussil	Tamil Nadu	Company
RSRTC	Rajasthan State Road Transport Corporation	Mofussil	Rajasthan	Corporation
SKNT	Sikkim Nationalised Transport	Hilly	Sikkim	Government Department
STPJB	State Transport Punjab	Mofussil	Punjab	Government Department
TPTC	Thanthai Periyar Transport Corporation Limited	Mofussil	Tamil Nadu	Company
TRPTC	Tripura Road Transport Corporation	Hilly	Tripura	Corporation
TTC	Thiruvalluvar Transport Corporation Limited	Mofussil	Tamil Nadu	Company
UPSRTC	Uttar Pradesh State Road Transport Corporation	Mofussil	Uttar Pradesh	Corporation

Source: CIRT (1995).

9.1.2 *Outputs*

At least two demand side measures (passengers carried and passenger kilometres effected) and two supply side measures (seat kilometres and vehicle seat hours) of output can be identified from a study of the literature. The supply side output measures may be alternatively considered intermediate outputs because not all of them may be used for service. Hence, demand oriented output measures are considered in this chapter. More specifically, being a composite measure of the passenger carried and the average lead travelled by passengers, passenger kilometres has been chosen for this chapter as a single measure of output of the bus operators. The details also are listed in Table 9.2. Note that similar input and output variables have been employed in the literature on performance measurement in road transport industry (*e.g.*, Hensher, 1992; Hensher and Daniels, 1995).

TABLE 9.2: Inputs and Outputs of the State Transport Undertakings

	Fleet Size	*Total Staff*	*Diesel*	*Passenger Kilometres*
Unit	*No.*	*No.*	*Kilolitres*	*Millions*
(1)	(2)	(3)	(4)	(5)
MSRTC	15,483	1,11,979	3,17,679	53,409
APSRTC	15,235	1,19,630	3,28,010	64,486
KnSRTC	9,899	63,712	2,16,159	37,460
GSRTC	8,945	59,706	1,86,557	29,485
UPSRTC	8,023	56,864	1,44,478	24,053
RSRTC	4,115	25,892	90,268	15,903
STPJB	2,368	12,551	54,411	7,633
CTC	1,290	8,338	42,117	8,147
PRC	1,150	8,992	34,971	6,939
TTC	940	8,733	49,813	7,559
NBSTC	947	6,707	19,637	2,500
OSRTC	954	7,223	18,244	2,435
TPTC	809	6,078	26,776	5,596
CRC	766	6,069	25,134	4,804
PATC	700	5,092	23,372	5,062
MPTC	700	5,268	23,394	4,819
MGRTC	661	4,902	20,220	4,411
RMTC	644	4,668	21,545	4,426
NTC	593	4,470	18,326	3,603
ASTC	584	4,116	19,163	4,394
HRTC	1,598	9,179	35,830	3,775
NGST	198	1,045	1,432	143
SKNT	198	1,114	1,030	57

(*Contd.*)

TABLE 9.2 (*Contd.*)

(1)	(2)	(3)	(4)	(5)
TRPTC	130	802	647	73
DTC	3,706	34,220	69,710	11,722
BEST	3,067	38,965	81,009	11,060
PTC	2,094	19,244	45,225	10,131
AMTS	753	6,105	11,815	1,795
KMTU	117	1,291	2,652	417

Source: CIRT (1995).

9.2 Results

The DEA analysis has been carried out using the software package from the University of Warwick (Windows version 1.03). Output maximising DEA has been employed.

9.2.1 *Efficiency Scores*

Efficiency scores have been obtained under both CRS and VRS assumptions. The efficiency scores of the STUs are shown in Table 9.3 along with the ranks. The most efficient STUs would get an efficiency score of 100 per cent in data envelopment analysis. The table shows that there is a high degree of agreement between the scores under CRS and VRS assumptions. The correlation coefficient is 0.83. However, the VRS scores tend be higher than the CRS scores. The average efficiency score under CRS assumption is about 75 per cent and 14 STUs have a score lower than this average. The average efficiency score under VRS assumption is about 84 per cent, with 10 STUs faring below this average figure.

Only two STUs are considered efficient under the CRS assumption, while more number of STUs are selected as efficient under the VRS assumption. ASTC and TTC are the STUs are the relatively most efficient STUs in terms of the CRS efficiency score, while APSRTC, ASTC, CTC, KMTU, KnSRTC, PATC, PTC, TRPTC and TTC have been rated as most efficient in terms of the VRS efficiency score. A deeper examination has shown that most of the STUs that received higher efficiency score under the VRS assumption compared to the scores under CRS assumption had high number of routes (this variable is used as a proxy for volume of operation).

A striking observation in the efficiency ratings based on CRS assumption is that the STUs operated as companies have received the highest ratings. However, though companies topped the list in terms of the VRS efficiency score, their domination is not so perfect.

TABLE 9.3: DEA Efficiency Scores (in percentages) and Ranks of STUs under Constant Returns to Scale (CRS) Assumption and under Variable Returns to Scale (VRS) Assumption

	CRS	*Rank*	*VRS*	*Rank*
AMTS	66.26	21	67.00	24
APSRTC	85.73	11	100.00	1
ASTC	100.00	1	100.00	1
BEST	59.54	23	71.52	23
CRC	83.35	13	89.38	16
CTC	91.52	7	100.00	1
DTC	73.33	16	79.01	21
GSRTC	68.92	19	85.08	19
HRTC	45.94	27	50.69	28
KMTU	68.54	20	100.00	1
KnSRTC	75.57	15	100.00	1
MGRTC	95.12	5	95.32	12
MPTC	91.31	8	95.17	13
MSRTC	73.32	17	87.86	17
NBSTC	55.53	25	55.58	27
NGST	43.45	28	55.66	26
NTC	85.73	11	85.80	18
OSRTC	58.20	24	58.25	25
PATC	95.93	4	100.00	1
PRC	86.53	10	97.08	11
PTC	97.69	3	100.00	1
RMTC	91.14	9	93.13	14
RSRTC	76.83	14	92.69	15
SKNT	24.13	29	35.06	29
STPJB	61.18	22	73.83	22
TPTC	91.84	6	99.46	10
TRPTC	49.30	26	100.00	1
TTC	100.00	1	100.00	1
UPSRTC	72.60	18	82.35	20

It is necessary to test the validity of the CRS or VRS assumption before we proceed with further analysis of performance of STUs using DEA. The regression exercise to be described later has shown that the efficiency scores (CRS or VRS) are not influenced significantly by the number of routes operated by a STU (considered as a proxy for the volume of operation). Hence, only the efficiency scores under the CRS assumption have been considered in the DEA analysis hereafter.

9.2.2 *Sources of Inefficiencies*

The DEA analysis also provides important information about the sources of inefficiencies of the STUs that do not have unit efficiencies. Obviously, the sources are identified by comparing the inefficient STU with the efficient ones. The targets and the reduction or improvement required in the performance of STUs to achieve the targets are listed in Table 9.4. For inputs, the target specifies the amount the STU in question ought to have consumed if it were to be rated efficient. Obviously, an inefficient STU would have consumed more inputs than the target. The extent of reduction needed is also listed in the table. Similarly, for the output, the target specifies the amount required to be achieved if the STU is to be rated efficient, and the extent of improvement needed is also listed for each STU.

We have seen earlier that both ASTC and TTC have been rated as efficient under the CRS assumption. Hence, their targets coincide with the actual achievements, and extent of reduction of inputs or improvement in output is zero. For others STUs, the targets are in general different from the actual performances. For example, the fleet size of AMTS has to be reduced from its present size of 743 to about 360 (that is by about 52%) in order that it qualifies to be an efficient STU. The least rated STU, namely SKNT, requires significant reductions (more than 80%) in fleet size or staff, or much more significant (more than 300%) improvement in output, to be rated efficient. Note that most STUs are using their fuel efficiently. But, the table shows that many of the inefficient STUs have excess capacities in terms of fleet size and staff. Of the two, overstaffing is more pronounced, which is a characteristic of public sector organisations in general.

An improved level of fleet utilisation is necessary for the STUs to be more efficient. This points to the need for efficient management of available non-human resources. If the STUs achieve higher output (passenger kilometres) with the same input, their efficiency score would improve. The extent of improvement needed in output for each STU is available in Table 9.4.

The STUs would do well if they properly utilise their human capital through better human resource management. This can be achieved through proper co-ordination, and motivation of the employees for extract better quality output.

9.2.3 *Identification of the Effect of Uncontrollable Factors on the Efficiency Scores*

The efficiency scores obtained using the DEA model described so far

TABLE 9.4: Targets in Original Units and Reduction/Improvement Needed (%)

UNIT	*Fleet Size*		*No. of Staff*		*Fuel Consumption*		*Passenger Kilometres*	
	Target	*Reduction*	*Target*	*Reduction*	*Target*	*Reduction*	*Target*	*Improvement*
AMTS	360	52.18	2,538	58.43	11,815	0.00	27,094	50.91
APSRTC	9,996	34.39	70,454	41.11	3,28,010	0.00	7,52,162	16.64
ASTC	584	0.00	4,116	0.00	19,163	0.00	43,942	0.00
BEST	2,469	19.50	17,400	55.34	81,009	0.00	1,85,761	67.96
CRC	766	0.00	5,399	11.05	25,134	0.00	57,635	19.98
CTC	1,183	8.29	8,338	0.00	38,819	7.83	89,016	9.26
DTC	2,125	42.67	14,973	56.24	69,710	0.00	1,59,852	36.37
GSRTC	5,686	36.44	40,071	32.89	1,86,557	0.00	4,27,796	45.09
HRTC	1,092	31.67	7,696	16.16	35,830	0.00	82,162	117.68
KMTU	81	30.94	570	55.88	2,652	0.00	6,081	45.89
KnSRTC	6,588	33.45	46,429	27.13	2,16,159	0.00	4,95,676	32.32
MGRTC	616	6.78	4,343	11.40	20,220	0.00	46,367	5.13
MPTC	700	0.00	4,981	5.45	23,394	0.00	52,779	9.52
MSRTC	9,682	37.47	68,235	39.06	3,17,679	0.00	7,28,471	36.40
NBSTC	599	36.80	4,218	37.11	19,637	0.00	45,031	80.09
NGST	44	77.98	308	70.56	1,432	0.00	3,284	130.13
NTC	559	5.82	3,936	11.94	18,326	0.00	42,024	16.64
OSRTC	556	41.72	3,919	45.75	18,244	0.00	41,835	71.82
PATC	700	0.00	4,978	2.23	23,372	0.00	52,774	4.25
PRC	1,066	7.32	7,512	16.46	34,971	0.00	80,192	15.56
PTC	1,378	34.18	9,714	49.52	45,225	0.00	1,03,706	2.37
RMTC	644	0.00	4,585	1.78	21,545	0.00	48,563	9.72
RSRTC	2,751	33.15	19,389	25.12	90,268	0.00	2,06,995	30.16
SKNT	31	84.14	221	80.13	1,030	0.00	2,363	314.49
STPJB	1,658	29.97	11,687	6.88	54,411	0.00	1,24,770	63.45
TPTC	809	0.00	5,727	5.77	26,776	0.00	60,931	8.88
TRPTC	20	84.85	139	82.67	647	0.00	1,484	102.82
TTC	940	0.00	8,733	0.00	49,813	0.00	75,589	0.00
UPSRTC	4,403	45.12	31,033	45.43	1,44,478	0.00	3,31,303	37.74

should be more appropriately termed as gross efficiency scores because they include the effects of certain variations in the inputs and outputs which are beyond managerial control of individual STUs. For example, a STU having older fleet will not be able to perform as well as the firms having younger fleet. Similarly, if a STU operates its bus services in hilly terrain, it is likely to consume more input for a given output. Without controlling for the effects of the factors beyond managerial control, any inference on efficiency of STUs is likely to be misleading.

DEA studies in the literature have recognised this problem, and have used different approaches to overcome the problem. For example, Majumdar (1997) has employed regression analysis to study the effect of several factors on the efficiency scores obtained for the U.S. telecommunication industry. Yeh (1996) has employed Principal Factor Analysis approach in his application of DEA for bank performance evaluation.

In this chapter, a regression based approach is employed for studying the effect on the DEA scores of the factors beyond managerial control but likely to affect the performance of STUs. Several factors, such as the following, have been considered for the regression analysis.

(a) Number of routes operated by a STU. This variable is a proxy for the volume of operation of a STU.

(b) Age of fleet (denoted as AGE). STUs with older fleet are likely to be less efficient compared to those with relatively younger fleet.

(c) Share of urban operations expressed as a percentage (CITY). In India, some STUs operate their services exclusively in urban areas, some exclusively in rural areas, while some operate services in both the areas. Urban services are likely to be more efficient because of higher capacity utilisation.

(d) The nature of the terrain. The STUs operating on a hilly terrain are likely to incur more expenditure, especially fuel, than those operating on a plain terrain. A dummy variable, denoted as HILL, is used to represent hill services.

(e) The average number of passenger per bus per day (PASSDENSITY). This is likely to indicate the capacity utilisation of a bus.

In addition to the above factors, several others, including deficit per passenger, ratio of labour to other inputs, average lead, etc. have also been used in the regression exercise. However, results with them were not satisfactory.

The first striking result emerging out of the regression exercise is the low statistical significance associated with the variable representing the number of routes. The same result has been obtained even with the efficiency scores under the VRS assumption. This supports the view that the efficiency scores are not affected by volume of operation. All other variables listed above yielded good results. Different combinations of these variables along with linear and logarithmic functional forms have been employed to generate four regression models. The results are given in Table 9.5.

TABLE 9.5: Results of the Regression Exercise with the Efficiency Score under CRS Assumption as the Dependent Variable

Regressor	*Linear*		*Logarithmic*	
	Model 1	*Model 2*	*Model 3*	*Model 4*
CONSTANT	97.221*	88.677*	5.002*	4.216*
	(17.886)	(14.851)	(42.620)	(15.387)
AGE	–4.538*	–3.831*	–0.422*	–0.383*
	(–4.152)	(–4.064)	(–5.752)	(–4.419)
HILL	–26.724*	–23.914*	–0.415*	–0.349**
	(–3.860)	(–3.449)	(–5.036)	(–2.763)
CITY	0.175**	—	0.028*	—
	(2.443)	—	(4.747)	—
PASSDENSITY	—	0.014*	—	0.117*
	—	(2.921)	—	(2.865)
R^2 adjusted	0.680	0.705	0.839	0.770

Note: *t*-values are shown in parentheses. *, ** represent that the corresponding coefficients are significant at 1 per cent and 5 per cent levels.

Note that AGE and HILL have come out to be highly significant consistently in all the models. They have the expected negative sign, which signifies that the efficiency score would decrease if the average age of fleet of a STU increases or if the STU operates on a hilly terrain. CITY has a positive sign, indicating an increase in efficiency for urban operations. Similarly, PASSDENSITY also has the expected positive sign.

9.3 Summary

The efficiency of operation of the State Transport Undertakings, who are the bus operators in the Indian public sector, has been assessed in this chapter using Data Envelopment Analysis. Three inputs representing capital stock, staff and material consumption, and one output have been employed for the purpose. Relative efficiency scores have been computed under the assumption that the operations of the bus operators are governed by constant returns to scale. Of the twenty nine operators considered, only two were found to be relatively efficient. Further analysis has shown that the inefficient units have to reduce their inputs and/or improve their performance in order to qualify to be efficient units. The exact quantum of the required reduction of input consumption or required improvement in output has been computed for each operator. This analysis has given results that are generally expected of a firm in the public sector—inefficiencies in the usage of capital stock and labour. It has been found that most of the operators are using their fuel efficiently, while large inefficiencies are observed in the usage of fleet (a measure of capital stock) and staff. However, the fact that the inefficient public sector units are compared only with their counterparts shows that there is a good scope for the inefficient units to improve their performance. Finally, the effect of certain factors beyond the managerial control of the bus operators on the efficiency scores have been assessed using regression. It has been found that the age of fleet has a negative influence on the efficiency scores. Efficiency scores tend to reduce if the area of operation happened to be hilly. City operations and operations with a higher passenger density per bus tend to increase efficiency scores.

It will be interesting to track changes in the efficiency scores of the bus operators over years. Unfortunately, such a study is difficult to carry out because of the frequent splits and mergers in the Indian bus industry in the past years. Similarly, inclusion of private operators in the analysis could have given valuable information on the productivity differences between private and public firms. Such a study could not be a part of the present chapter due to several problems. For example, while public operators have on an average about 5000 fleet per firm, about ninety per cent of the private operators are single bus owners. Uniform and systematic data are not available on the performance of private operators. If these problems are solved and data on the private bus operators are also included in the analysis, it could have helped in getting information on the effect of management structure and nature of regulation. These provide directions for future research.

PART III

POLICY

This part has three chapters. Chapter 10 provides a scenario analysis to identify alternatives for reducing energy consumption and emissions due to Indian transport operations in future. A policy analysis, describing the problem areas and possible policy actions, for improving the performance of various transport modes is presented in Chapter 11. The last chapter is devoted to a discussion on urban transport policy in India.

10

ENERGY AND ENVIRONMENTAL IMPLICATIONS OF GROWTH OF INDIAN TRANSPORT

In the last few chapters, several analysis of trends in the transport sector in India have been carried out. In this chapter, some of the results of the analyses presented in previous chapters are synthesized to derive useful policy conclusions regarding the energy and environmental implications of the future growth of transport sector in India. Specifically, the future levels of transport performance are obtained using the cointegration model developed in Chapter 6, and the future modal split of transport performance will be estimated using the logistic substitution model developed in Chapter 4.

10.1 Projecting the Future Transport Requirements

A cointegration econometric model for projecting the long-term growth of transport performance in India was developed in Chapter 6. For ease of exposition, the models developed in that chapter are repeated below, with the numerical values of parameters corresponding to the general equations listed in Chapter 6.

$$\begin{aligned} PKM_t = {} & \underset{(0.114)}{0.684} + \underset{(4.105)}{1.147}\, Y_t + \underset{(2.606)}{4.414}\, NR_t - \underset{(-1.381)}{0.209}\, P_t + V_{1t} \end{aligned} \tag{10.1}$$

$$\begin{aligned} \Delta PKM_t = {} & \underset{(2.20)}{0.060} + \underset{(0.66)}{0.122}\, \Delta Y_t + \underset{(0.29)}{0.464}\, \Delta NR_t - \underset{(-0.09)}{0.010}\, \Delta P \\ & - \underset{(-2.46)}{0.345}\, V_{1(t-1)} + \underset{(0.48)}{0.098}\, \Delta PKM_{t-1} + U_{1t} \end{aligned} \tag{10.2}$$

$$TKM_t = \underset{(10.15)}{1.241} + \underset{(15.69)}{1.183}\, I_t - \underset{(-4.16)}{0.188}\, P_t + V_{2t} \tag{10.3}$$

Note: This chapter is based on Ramanathan and Parikh (1999).

$$\Delta TKM_t = \underset{(-1.68)}{-0.044} + \underset{(3.174)}{0.994\,\Delta I_t} + \underset{(0.91)}{0.072\,\Delta P_t} - \underset{(-2.01)}{0.400\,V_{2(t-1)}} + \underset{(1.61)}{0.331\,\Delta TKM_{t-1}} + \underset{(1.56)}{0.295\,\Delta TKM_{t-2}} + U_{2t} \quad (10.4)$$

where the notations PKM, TKM, Y, NR, I and P stand for passenger kilometres, tonne-kilometres, gross domestic product, ratio of urban to total population, index of industrial production and price of mineral oils respectively. Figures within parentheses are the *t*-values. Data for the period 1956-89 were used in the construction of the model. We could not use data till 1993-94 because a regular time-series data on PKM and TKM are not available beyond 1988-89.

Models (10.1) and (10.2) have been used for forecasting PKM using the procedures explained in Section 6.3.1. Similarly, future TKM levels have been projected using the cointegrating Model (10.3) and its ECM (Model 10.4). The forecasts for the year 2020-21 have been estimated. The results are plotted in Fig. 10.1.* The average annual growth rates during 1990-2021 are 8.41 per cent for PKM and 5.41 per cent for TKM.

With a view to analysing the implications of these forecasts on the sustainability of this sector in India, a scenario analysis has been performed. The details are presented below.

10.2 Energy Requirements and Carbon Dioxide Emissions upto 2020-21: A Scenario Analysis

For policy purposes, it is necessary to identify the implications of alternate courses of action so that the future can be shaped to ensure sustainable development. The impact of the Indian transportation sector is likely to be felt mainly on two important areas—energy requirements and CO_2 emissions. Assuming that the PKM and TKM projections made in the previous section will materialise, their likely impacts and the effects of alternate courses of action have been analysed using four scenarios. Table 10.1 describes the scenarios in terms of annual average growth rates for the period 1990-2021. These may be compared with the growth rates of PKM and TKM for the period (8.41% and 5.41%

* Note the kink observed in the figure during 1985-86 for both PKM and TKM. The kink occurs in the actual published data. Such a kink is due to the published data on the performance (PKM and TKM) of road transport. However, no sharp increase in related data such as the number of road transport vehicles or road transport energy consumption. See Chapter 2 for more discussion.

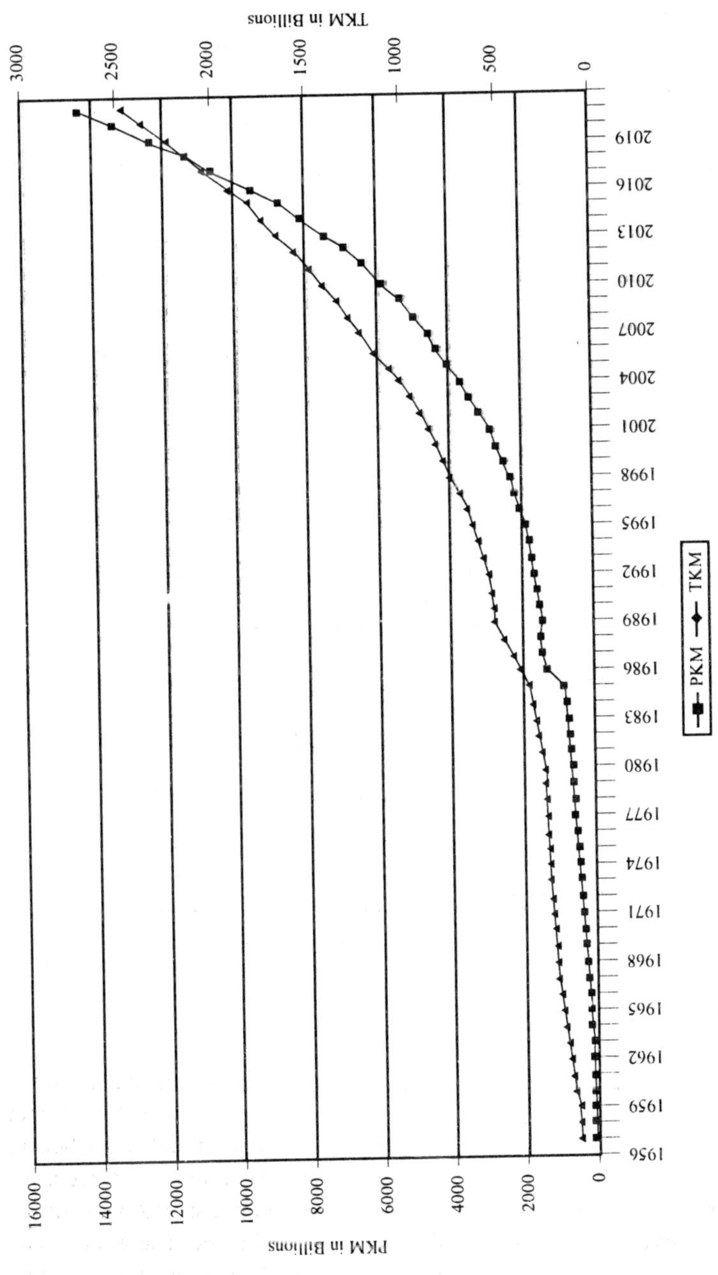

FIG. 10.1: Forecasts of Passenger Kilometres and Tonne-Kilometres in India. The Plots show Actual Values till 1989

respectively). The results of the scenarios are also plotted in Fig. 10.2 (for energy requirements) and Fig. 10.3 (for CO_2 emissions).

TABLE 10.1: Growth Rates Obtained for the Scenarios (in % per annum for the period 1990-2021)

Scenarios	*Energy Requirements*	*CO_2 Emissions*
Business as usual	5.96	5.72
Efficiency increase	4.88	4.65
CNG and Electric vehicles	4.88	4.65
High share of mass transport	3.42	3.68

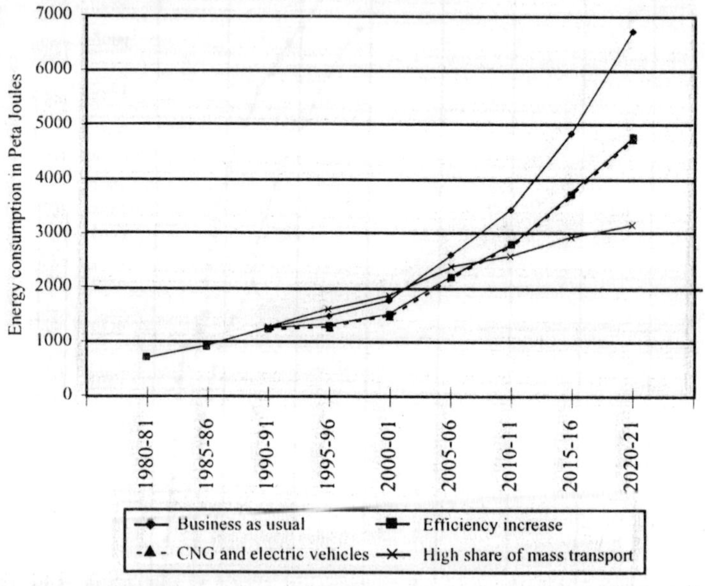

FIG. 10.2: Projections of Energy Consumption due to the Transport Sector in India under Different Scenarios

10.2.1 *Scenario 1: Business as Usual (BAU)*

In this scenario, existing historical patterns have been assumed to continue in future. The trends in the past modal splits have been used to project future modal splits using the logistic substitution model described in Chapter 4. Based on their performance in the previous decade, an increase in the efficiencies of road transport equipment by 2 per cent per annum over the prevailing values in 1990-91 has been assumed. The efficiencies of rail and air transport equipment have been assumed to be the same as those prevailing in 1990-91.* Based upon these assumptions, the energy requirements and CO_2 emissions till 2005-06 have been projected. The energy requirements in 2020-21 is projected to be about 6837 Peta Joules (PJ) (Fig. 10.2), which is more than 5.5 times the consumption in 1990-91. CO_2 emissions have also recorded a similar rise (Fig. 10.3). Such a sharp increase is obvious considering the fact that the energy and carbon intense modes of transport (gasoline vehicles and trucks) have been assumed to satisfy the additional transport demand during 1990-2021. It is necessary to reduce such a high growth using policy options. An analysis of such options is presented below.

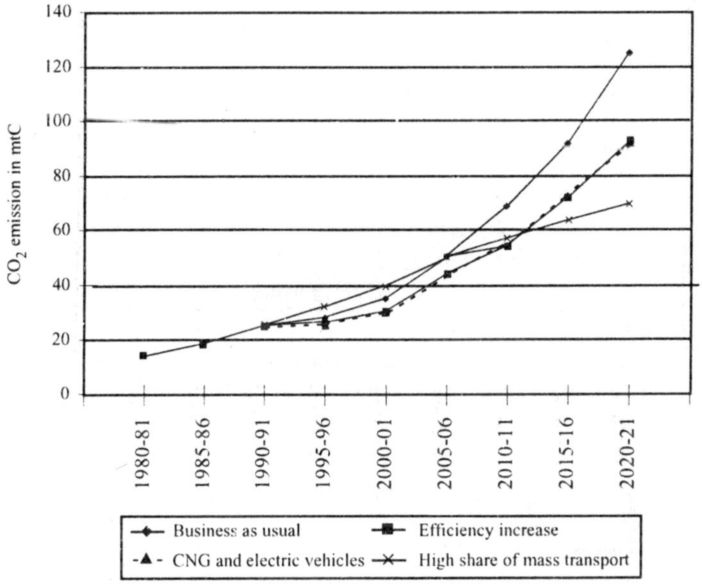

FIG. 10.3: Projections of CO_2 Emissions due to the Transport Sector in India under Different Scenarios

* The analysis with actual data has revealed that the specific energy consumption in the past decade for rail and air traffic did not show any specific trend, and hence the efficiencies prevailing in 1990-91 were assumed in this scenario. From the data available for road transport, it appears its efficiency has increased. The total energy consumption of this transport has increased at a rate of about 8 per cent per annum during 1980-90, whereas PKM and TKM by road have risen at about 11 per cent and 12 per cent respectively. Fuel efficiency of road transport, on an average, may therefore have increased by about 4.5 per cent per annum. Hence assumption of 2 per cent efficiency increase is quite conservative.

10.2.2 *Scenario 2: Emphasis on Efficiency Improvements (EFFICIENCY)*

The assumptions of the previous scenario have resulted into a huge increase in energy requirements and CO_2 emissions. Emphasis on efficiency improvements can reduce this unhealthy trend. Hence, in this scenario, it has been assumed that there will be enhanced efforts to increase the efficiencies of transport equipment. An increase in efficiency by 1 per cent per annum for rail and air transport, and about 3 per cent per annum (*i.e.*, 1% over and above the expected efficiency improvements) for road transport* have been assumed. Energy requirements and CO_2 emissions in 2020-21 have been estimated to be about 5041 PJ and 96 million tonnes of carbon equivalent (mtC) respectively. These values represent a significant (more than 26%) reduction compared to the corresponding figures of the previous (BAU) scenario.

10.2.3 *Scenario 3: Introduction of Alternate Transport Fuels (ALTFUEL)*

In addition to efficiency improvement, introduction of alternate transportation fuels can further reduce energy requirements and CO_2 emissions. In this scenario, the effect of introducing these fuels *over and above efficiency improvements* has been examined.

At present virtually all (99%) fuels consumed in road transport in the world are being produced from crude oil. The market share of other non-oil transport fuels such as bio-ethanol, methanol and Compressed Natural Gas (CNG) is very minor (Okken, 1991). Other non-oil alternative fuels (hydrogen and electricity) are still in the research and development stage (OECD, 1993).

Of these non-oil fuels, the most relevant one for India is the CNG. CNG vehicles are more efficient and cleaner as compared to their gasoline counterparts. It has been estimated that the CNG vehicles will emit only 80 per cent of CO_2 (full fuel cycle) compared to gasoline

---

* The average fuel economy of cars at present in developing countries in Asia is about 9 to 10 litres per 100 kilometres. For developed countries the value is about 8. However, new technological improvements have resulted in small cars which have a fuel consumption as low as 5 litres per 100 km. If one assumes that these types of cars will be commercially available in developing countries in about 30 years (Okken, 1991), it amounts to a cumulative efficiency increase of about 2.5 per cent per year. Hence, the assumption of 1 per cent in efficiency increase in road transport (which also includes buses) is not unrealistic. For other transports, the assumption of 1 per cent efficiency improvement per year is quite conservative.

engines (Okken, 1991). A technology assessment has identified fruitful utilisation of the natural gas available in India for transportation purposes (Parikh and Painuly, 1991; Painuly and Parikh, 1993). Calculations using available data reveal that CNG vehicles are expected to consume about 0.4683 MJ and emit 7.8 grams of Carbon equivalent of CO_2 for every PKM.

Pressure on cleaner environment especially in urban areas is expected to stimulate the introduction of electric vehicles in India. Both Battery Powered Electric Vehicles (BPEV) and Hydrogen Fuel Cell Electric Vehicles are not yet commercially available (Williams, 1993), with the former being in a relatively more advanced stage of development. Hence, except for a few studies (Wang and DeLuchi, 1992; Mac Kenzie, 1994), details on their technical performance is not available. Their performance vary from 0.3 to 0.4 kWh per mile (Wang and DeLuchi, 1992). A battery powered EV (BPEV) emits only 56 per cent of greenhouse gases compared to a gasoline vehicle, if the battery is charged using the average US electricity. The corresponding CO_2 emissions for a fuel cell powered electric vehicle is quite low and depends upon the fuel used in the fuel cell (Williams, 1993). It is usually as low as 8 per cent of the corresponding value for gasoline vehicles (Okken, 1991). The electric vehicles are expected to consume about 0.2283 MJ/PKM. BPEVs emit about 5.9 grams of Carbon equivalent of CO_2, while fuel cell powered electric vehicles are expected to emit about 0.8 gram.

For the purpose of this scenario, a diffusion of CNG and electric vehicles in 2020-21 along the S-shaped logistic pattern has been assumed. It is assumed that both the CNG vehicles[*] and EVs will diffuse to account for 10 per cent (each) share in the new vehicles registered in 2020-21.[**] The level of market penetration has been assumed to be uniform for both these EVs.

---

[*] This share of CNG vehicles may be optimistic because as per the present Indian natural gas policy, fertiliser has the first priority use for natural gas. In fact, its use as CNG for transportation has a much lower priority. However, we assume a high level of use of CNG for transport as we hope that there will be a change in the natural gas policy towards transportation. Our optimism is based upon two facts. We feel that the pressure on reducing the CO_2 emissions will force the government to encourage the use of CNG vehicles. Also, with the new joint ventures for setting up Indian fertilizer plants in West Asia coming up, the need for fertilizer production in India using indigenous natural gas is expected to decline.

[**] Electric vehicles are expected to occupy 25 per cent share in the Total Motor Vehicle sales in the United States in the year 2010 AD (Mac Kenzie, 1994). Hence, this assumption seems to be conservative. Due to the large amount of uncertainty regarding the development of EVs, a more optimistic assumption may not hold the realistic view.

Surprisingly, the results have not shown much variation from those of the previous scenario (EFFICIENCY). This is because, under the stated assumptions, the share of the alternate fuel vehicles in the total number of vehicles expected in 2020-21 has been quite low (1.24% for each). This means that if the alternate fuel vehicles are to make any appreciable effect on reducing energy consumption and the CO_2 emissions, they have to be encouraged very vigorously. Otherwise, their likely impact is expected to be very minimal in terms of CO_2 emissions.

However, introduction of alternate fuel vehicles can be beneficial from the point of view of local pollution, as they have the potential to reduce the emissions of carbon monoxide, nitrogen oxides, particulates etc. Also, the benefits of the alternate fuel vehicles can be significant in urban areas. The major eleven metropolitan cities of India accounted for about 30 per cent of the all vehicles in India in 1980-81. The share declined to about 24 per cent in 1993-94. The share of 23 metropolitan cities, which include additional cities recognised as metropolitan cities after the 1991 census, in all vehicles in India was about 33 per cent in 1993-94. Alternate fuel vehicles are more likely to be useful in urban centres, which face severe problems due to local pollution. Also, the diffusion of these vehicles can be smooth if they are concentrated in urban areas, where the necessary infrastructure (such as CNG pumping stations, battery charging stations, etc.) can be provided relatively easily and efficiently. Assuming that the major urban centres will account for about 30-40 per cent of total vehicular population in 2020-21, the likely share of alternate fuel vehicles in the vehicles in these urban centres is likely to be higher at about 3-5 per cent. Obviously, this can lead to a relatively more significant reduction in the emission of local pollutants.

10.2.4 *Scenario 4: Desired Modal Split (MODSPLIT)*

The modal split employed in the previous three scenarios is the expected pattern based on past trends (using the logistic substitution model developed in Chapter 4). The modal split is shown in Table 10.2 for the years 1990-91 and 2020-21. This modal split is however highly undesirable as it favours energy inefficient and CO_2 intensive modes. For example, in 2020-21, gasoline vehicles have been assumed to meet more than 36 per cent of the PKM demand. The share of rail has been assumed to be less than 5 per cent.

However, rail is highly energy efficient and less carbon intensive mode (see Table 3.4). Hence, there is a strong case for increasing the share of railways in the modal split. Many planning studies on Indian transportation sector have also opined that railways should account for a major share of PKM and TKM as they are more energy efficient. The National Transport Policy Committee (NTPC, 1980) has recommended that the railways should plan to carry 72 per cent of the total land freight traffic by 2000 AD.

TABLE 10.2: Modal Splits (%) for Passenger and Freight Transport

Mode	*Passenger Transport*			*Freight Transport*		
	1990-91	*2020-21 (projected)*	*2020-21 (desired)*	*1990-91*	*2020-21 (projected)*	*2020-21 (desired)*
Rail						
—Coal	5.2	0.02	0.0	0.6	0.02	0.0
—Diesel	11.5	3.1	18.0	30.7	9.0	24.0
—Electricity	4.3	1.5	12.0	14.26	7.8	36.0
Rail Total	**21.0**	**4.6**	**30.0**	**45.56**	**16.82**	**60.0**
Road						
—Gasoline	17.1	36.0	3.4	—	—	—
—Diesel	60.9	54.0	50.6	54.42	82.6	39.9
—CNG	0	1.2	6.8	—	—	—
—EV	0	1.2	6.8	—	—	—
Road Total	**78.0**	**92.4**	**67.5**	**54.42**	**82.6**	**39.9**
Air	**1.0**	**3.0**	**2.5**	**0.02**	**0.58**	**0.1**
Grand Total	**100.0**	**100.0**	**100.0**	**100.00**	**100.00**	**100.0**

Source: Values computed by the author.

Hence, this scenario has been constructed to identify the effects of encouraging more desirable travel modes in terms of energy consumption and CO_2 emissions. The details are also provided in Table 10.2. Specifically, this desired modal split assumed a more share for rail in total PKM and TKM, for buses and alternate fuels in passenger road transport, and for electric traction in railways.*

The results have shown a much larger reduction (nearly 45% compared to the BAU scenario) in energy requirements and CO_2 emissions (3306 PJ and 72 mtC respectively). Thus this scenario has shown that it is possible to have a reasonably low increase in energy

* All these assumptions have their own financial implications. For example, to increase their share, the railways have to substantially invest on new capacity generations, as many of its important routes are already nearing saturation limits. However, we do not analyze this aspect further in this chapter.

requirements and CO_2 emissions, and hence points to the best strategy for sustainable transport development in India.

10.3 Policy Implications

The scenarios have shown that the energy requirements and emissions need not follow the same rate of increase of travel demands. They show that it is possible to reduce the energy demands of transportation by more than 26 per cent by efficiency improvements. The best available technologies should be commercialized at the earliest. Vehicles should be made to run at optimal speeds, and at full capacities. Enforcing minimum standards on efficiency, capacity per vehicle, and speed limits, can help promote conservation among vehicle owners.

It has been shown that if the market mechanisms are allowed to operate so that CNG and electric vehicles form 10 per cent each of the total vehicles registered in 2020-21, the extent of diffusion in the Indian market is only marginal (1.24% each). It has been shown that such a low diffusion will not result in any tangible progress towards sustainability, though there is likely to be a reduction in the emission of local pollutants in urban areas. Hence efforts must be made to promote them as fast as possible. Subsidies may be provided on the capital and fuel costs of these vehicles, exclusive roads and parking spaces may be constructed, investments can be preferentially allotted for developing the necessary infrastructure (such as fuel rechargers for battery operated electric vehicles, CNG filling stations, etc.).

11

SOME POLICY ASPECTS PERTAINING TO INDIAN TRANSPORT SECTOR

In this chapter, using the performance data presented in Chapter 2, bottlenecks affecting the performance of Indian transport sector are analysed and important policy directions for future planning are specified. Some of the important policy options have already been initiated by the government in the nineties. Some of the recent developments are discussed and further policy directions are specified.

11.1 Rail Transport

The productivity of Indian Railways as measured by the Average Capital Output Ratio (ACOR) showed a favourable trend (*i.e.*, reduced) till 1986-87, but increased since then. It declined from 9.86 in the year 1965-66 to 7.17 in 1986-87, and then increased to 7.8 in 1990-91 (RITES, 1993).

Indian Railways have been registering excess revenue over expenses in the last few years. The excess was Rs. 441.05 crore for the year 1992-93, which quadrupled to Rs. 2,446.40 crore in 1994-95. Freight traffic accounted for a major portion of earnings in 1993-94 (68.8%).

11.1.1 *Problem Areas*

Reducing share in modal split: The National Transport Policy Committee (NTPC, 1980) has envisaged a preferred modal split of 72 per cent and 28 per cent for railways and roadways respectively for long distance freight traffic. Railways are also one of the least consumers of energy (excluding coal traction) and least emitters of carbon dioxide (CO_2) per PKM or TKM effected (see Table 3.4). However, the trends in the last

Note: This chapter is partly based on Ramanathan (1997) and Parikh, K. and Ramanathan (1997).

decade point to a gradual reduction in the performance of railways. There are many reasons for this unhealthy trend—shortage of track capacities especially on trunk routes, and lack of sufficient resources for capacity augmentation, and superiority of road transport in terms of flexibility and convenience due to door-to-door delivery. Unlike roadways, where investment is made by different agencies (investment on roads by the government, and investment on vehicles by users), so far all the investment in railways had to be made exclusively by the government.

Paucity of resources: The shortage of capacities in railways and very high traffic density on major routes point to the urgent need for augmentation of rolling stock capacity and expansion of track. It has been estimated that it is necessary to double the capacity of Indian Railways to meet the transport demands by the year 2000 AD. Obviously, this requires huge investment. The total investment in Indian Railways was about Rs. 32,000 crore at the end of 1993-94 (book value). Assuming conservatively that about 60 per cent of this investment is required for a further doubling of capacities, about Rs. 20,000 crore would be needed to be invested in railways by the year 2000. This may be compared with the total plan investment of just Rs. 7,500 crore as per the 1995-96 budget. Of this, the budgetary provision is only Rs. 1,150 crore. The budgetary support to Indian Railways has been decreasing over the past five year plan periods. A review of plan investments in the past indicates that the outlay on railway sector as a percentage of total plan outlay came down from 6.9 per cent to 5.9 per cent in the last four plan periods from about 11.1 per cent to 15.5 per cent in the first three plan periods. Thus, the railway sector is forced to look into alternate sources of financing such as market borrowing and private participation. The gap between the plan investment (Rs. 7,500 crore) and budgetary provision (Rs. 1,150 crore) in the railway budget 1995-96 has to be financed by Indian Railways through internal resources (Rs. 4,100 crore), market borrowing through Indian Railway Finance Corporation (IRFC) (Rs. 2,250 crore) and private investment through *Build-Operate-Lease-Transfer* (BOLT) and *Own-Your-Wagon schemes* (Rs. 577 crore). The balance will be provided by IRFC through taxable and tax-free bonds.

Subsidies in operations: Social obligations of Indian Railways force it to provide certain services below the cost of operation. Essential commodities of mass consumption like sugarcane, salt, edible oils, etc. are carried at low rates below cost. These operations resulted in a loss of Rs. 46.66 crore in the year 1994-95. As many as 119 low traffic branches have resulted in a loss of Rs. 166 crore in 1993-94 as against their original investment of Rs. 153 crore. Fares of the short distance second ordinary class and season tickets are much below their costs. In addition, special concession are extended to certain categories of people. They resulted in a loss of Rs. 1,927.10 crore in 1994-95. About 11 per cent this loss was due to the suburban train operations in Mumbai, Kolkata and Chennai. Thus we see that subsidised passenger fares are resulting in huge losses in Indian Railways.

11.1.2 *Recent Developments*

In order to encourage more private participation in resource generation and win away the growing share of road freight transport, Indian Railways have devised a new marketing strategy following the process of liberalisation. The main features of this strategy are described in Table 11.1.

TABLE 11.1: Main Features of Indian Railways' New Marketing Strategy

- The Container Corporation of India (CONCOR) will provide door-to-door services for domestic users, transportation in bulk for small customers and international transport in ISO containers.
- Brake van space is leased to customers so that they can have assured transportation between fixed points.
- *Own Your Wagon* scheme is introduced to invite private sector investment for the ownership of railway wagons. The railways have already sought private investment to operate the eight tourist circuits and rolling stock under this scheme. The scheme has further been modified in June, 1996 in favour of private parties. Wagons will now be allocated to their sister concerns also.
- Long distance special parcel service is introduced between important cities.
- Rules are simplified for faster processing. These include free acceptance of indents, supply of wagons, single window booking systems and faxing of invoices to the destination.
- A rebate is provided for carrying freight in the empty flow direction.
- Yards are closed to facilitate faster movement.
- Private participation through Build, Operate, Lease and Transfer (BOLT) scheme has been introduced. Projects costing Rs. 555 crore have already been finalised and another Rs. 1,175 crore worth of investment proposals are under various stages of consideration.

Source: *Economic Survey*, 1995-96, and Monthly Review of the Indian Economy (Jan-Sept. 1996 issues), published by the Centre for Monitoring Indian Economy, Mumbai.

The convenience of assumed door-to-door delivery that trucks provide and the significant fuel efficiency and cost reduction that railways provide for long distance freight transport can be combined. This needs proper inter-modal connections between railways and road vehicles. The proposed door-to-door services by CONCOR is a step in the right direction. However, the operations of CONCOR should be properly regulated. To ensure economic efficiency, competition should be encouraged.

11.1.3 *Further Policy Directions*

Thus the recent efforts made by Indian railways indicate their willingness to reemerge as the dominant transport industry in India. It requires some more time to test the effects of the efforts outlined in Table 11.1.

Encourage more private parties for providing door-to-door services: In the long run, it is necessary to encourage private parties also for providing door-to-door services and end the monopoly of CONCOR. Private parties can own wagons in which they can transport containers, and carry them through trucks to the warehouses of their customers. Enactments similar to the Multi-Modal Transportation Act, 1993 should be made for guiding these operations.

Avoid delays and make projects more attractive: In spite of the flexibilities offered, it has been reported that the *Own-Your-Wagon* scheme has not attracted many private parties. Similarly, many of the projects proposed under the BOLT scheme (*e.g.*, quadrupling of the railway lines between Borivli and Virar near Mumbai) have not received enthusiastic response from private entrepreneurs. Unnecessary delays due to procedural formalities and uncertain return on income are the reasons. The delays add to the cost, thus reducing the profitability of the projects. It may be necessary for the railway authorities to make the projects more profitable by offering the development of auxiliary facilities to private parties. If the profitability of the projects are still in doubt, then government-private partnerships may be created to instill confidence in the private parties. Once projects become sufficiently profitable, government may divest and re-invest the money on other risky projects.

Run reliable, punctual container trains: To capture growing road freight traffic, it is necessary to run train services punctually and according to pre-specified schedules. The marketing strategy proposes such special parcel services. These should be operated on a scheduled guaranteed time delivery basis. If the services are convenient, time guaranteed and profitable to private truck operators, they will prefer these trains to running the energy inefficient trucks for long distances. Using trains, they can then provide door-to-door freight services with guaranteed time delivery. This will capture a lot of long distance road freight traffic. There will also be phenomenal savings in diesel as train consumes only one-ninth as much diesel as a truck per TKM. In the long run, competition should be encouraged by allowing private entry to operate such container trains.

Rationalise railway passenger fares: The excess of railway earnings over expenses is much smaller compared to the investment needs. The excess during 1994-95 (Rs. 2,446.40 crore) was just 9 per cent of the investment required by the year 2000. Obviously, earnings of Indian Railways have to be improved. As indicated earlier, a major portion of the losses in earnings occur in the subsidised second class and season ticket passenger fares. Hence, a more rationalised cost based fare structure, especially in the suburban train operations, should be attempted.

Provide more differential services at differential prices: At present, only two services are offered in suburban train services. It may be worthwhile to attempt to provide further differentiated services to cater to different sections of commuters. This will help railways to best utilise the consumers' surplus. This differential service can also be used to provide cross-subsidisation in passenger fare structures. Similar attempts may also be made in non-suburban services.

Create a long-term fund for capacity additions: A nominal percentage may be charged in fares which may form part of a long-term fund for railway capacity additions. For example, the gross traffic receipts by railways for the year 1994-95 were Rs. 20,101 crore, whereas the minimum investment required for new capacity addition by the year 2000 is estimated as Rs. 20,000 crore. Assuming a minimum of this gross traffic earnings for all the years during 1996-2000, charging an additional 15-20 per cent increase in fares and earmarking such increased earnings for capacity additions can meet the investment requirements of railways. If additional resources are available for capacity augmentation, the percentage can be accordingly adjusted.

Avoid encroachments of railways by long-term lease: Encroachment of railway land near the railway lines by slum dwellers affects the profitability of railways. Railways will not be able to exploit the commercial value of these encroached land. Augmentation of railway lines becomes difficult. To avoid these difficulties, the land should be leased for commercial purposes, or given on a long-term lease for the development of telephone/electric lines or roads, if feasible.

Joint implementation for attracting foreign funds: In addition, we wish to highlight one important policy direction for financing capacity augmentation in Indian Railways. This involves identifying the opportunities for Joint Implementation (JI) (Parikh, J., 1994) in the context of global climate change for attracting investments from developed countries in Indian Railways. (See Table 11.2 for details.)

TABLE 11.2: Joint Implementation Possibilities in Indian Railways

It has been reported that more than 50 per cent reductions in energy consumption and CO_2 emissions can be achieved if the future modal splits in India are channelised in favour of railways (see Chapter 10, specifically Figs. 10.2 and 10.3). Much more reductions of CO_2 emissions are possible if a part of the growing air traffic (which is a maximum emitter of CO_2) is captured by high speed luxury trains. Thus development of railways is vital for sustainable transport development in India. These superior characteristics of railways may be advantageously exploited for attracting foreign funds. Obviously, if the growing road transportation is captured by the more efficient railways, a sharp reduction in CO_2 emissions may be expected. This can act as an incentive for the developed countries for investment in Indian Railways. This will be beneficial to the investing countries as they can claim an equivalent amount of global CO_2 reductions as per the procedures followed for implementing projects for Joint Implementation. This will be equally beneficial to India on at least three counts: the transport infrastructure will be improved, the shift in transportation from roadways to railways will help in reducing transport energy consumption and pollutant emissions, and the domestic resources thus saved can be fruitfully diverted to other important activities, such as the social sectors, where private sector and foreign countries may not be interested in investing.

Further general aspects of privatisation of infrastructural projects are discussed in Section 11.6. As explained in that section, improvements in capital markets, development of innovative financial instruments, and provision of fiscal incentives should also be attempted to encourage more private sector participation, that will increase the financial options available to Indian Railways. Some specific details on private sector participation, more in line with the discussion to be made in Section 11.7, are provided below.

11.1.3.1 *Private Sector Participation*

Unbundling of the railway infrastructure: A necessary condition before attracting private participation is unbundling the railway infrastructure in logical sub-activities (modules) which can each be privatised separately to enable private parties not to have to bite more than what they can chew. A recent example of the unbundling of the British Railways could be a model. A framework to do this is suggested in Table 11.3. The broad activities are creation of infrastructure and provision of services.

The latter includes maintenance, operations and customer services. Possibilities of private participation may be explored in each of these activities.

TABLE 11.3: Unbundling Possibility for Indian Railways

Infrastructure	*Responsibility of*
1. Asset Creation	
—Right of Way	Indian Railways (IR)
—Terminals	IR
—Tracks	IR/Private Parties (PP)
—Rolling Stock and Equipment	IR/PP
Services	
2. Maintenance	
—Right of Way	IR
—Terminals	IR/PP
—Tracks	IR
—Rolling Stock and Equipment	IR/PP
3. Operations	
—Terminals	IR/PP
—Rolling Stock and Equipment	IR/PP
4. Customer Services	
—Basic Services	IR
—Special Services	IR/PP

Source: Ramanathan (1997), based on Pangotra and Raghuram (1995) and Raghuram and Padmanabhan (1992).

Frame agreements properly: Encouragement of private parties to partially take part in railway functioning is an important feature of the new strategy of Indian Railways. Agreements with private parties should be framed without ambiguity to avoid difficulties later. For example, allocation of risks should be clearly specified. It may require framing of additional rules in due course depending upon the then emerging scenario.

Avoid delays and make projects more attractive: In spite of the flexibilities offered, it has been reported that the Own-Your-Wagon scheme has not attracted many private parties. Similarly, many of the projects proposed under the BOLT scheme (*e.g.*, quadrupling of the railway lines between Borivli and Virar) have not received enthusiastic response from private entrepreneurs. Unnecessary delays due to procedural formalities and uncertain return on income are the reasons.

Delays add to project cost, thus reducing the profitability of the projects.

If the projects are non-viable for private parties, different components of the projects can be made modular, and each sub-module should be made open for private entry. This can help private parties to take up only the projects which are within their financial capability.

Further, it may be necessary for the railway authorities to make the projects more profitable by offering the development of auxiliary facilities to private parties.

If the profitability of the projects is still in doubt, then government-private partnerships may be created to instill confidence in the private parties. Once projects become sufficiently profitable, government may divest and re-invest the money on other risky projects.

Legal issues: As stated earlier, the first and foremost requirement would be to set up such a legislation for project formats such as BOLT. This legislation may be applicable to projects in all infrastructural sectors.

A more consumer oriented legal system can also improve the standards of services provided by Indian Railways. Many of the traders of bulk commodities prefer trucks to railways for transporting their goods. Their main concern seems to be the uncertainty and enormous delay associated with railways, which are the main reasons for the lukewarm response of the Own-Your-Wagon scheme. If, by legislation, Indian Railways are made to operate their services according to pre-specified (and published) schedules and legal provision is made to penalise railways for delays, more traders will be willing to use railways, which are cheaper than road transport. The trader should be able to get a fair compensation with minimum hurdles.

Dispute resolution: As said earlier, a special legal system should be developed to resolve disputes related to private sector participation.

11.2 Roads and Road Transport

Because of its inherent flexibility and the advantage in connecting the remote hilly rural areas, road transport is projected to increase in future. It is estimated that this mode of transport, which presently accounts for 83 per cent of passenger traffic and 57 per cent of freight traffic, will account for 87 per cent and 65 per cent of passenger and freight traffic by the year 2000. Results of econometric studies discussed in Chapter 6 reinforce this view.

11.2.1 *Problem Areas*

Saturated road network: Paucity of resources has been the most important bottleneck in the progress of the road transport sector. Many of the important roads are saturated. For example, the National Highways network, which constitutes less than two per cent of the total road network, carries nearly 40 per cent of the total road traffic. Only 2 per cent of the National and State Highways have four lanes, 34 per cent two lanes and the remaining 64 per cent have only single lane. The road network increased from 4 lakh km in 1951 to 20 lakh km in 1991, but vehicle population rose from 3 to 219 lakh during the corresponding period, clearly exposing the lack of a highway system to meet the road user demand.

Consequent to liberalisation, the car manufacturing sector has been delicensed in June, 1993. A number of tie-ups of Indian companies with international giants (*e.g.*, DCM-Daewoo and Peugeot-Premier Automobiles) have taken place since then and many more are still expected. A recent survey by the Confederation of Indian Industries has estimated that if the GDP grows at the rate of 8.5 per cent, car purchases will increase by 20 per cent per annum, taking the annual demand of cars to 6,50,000 cars by the turn of the century. This number is more than triple the number of cars sold during 1993-94 (210,672 cars). The existing infrastructure is poorly equipped to carry such a volume of traffic.

Inadequate road network has led to higher transportation cost, which has severely eroded international competitiveness of the Indian economy. Commercial vehicles in India are able to run only 200-250 km per day, as compared to 500-600 km per day in developed countries. In addition, congestion leads to enormous economic losses. We consider an example to illustrate this point. It has been reported that, during peak hours, it takes about two hours to cover the 40 km stretch between Bangalore and Hosur, which is more than double the expected travel time. Assuming conservatively that about 4000 people travel on the road for work per day and a cost of just Rs. 25 per hour for all these people, the loss of one extra-hour of production time can be calculated as Rs. one lakh per day, or Rs. 3.6 crore annually. In addition, poorly maintained roads increase fuel consumption and pollution. Obviously, the cost of proper maintenance of the road would be a small fraction of this social cost.

The total economic losses due to the bad condition of roads have been estimated to be of the order of Rs. 20,000 to Rs. 30,000 crore.

Poor quality and maintenance of roads: Economic losses arising from the wastage of large amount of scarce resources due to poor maintenance of existing roads can be avoided by proper policy action. According to a study conducted near the location of the Indira Gandhi

Institute of Development Research in Goregaon, Mumbai (Ramanathan, 1997), the social cost of not repairing a 2 km road would be as high as Rs. 6 lakh as against Rs. 50,000 needed for repairing the road. Supposing that a private party is entrusted with the responsibility of maintaining the road and is allowed to charge a nominal fee of Rs. 0.10 per bus trip, Rs. 0.05 per car trip, Rs. 0.01 per scooter trip and Rs. 0.10 per trip by other vehicles, the expected revenue to the private party would be Rs. 200 per day. This means that the private party would be able to get back the investment in just 8 months. Road users would also be quite willing to pay the nominal fee to save time and the unnecessary wastage of fuel.

Poor financial structure of State Road Transport Undertakings (STUs): STUs, with a few exceptions, face serious financial constraints. They have been incurring losses in their operations (Table 11.4). This situation is due to various factors such as social commitment to operate even on uneconomic routes, absence of rationalised cost-based fare structures, overstaffing, etc.

TABLE 11.4: Financial Performance of Selected State Transport Undertakings Operating City Services as on March, 1994

(*Paise per km*)

Name	*Total Cost*	*Earning*	*Profit or Loss*
Delhi Transport Corporation	1758.7	657.5	–1,101.20
Bombay Electric Supply & Transport Undertaking	1732.7	1493.9	–238.80
Calcutta State Transport Corporation	1457.2	676.1	–781.10
Pallavan Transport Corporation Limited (Chennai)	1001.4	984.3	–17.10
Ahmedabad Municipal Transport Service	1256.3	1046.3	–210.00
Poona Municipal Transport	1065.5	1033.4	–32.10
Chandigarh Transport Undertaking	652.2	622.3	–29.90
Pimpri-Chinchwad Municipal Transport	877.4	859.1	–18.30
Kolhapur Municipal Transport Undertaking	1039.0	1000.2	–38.80
Thane Municipal Transport Undertaking	1177.6	1560.8	+383.20

Source: Report (1996a,b).

11.2.2 *Recent Developments*

Huge investments are needed in constructing new roads. We have seen that the social costs associated with poor maintenance and the costs of congestion due to inadequate roads are quite high. To obviate these difficulties, private entry into road maintenance, road construction and road transport operation is necessary. It is equally necessary to induce competition in order to achieve economic efficiency.

To generate additional resources, the Union government has already amended the National Highway Act and declared the roads sector as an industry. Levying a fee on selected sections has been permitted. Private sector has been invited to finance, construct, maintain and collect toll taxes on highway and bridge projects. The government identified 27 road projects consisting nine each of expressways, bridges and bypasses. These involve a large investment amount of Rs. 14,213 crore.

Following the process of liberalisation, the government has announced certain reforms in road sector and is contemplating some more in the near future. These reforms are highlighted in Table 11.5.

TABLE 11.5: Reforms in Road Sector

- Entry taxes such as Pathkar and Octroi have been abolished by all or many State governments to enable free flow of traffic.
- The Motor Vehicle Act, 1988 has been amended to simplify procedures.
- Road sector has been declared an industry to facilitate borrowing on easy terms and to permit floating of bonds.
- MRTP provisions have been relaxed to enable large firms to enter the highway sector.
- National Highways Act has been amended to enable levy of a fee.
- Customs duties on construction equipment have been reduced and the procedures have been streamlined.
- Provision has been made for the development of a Highway Development Fund. It will be based on the tolls collected from the upgraded national highways. The money will be utilised for regular maintenance and further upgradation of new stretches of highways.

Reforms Contemplated

- Participation of private sector and foreign investors will be sought.
- The land acquisition and removal of utilities will be done by the government.
- To enhance the viability of the project by private entrepreneurs, development of auxiliary facilities (restaurants, motels, fuel stations, parking areas, etc.) would be allowed.
- A Central Road Fund, based on a levy of 5 per cent of the basic price of petrol and diesel sold, has been proposed.
- A foreign equity participation of 74 per cent in road projects would be allowed.

Source: *Economic Survey*, 1996-97, and focus issue on new road policy, in the *Economic Times*, dated 18 November, 1996.

So far, the response of the private sector towards the privatisation process in the road sector has been relatively lukewarm. Private parties appear to be concerned about the low or uncertain return on investment, cost escalations caused by uncontrollable administrative delays and lack of consistent and committed policies by the authorities. The cost of the Rau-Pithampur link road, India's first private sector infrastructure project, escalated from Rs. 2 crore at the beginning of the project to Rs. 7 crore mainly due to a delay of two years. In many other projects, the private parties were forced to carry out their own feasibility study rather than relying solely on government data. This has added to the delay and to the pre-project cost.

Similarly, the Mumbai-Pune expressway (supernational highway) is being delayed by more than one year, which has led to cost escalations. Once estimated to cost Rs. 800 crore, the estimates at present have gone up to Rs. 2,000 crore. Of late, government has started to widen and improve the existing highway, as its policy has now shifted from building new expressways to improving existing highways. The bidders of the expressway project are concerned about the reduction in the traffic volume in the proposed expressway, which will affect the profitability of the project. They are also reported to have expressed concerns about the traffic projections made by the government. Their main concern has been on the profitability of the project, in spite of the offer of about 1030 hectares of land by the government for development of auxiliary facilities.

In addition to private investment, additional budgetary support is also being obtained through loan assistance from International agencies. Asian Development Bank is funding the conversion of 330 km stretches of various National Highways from two to four lanes in Haryana, Rajasthan, Andhra Pradesh, Bihar and West Bengal, which is estimated to cost Rs. 771 crore. These externally funded projects will be implemented by the National Highways Authority of India. A budgetary allocation of Rs. 200 crore has been provided in the 1996-97 Union budget to strengthen its capital base.

11.2.3 *Further Policy Directions*

Financing options: The expert group on the commercialisation of infrastructure projects (IIR, 1996) has estimated a resource requirement of Rs. 41,000 crore for the construction and maintenance of National, State and Supernational Highways for the period 1996-2001. Apart from obtaining budgetary support, there are at least four sources available for obtaining such an investment: allocation from existing user taxes, creation of an earmarked fund through levies, collecting tolls from users and private sector participation. A Highway Infrastructure Savings Scheme (HISS) has been proposed by the working group on commercialisation of infrastructure projects (IIR, 1996) to provide assured funds for commercial roads. As transport demand is created by the operations of commercial establishments and industries, the working group on urban transport (Report, 1996a,b) has suggested that these establishments may be asked to pay a nominal transport cess on sales tax.

Technical options: It has been shown in the previous chapter that investment in efficiency improvements in road transport vehicles can fetch a saving of 26 per cent in energy consumption. This may be considered a least cost option and vigorously pursued.

Private participation—transparency in bidding: It is necessary to follow competitive bidding and benchmarking for private investment in road projects. Bidding process should enable provision of service at minimum cost to users. For example, bidders may asked to bid for the toll rate, and the minimum bidder may be awarded the contract. If it is a free access road where no toll is to be charged, bids may be awarded on the basis of minimum area of compensatory land for development. There are several issues to be considered for encouraging private investment. These are discussed in Section 7 of this chapter.

Avoid delays: To avoid unnecessary delays, the government should first carry out a detailed techno-economic study of the projects before inviting private parties. It should also follow committed and consistent policies. In the case of risky projects, new government-private partnerships should be formed to instill confidence in private parties.

Market oriented, demand driven approach: Road projects should be identified based upon user demand. Toll collection is the main source of revenue for private roads, and the projects should be selected only when the users feel an acute need for such a road. Government should not fix any cap for the toll and let the market decide the toll.

Make STUs autonomous and profit oriented: It is necessary to make the STUs autonomous in order to enable them to charge rationalised cost based fares. Only this will improve their financial standing. Due to their social obligations, STUs are forced to operate services on uneconomical routes. The losses accrued to STUs in such cases should be compensated by allocating a suitable amount from the profits due to operations in profitable routes. In case private operators run only on profitable routes, they should be asked to provide a specific percentage of their earnings to STUs to make up these losses.

11.3 Urban Transport

For the sake of completion, the case of urban transport is discussed briefly here. Policy aspects of urban transport will be discussed in more detail in the next chapter. The urban population in India has increased from 62.4 million in 1951 to 217.2 million in 1991, nearly 3.5 times. While the population in major metropolitan cities in India has doubled in about twenty years in the past, the travel demand within them has increased by four to eight times. An increase of 66-200 per cent in travel demand in five major metropolitan cities in India has been projected for 2001 AD (NCU, 1988).

11.3.1 *Problem Areas*

The exponential growth in personalised vehicles and the slow growth in the urban road network have resulted in choking congestion and air pollution in Indian cities. Growth of fuel inefficient personalised vehicles have also led to very high increase in oil consumption, straining seriously India's balance of payments.

According to the working group of urban transport (Report, 1996a,b), the important problems affecting the urban transport sector are the following.

- High accident rate, poor road safety and limited road space.
- Lack of integration of transportation and land use.
- Critical parking conditions, specially in the down town or CBD areas.
- High air pollution and noise level in different parts specially along the high traffic density corridor.
- Unsustainable and low capacity road based public transport system.
- High increase of personalised vehicles and unregulated growth of Intermediate Passenger Transport (IPT) modes.
- Shortage of fund for long-term transport plan and programmes which are capital intensive and have low return and long gestation periods.
- Deregulation, privatisation and disinvestment of public transport undertakings.
- Multiplicity of agencies/authorities.
- High energy consumption.

As resource shortage is the main problem affecting the smooth performance of urban transport, the working group has made several recommendations. The following are the salient features:

- Dedicated levy and taxes from beneficiaries: the property owners, flat owners, builders, etc. should be asked to pay one time transportation tax at 2 per cent of the property tax and 1 per cent stamp duty. Cess of 5 paise per litre on petrol and diesel should also be charged. Commercial establishments and industries should be asked to pay 2 per cent transport cess on sales tax.
- Commercial exploitation of immovable property of State Transport Undertakings (STUs).
- Revision of fare structure of STUs to cover the cost of operations.
- National/International loans/grants.
- Establishment of appropriate institutional framework.
- Multiplicity of agencies in urban transport development to be replaced by Unified Metropolitan Transport Authority.
- An Urban Transport Development Bank of India be set up to provide loans on commercial basis. The bank can mobilise funds from the capital market by issuing bonds, debentures, shares and accepting fixed deposits from the public.
- Privatisation and de-regulation of urban transportation system.

11.3.2 *Recent Developments*

There have been some interest in private investment in urban transport sector. The Karnataka government has approved Rs. 4,200 crore bid made by the U group led consortium for an elevated light rail transit system in Bangalore. The project will be on Build-Own-Operate-Transfer basis and would be handed over to Bangalore Mass Rapid Transit Ltd. after a 30-year lease period.

In order to raise the necessary resources for investing in infrastructure, a levy of 2 per cent as special customs duty on selected imports has been proposed in the 1996-97 Union budget.

11.4 Further Policy Directions

Improve mass transport systems: Mass transport systems provide the least energy consumption, CO_2 emissions, and cost per PKM or TKM. They also reduce the level of congestion in cities. Hence, they should be encouraged wherever possible. It is necessary to improve the speed, comfort, and reliability of public transportation. To increase competition, private bus operators should be encouraged. To win away sizeable commuter traffic from private cars and the growing intermediate public transport modes such as taxis and auto-rickshaws, fast and luxury bus services should be provided at a reasonable price. Services of differentiated qualities may also be offered at a range of prices to best utilise the consumers surplus.

Rationalise fare structure and make-up subsidies through levies and cess: Unlike the mass transport systems of developed countries which incur losses due to under-utilisation, the losses incurred by the systems in India are mainly due to the subsidised fare structure. There exists ample scope for improving the performance of public transportation in India, which are presently overcrowded and inadequate to meet growing travel demands. Rationalised fare structure based on long run marginal cost principles and without subsidies has tremendous potential to improve the performance of these systems and to augment capacities in the long run. However, we must recognise that almost all urban transportation systems in the world are subsidised. The level of subsidies in India is quite high, and hence needs to be brought down. One strategy for bringing down the subsidy would be to charge a *pollution* cess on private vehicles and transfer it to finance part of the subsidy.

Encourage private operators: To ensure efficient functioning of mass transport systems, a number of private operators should be encouraged. If private operators prefer only profitable routes, agreements should be framed to make them contribute towards the cost of providing services on other uneconomical routes. See Section 7 of this chapter for further discussion on private participation.

Joint Implementation: Further, foreign investments in the form of Joint Implementation may be pursued by exploiting the CO_2 emission reduction potentials of the mass transport systems. In this context, the arguments of Table 11.2 are equally applicable for mass transport systems.

Promote technological options vigorously: In view of serious problems for intra-city movement and wastage of energy as well as adverse consequences of vehicular pollution, more and more use of non-conventional energy like CNG, battery, electricity for vehicles and multi-modal transport systems with low energy consumption and pollution, are necessary. However, the analysis presented in the previous chapter has shown that when market conditions are allowed to operate, the diffusion of these technologies will be so low that it will not cause any appreciable benefit in the next twenty years. Hence, a more vigorous promotion of these alternate clean technologies by the government is required.

A more prudent move to achieve a sustainable (urban) road transport would be to *reduce the volume of travel demand* itself. Some of the strategies for policy purposes include the following:

- Raising the occupancy ratios of vehicles.
- Substituting motorised means of transport by non-motorised means such as bicycling and walking. Planning of new urban areas (extensions of existing metros and newly developing towns) should favour low cost solutions in the form of development of activities within walking distance or by providing exclusive pedestrian paths and cycle track.
- Substituting passenger transport by better communication facilities.
- Instilling an awareness of sustainable development among the travelling public by educational and training programmes.

11.5 Civil Aviation

11.5.1 *Problem Areas*

The civil aviation sector is a key element which must be able to cater to the surge in air traffic that the rapid economic growth in India will cause. This requires investment in increasing the capacities of airlines, and in the development of airports and allied facilities.

The net profit of Air India for the year 1994-95 was Rs. 41 crore, which is quite low compared to the profit of Rs. 200 crore recorded in 1993-94. The net profit of Pawan Hans Limited increased to Rs. 40 crore in 1994-95, which is an improvement compared to Rs. 33.6 crore registered in the previous year. AAI is reporting profits in the last few years. Net profit of its International Airports Division has been Rs. 97.7 crore while that of its National Airports Division has been Rs. 94.15 crore for the year 1994-95.

Indian Airlines has been incurring losses. Its net loss was Rs. 188.73 crore in 1994-95, which is lesser than the loss of Rs. 258.46 crore in 1993-94. Indian Airlines seems to be the most affected by the deregulation and consequent private entry in domestic air services. The details are discussed below.

11.5.2 *Recent Developments*

Airport infrastructure demands heavy investment, large expenditure on servicing, replacements and renewals. For example, it has been reported that IAAI's (prior to merger) eighth plan budget is only US$ 550 million for five airports, whereas Delhi alone would need an immediate investment of around US$ 400 million. The cost of development of a new international airport has been estimated to be of the order of Rs. 7,000 crore. With just Rs. 100 crore as the profit of the international division of AAI, it is obvious that such airports cannot be constructed exclusively by AAI. Hence, domestic and foreign private investors have been invited to participate in the development of new international airports and the expansion of infrastructural support at the domestic airports. It has been suggested that procedural formalities should be simplified to enhance private investment in airports.

Recently, private parties have shown interest in developing airports in India. The Central government has cleared the construction of airports at Bangalore and Cochin in the private sector. A consortium led by the Tata group formalised an agreement with Karnataka State Industrial Investment and Development Corporation to build an international airport at Devanahalli, near Bangalore. The project costs about Rs. 7,000 crore. The project will be on BOT basis. Cochin International Airport Ltd. (CIAL), India's first private airport, is planning to launch a public issue of Rs. 140 crore. This is the first time that an airport development organisation will be approaching the capital market for funds. In a bid to enhance efficiency and decongest airports, AAI has decided to privatise ground handling at Delhi and Mumbai airports. In addition, some innovative steps have been initiated by the ATOs in order to increase their market share. The NEPC airlines has proposed to provide air-rail combined ticket booking facilities at major railway stations and airports in all the metropolitan cities of the country. This may be followed up by other airlines, which will increase the quality of domestic air services.

Regarding the post-liberalisation scenario of the domestic air industry, it is necessary to modify policies to encourage competition in the real sense of the term. At present Indian Airlines is running into huge losses, the private companies do not seem to be comfortable either. Damania Airlines has been taken over by NEPC Airlines and operations of Raj Air have been grounded. High sunk costs and inadequate infrastructural facilities is making it difficult for the small operators to survive in this market. On the other hand, the government has strictly restricted entry of big players. The proposed entry of Tata-Singapore Airlines had been thwarted by introducing a ban on entry till 1996 with the alibi that airports were unable to bear the load of increasing traffic. With restrictions on import of aircraft by existing operators, we find that the private companies are purchasing smaller planes (17 and 19 seaters) and concentrating on shorter feeder routes where there is minimum competition.

11.5.3 *Further Policy Directions*

The primary step would be to enlarge and upgrade airports and allied infrastructural facilities. Adequate availability of these facilities is mandatory in order to encourage competition among airlines. However, the projects for creation and upgradation of airports and related infrastructure (such as the air traffic control) are extremely capital intensive, and have low return and long gestation periods. They require innovative solutions for financing and execution.

As with the discussion on railways and roadways, the following discussion draws heavily from the section on private sector participation, available later in this chapter.

Financing options: A combination of strategies, such as pricing, domestic financing through capital markets, private participation and attracting foreign investment, should be adopted to develop the infrastructure.

Pricing of airport services: The existing pricing schemes in airports require reforms. First of all, all airports should be made to operate autonomously, creating a level-playing-field in which both Indian Airlines and other private operators are made to compete equally. As suggested earlier, the pricing strategy should aim at maximum utilisation of the capacity of airports, and should aim at forcing airlines to formulate schedules and fares related to demand densities on a route basis. Peak and off-peak pricing is one such strategy. Higher charges may be made for the operation of aircraft during peak hours (*i.e.*, morning and/or evening flights), and excursion fares may be charged for off-peak hour operations. This strategy can ensure that the airport facilities are used evenly throughout the day/night.

Domestic financing: The domestic finance for airport infrastructure projects will typically come from debt finance. In developed countries, infrastructure projects raise financing from institutional investors (insurance companies, pension funds, endowments, etc.) either through bond markets, or through direct private placements. In India, institutions such as LIC, GIC, PFs, EPF, other charitable and religious trusts, mutual funds, commercial banks and other financial institutions can provide the required finance. However, their efficient utilisation calls for substantial reform in the debt market. In this connection, a stock exchange type clearing house for transparent trading of debt instruments of different varieties has been recommended by IIR (1996).

At present, the insurance, pension and provident funds are entirely under the control of government, which pre-empts the use of their funds. However, it is necessary to privatise in these areas so that these contractual savings are brought to the capital market.

Long-term debt instruments, in the line of the recent issues of deep discount bonds by the financial institutions such as IFCI and IDBI, should be developed. However, these bonds had an interest rate much higher than the rates reported to be suitable for long-term infrastructure investment (about 10% in real terms). Issuing tax free bonds, such as those Konkan Railway Corporation, can be considered. This further requires credit enhancements of borrowing entities through bond insurance, provision of guarantees, credit rating of infrastructure projects and companies, funding of feasibility studies, etc.

In addition, fiscal incentives may be offered to attract equities in infrastructure projects. In India, a five year tax holiday is available under Section 80-IA of the Income Tax Act to enterprises engaged in developing, maintaining and operating infrastructure facilities such as roads, highways, bridges, new airports, ports and rail systems. In the 1996-97 Union budget any dividend, interest or long-term capital gains arising out of infrastructure funding have been exempted from income tax. Investment in approved debentures or equity shares of public companies have been made eligible for tax rebate under Section 88 of the Income Tax Act, if the proceeds of such public issues are applied to create a new infrastructure facility or to generate or distribute power. In the case of such investment, the limit of Rs. 60,000 under Section 88 has been raised to Rs. 70,000. In addition to these reforms, further tax reliefs similar to the erstwhile 80CC provision may also be contemplated.

Special footing for attracting foreign investment: Foreign investment not only bring the much needed finance, but also the crucial technological know-how and managerial skills. They have to be attracted by placing them on a preferred footing. Special channels for such funds should be opened, with minimum administrative hurdles.

Private sector participation: To achieve the required capacity of airports in the near future, private investment should be encouraged, for which it is necessary to minimise procedural formalities. Agreements should be framed with these parties without ambiguity to avoid confusions after the projects have been initiated.

It has been reported that private investment in several large and medium projects have been delayed due to several constraints. A viable and transparent policy framework should be formulated to avoid unnecessary delays at crucial stages of private participation. It is necessary to follow competitive bidding and benchmarking, and simplify legal and procedural formalities to encourage private investment.

Airport projects are highly capital intensive, which may not be within the reach of many private parties, even after considering financial assistance from capital markets. For example, in spite of its proposed public issue, it has been reported that CIAL is scaling down its original investment plans for the construction of the Cochin International Airport. It has been reported that it is now planning to have manual methods of Air Traffic Control (ATC), when many of India's existing airports are planning to automatise further. The main problem is the lack of sufficient funds to the private agency (CIAL). To avoid such difficulties for future airport infrastructure projects, it is necessary to modularise the activities of airport development (such as runway construction, runway maintenance, ATC construction, etc.), and allow private entry to different modules of airport development. If the profitability of the projects are still in doubt, then government-private partnerships may be created to instill confidence in the private parties. Once projects become sufficiently profitable, government may divest and reinvest the money on other risky projects.

Legal issues: Private investment in airport infrastructure is usually obtained through the Build, Operate and Transfer (BOT) format. At present, there exists no Act in India which defines the principles, procedures and rules to be followed for such a format. Hence, the first and foremost requirement would be to set up such a legislation, which is generally applicable to projects in all infrastructural sectors.

- The BOT approach was developed at the end of the 1970s as a way for countries with severe budgetary restrains to acquire needed infrastructure. The salient characteristics of these projects have been discussed later.

Dispute resolution: A special legal system should be developed to resolve disputes in infrastructure projects very fast. Conventional legal procedures, which start with lower courts, take a very long time and the delays can be detrimental for the development of infrastructure owing to cost escalations (example, the ENRON project). Special courts should be formed for resolving disputes related to infrastructure projects.

11.6 Water Transport

Waterways of transport is an important mode of transport for both passenger and cargo traffic in India. They include Shipping, Ports and Inland Water Transport.

11.6.1 *Shipping*

The Shipping Corporation of India (SCI) registered a net profit after tax of Rs. 201 crore in 1994-95, which represents an increase by 19 per cent compared to the previous year. The other two shipyards, *viz.* Cochin Shipyards Ltd. and Hindustan Shipyards Limited, which have been incurring losses till the year 1993, have registered profits in 1994-95. Their profit stood at Rs. 11.2 crore and Rs. 33.4 crore respectively.

Recent developments: India's shipping policy aims at increasing self reliance in the carriage of country's overseas trade and reserving 100 per cent coastal trade to national shipping. Following the liberalisation process, for promoting the development of Indian shipping, a new shipping policy was initiated in 1990-91. Its salient features are summarised in Table 11.6.

TABLE 11.6: Reforms in Shipping Sector

- Automatic approval is now given for acquisition of all but a few selected categories of ships.
- No approval is required for sale and acquisition of ships from an Indian shipyard.
- Shipping companies are allowed to retain sale proceeds of their ships abroad and utilise them for fresh acquisition.
- They are given freedom to time charters out Indian ships.
- They are allowed to acquire vessels through bare boat charter-cum-demise method.
- They are permitted to get their ships repaired in any shipyard without seeking prior approval from the government.
- Quarterly Block Allocation Scheme for repair of ships has been dispensed with entirely, and the Reserve Bank of India now releases foreign exchange for ship repair/drydocking and spares for imported capital goods without any value limit.
- Certain sections of Merchant Shipping Act have been amended to facilitate Indian shipping companies to raise external commercial borrowing for foreign ship acquisitions.
- As per the recent amendments to Section 42 of the Merchant Shipping Act, 1958, from October 1993 no prior permission from Directorate General of Shipping is required for sale of vessels either for further trading or scrapping by the Indian shipping companies.
- The Multimodal Transportation of Goods Act, 1993 was introduced to facilitate the exporters and give them a sense of security in transporting their goods. Door-to-door delivery is ensured by this Act, which reduces the logistic costs to the exporter, making his products more competitive in international market.

Source: Economic Survey, 1996-97 and *Annual Report* (1995).

Further policy directions: Competition and private participation should be more seriously encouraged in the shipping sector. It has been reported that the "cost plus" formula adopted by the SCI for pricing its services (especially to the oil industry) requires modification as it conceals inefficiencies of operation. The inefficiencies are revealed by the continuous losses suffered by SCI when it was forced to use its tankers in the open markets. It is necessary to encourage competition to overcome this situation. To ensure best service at least cost, foreign collaborations and investment should be pursued. More private parties should be encouraged to register as Multimodal Transportation Operators.

11.6.2 *Ports*

In 1993-94, all major ports have generated operating surpluses. Port productivity has improved in recent years. The average ship turnaround time during April-October, 1994 was 7.6 days, as against the 7 days for the corresponding period in 1993. However, in contrast to port productivity, labour and equipment productivity levels are low due to surplus labour in ports, outdated equipment and operational constraints.

Bottlenecks and Recent Developments: The key problem facing Indian ports is their low productivity. Major factors contributing to this include the following:

- Obsolete and overage equipment. They result in operational constraints such as frequent breakdown of cargo-handling equipment. Non-optimal deployment of equipment add further to the inefficiency.
- Inadequate dredging and container-handling facilities.
- Draft limitations.
- Inadequacy of container handling facilities.
- Unionised labour.
- Labour intensive methods of bulk handling of sensitive commodities like thermal coal.
- Lack of proper coordination in the entire logistics chain.

It has been estimated that, in 2000-01, the overall port capacity required would be 325 million tonnes and the overall port traffic would be 390 million tonnes (IIR, 1996). These represent an increase of about 86 per cent and 97 per cent compared to the existing capacity and traffic respectively in 1995. About Rs 10,000 crore is expected to be needed for increasing the capacities of Indian ports. Of these, internal accruals of the ports are expected to be about Rs 6,000 crore. The remaining Rs 4,000 crore should be generated from outside such as by encouraging private participation.

Port capacities can be increased by developing many small or big ports. Privatisation of ports is relatively easier as development of one port is independent of the development of another. This has been recognised by the government. In order to attract private investments along with modern technology, the process of privatisation of port facilities has started with the announcement of the new economic policy. Broadly, the following areas have been identified for private sector participation in port sector (CMIE, 1995).

- Operation/setting up of container terminals.
- Setting up of warehousing and storage facilities.
- Operation and maintenance of various cargo handling terminals.
- Operation and maintenance of floating crafts.
- Provision of pilotage, dredging and carnage services.
- Maintenance of other miscellaneous services.

Some of the measures introduced for encouraging private sector participation in ports include the following:

- Relaxation of Cabotage law.
- Enactment of the Multimodal Transportation of Goods Act, 1993.
- Berth reservation facilities in ports.
- Leasing of berths to private entrepreneurs.
- Leasing of land and water front for setting up ship repair facilities.
- Creation of storage facilities.
- Privatisation of dry docks and liberalisation of licensing procedures.

The results of the above efforts are beginning to yield results. Two dry docks at Calcutta dock system have been privatised. At Haldia complex, two berths have been leased out to the Steel Authority of India Limited and the Tata Iron & Steel Company Limited. Maharashtra government has decided to have 11 per cent equity participation in the construction of seven of the total 48 minor ports. The development of the 41 other ports would be on BOLT basis. The assets will be transferred to the State government after 30 years. The Government of Andhra

Pradesh has cleared the privatisation of Krishnapatnam port to develop it into a road-rail-port complex. Hyderabad based NATCO group has been awarded Rs. 1,300 crore project. The Gujarat government is developing ten ports under its modernisation programme. Of these, six ports would be developed by private companies.

Further policy prescriptions: Indian ports have the potential for emerging as Asian hubs. This requires an immediate upgradation of their handling technology, and modernisation of their equipment and management. These demand commercialisation and privatisation of ports.

The first requirement is to make the ports more autonomous and reduce existing legal formalities.

Autonomous port authorities should be made to operate on commercial lines so that they can raise resources from the primary market by way of equity and debt and from financial institutions. They should also be allowed to fix tariffs so as to cover their debt obligations and earn a reasonable return on equity. Port authorities should be delegated powers to create new technical posts required for modernisation.

At present, the port trusts have powers to incur expenditure up to Rs. 5 crore only. This limit may be raised to enable them to create more assets. Further, projects to be executed through private participation involving no investment by the ports should not require the approval of the Expenditure Finance Committee or the Public Investment Board.

It has been reported that the recent reforms in ports sector do not provide for construction of additional facilities through private investment, which has led to no significant capacity generation in ports. Hence, amendments to the Act are necessary to permit projects to be taken up on a BOT basis in ports.

Training institutes should be set up to improve the technical skills of the existing labour in line with modernisation of ports. To minimise the unionised labour problem, especially with regard to privatisation, voluntary retirement scheme should be vigorously pursued.

Government may give fiscal incentives for private sector participation in ports. The ports may be exempted from paying corporate tax, while investment by the private parties may be given further tax relief.

In addition, privatisation involves consideration of various issues. They are discussed in detail later in this chapter.

11.6.3 *Inland Water Transport*

The performance of CIWTC has been improving over the years. During

April-September, 1994, the average monthly traffic handled was about 25,000 tonnes and about 95 lakh TKM. This is better than the performance of 20,000 tonnes and about 86 lakh TKM recorded for the whole financial year of 1993-94. Its average monthly freight earnings during April-September, 1994 were about Rs. 59 lakh, which is quite high compared to the earning of about Rs. 46 lakh registered for the whole of 1993-94.

Recent developments: The government is promoting IWT in the form of interest subsidies and inducing private investment. IWT entrepreneurs are granted an interest subsidy in the form of subsidised interest rate of 5.5 per cent on the loans obtained from banks/financial institutions. For promoting the use of this mode by private operators, they are encouraged to use CIWTC vessels free of hire charges.

Further policy directions: IWT is a cheaper and more energy efficient mode. It has been estimated that IWT movement of cargo would cost around Rs. 0.65 per TKM for a distance of above 1000 km, which is cheaper than road freight transport. Movement through IWT is also the best mode from the point of view of ecology preservation. Hence, IWT has a good potential to be exploited wherever possible, and efforts should be made in this direction. Passenger transport should be more vigorously encouraged. Intermodal connections with shipping, railways and roadways can improve the performance of IWT and hence encourage better utilisation of this mode of transport.

11.7 Issues related to Private Sector Participation*

Power, telecommunication, roads, civil aviation, ports, urban transport and airports are the main sectors where restructuring has recently been initiated. Private sector participation is now encouraged in these sectors.

11.7.1 *Need for Private Sector Participation: Resource Crunch*

The expert group on the commercialisation of infrastructure projects (IIR, 1996) has estimated a total infrastructure (in power, telecom, roads, ports and urban infrastructure) investment requirement of Rs. 4,00,000 to Rs. 4,50,000 crore during the next five years. As much as 85 per cent of this investment is expected to be made using domestic resources. This should be compared with Rs. 1,27,000 crore (approx.) invested in these sectors over the eighth plan. Looked at it differently, this is 45 per cent to 50 per cent of our GDP for the year 1995-96.

* This section draws from IIR (1996) and Parikh and Ramanathan (1997).

It has been realised that the public sector alone cannot come up with the finances needed for the infrastructure sectors. This calls for tapping the resources of the private sector. The share of private investment in infrastructure (power, telecom, roads, ports and urban infrastructure) is expected to rise from the current Rs. 12,000 crore per year to Rs. 38,000 crore in 2000-01.

This has transformed the policy of financing the infrastructure development entirely from government resources to promoting private sector participation.

11.7.2 *Need for a Well-Defined Policy for Private Sector Participation*

Absence of a clear cut policy on private sector participation is the most vital issue affecting the progress of the reforms. The recent chaos encountered in restructuring the telecommunication sector illustrates this point. Owing to the huge costs of delays in infrastructure projects, a well defined policy is a must for timely decision making. The policy should provide clear guidelines for moving from a completely government controlled regime to a regime where private sector participation is significant and control is exercised by market forces. Specifically the policy should cover the following aspects.

11.7.2.1 *Unbundling*

Most of the infrastructure services are natural monopolies. They require a co-ordinating mechanism to ensure efficient operation. However, parts of the service can be operated by small independent operators under well defined agreements with the Central Management. In a restructured economy, the monopoly services can be subjected a regulatory framework, while the non-monopoly services can be opened to private parties for competition. For example, in the operation of railways, track management is a monopoly service, while railway operation and provision of other services (such as maintenance of railway stations) are the non-monopoly services. This type of dividing the operations of an infrastructure is called "fragmenting" or "vertical unbundling." The increased competition and the resulting economic efficiency will ensure a better service to the consumers.

Several infrastructure services which have long been thought of as natural monopolies no longer hold the characteristic, thanks to technological progress (*e.g.*, telecommunications.) Vertical unbundling can provide the scope for private participation in such sectors.

Even when an infrastructure is highly monopolistic and it is not desirable to disturb that setting, "horizontal unbundling" can be adopted to ensure competition. In this case, the geographical area is divided into different zones and different agents provide infrastructure service to the zones. The performance can then be gauged by comparing the operations in different zones and by way of "Yardstick competition."

An example for this type of unbundling is the privatisation of the Japan National Railways (JNR) (Okano, 1990; Kikeri, Nellis and Shirley, 1992). In the eighties, it was recognised that the inbuilt inflexibility, bureaucracy, overmanning and low productivity of a large public sector monopoly were causing mounting losses to JNR. To overcome the problems, the JNR was restructured and six passenger and one freight railway companies were created in 1987. The performance of these companies are reported to be much better than expected—both in terms of finance and quality of service. However, the experience in Japan shows that two preconditions are necessary for such horizontal unbundling to be successful—regulation and market competition. Without regulation, even a privatised enterprise cannot improve its managerial efficiency because operational strategies are limited. Without competition, a privatised enterprise has no strong incentives to improve managerial efficiency.

Even if it is established that some components can be effective only as a monopoly, competition can be introduced for operating such a monopoly through franchising and competitive bidding.

11.7.2.2 *Framing of Agreements*

Inviting private investment is fraught with certain risks. They may try to extract unreasonable concessions. They may operate only on profitable routes or may serve only select customers, thus compromising the social merit good aspect of infrastructure. Due care has to be taken while framing agreements with private parties to avoid these problems. They should be framed without ambiguity to avoid difficulties later. For example, it is necessary to clearly demarcate and allocate risks to different stakeholders as the tendency of each stakeholder is to shift the risk to others. Privatisation policy should provide adequate guidelines for framing agreements, which may be sector specific.

Guidelines should be provided for tackling different kinds of risks which concern private parties. Commercial risks (*e.g.*, cost overruns, delays, and shortfalls in project revenues) are usually within the control of the private parties, while political risks (*e.g.*, expropriation of assets and civil unrest,) are not. The former can be mitigated through a clear agreement about marketing the product. Another major kind of risk arises due to lack of adequate legal, institutional and regulatory systems. This makes it possible for government to take unpredictable actions, which can seriously erode profitability of projects (Razavi, 1996). Counter-guarantees from government can be used against these kinds of risks.

11.7.2.3 *Transparency*

In our democratic system, it is absolutely essential that a transparent policy framework should be formulated to avoid unnecessary delays at crucial stages of private participation. It is necessary to follow competitive bidding and benchmarking, and simplify legal and procedural formalities to encourage private investment.

11.7.3 *Financial Options*

As said earlier, the infrastructure investments require huge finances, most of which have to come from domestic sources. How can infrastructure firms raise the needed finances? It requires first of all an improvement in their financial performances. In addition several innovative approaches will be needed to improve capital markets, to develop new instruments and to create new institutional arrangements. These are discussed below.

11.7.3.1 *Performance Improvement*

Improving the performance of existing infrastructure services provides the least cost solution for meeting future infrastructure demands. This will not only reduce the need for new capacities but also improve the financial performance and credit rating of infrastructure firms. Performance can be improved in many ways. Capacity utilisation should be improved. For example, more reliable and punctual train services can attract the growing demand of freight transport, and a rational utilisation of existing tracks and wagons can handle the increased demand without much increase in the investment requirements. More rationalised, cost based fare structure can also improve the financial performance and help meeting future investment needs.

11.7.3.2 *Capital Markets*

Privately financed infrastructure projects need well-developed domestic capital markets. The total funding requirements for infrastructure to be financed from the domestic capital market is projected to rise from the current Rs. 25,000 crore to Rs. 42,000 crore per year by 2000-01. Since the level of retained earnings (after meeting costs of capital-service, tax and statutory capital reserve requirements) over and above the depreciation provision is low, infrastructure firms typically fund projects through debt finance (IIR, 1996).

In developed countries, infrastructure projects raise finance from institutional investors (insurance companies, pension funds, endowments, etc. which are willing to invest in long-term debt instruments) either through bond markets, or through direct private placements. In India, institutions such as LIC, GIC, PFs, EPF, other charitable and religious trusts, mutual funds, commercial banks and other financial institutions can provide the required finance. However, their efficient utilisation calls for substantial reform in the debt market. At present the debt market is not well developed. In this connection, a stock exchange type clearing house for transparent trading of debt instruments of different varieties has been recommended by IIR (1996).

At present, the insurance, pension and provident funds are entirely under the control of government, which pre-empts the use of their funds. However, it is necessary to permit private entry in these areas so that some of these contractual savings are brought to the capital market.

11.7.3.3 *Financial Instruments*

Long-term debt instruments should be developed. The recent issues of deep discount bonds by the financial institutions such as IFCI and IDBI is a welcome step in this direction. However, these bonds had an interest rate much higher than the rates reported to be suitable for long-term infrastructure investment (about 10% in real terms). This requires credit enhancements of borrowing infrastructure firms through bond insurance, provision of guarantees, credit rating of infrastructure projects and companies, funding of feasibility studies, fiscal incentives, etc.

11.7.3.4 *Fiscal Incentives for Equity Capital*

In addition, fiscal incentives may be offered to attract equities in infrastructure projects. In India, a five year tax holiday is available under Section 80-IA of the Income Tax Act to enterprises engaged in developing, maintaining and operating infrastructure facilities such as roads, highways, bridges, new airports, ports and rail systems. Along with the accumulated depreciation that can be claimed from the 6th to 10th year, firms in effect pay no tax for 10 years.

In the 1996-97 Union budget any dividend, interest or long-term capital gains arising out of infrastructure funding have been exempted from income tax. Investment in approved debentures or equity shares of public companies have been made eligible for tax rebate under Section 88 of the Income Tax Act, if the proceeds of such public issues are applied to create a new infrastructure facility or to generate or distribute power. In the case of such investment, the limit of Rs. 60,000 under Section 88 has been raised to Rs. 70,000.

11.7.3.5 *Foreign Investment*

We can accelerate infrastructure development if foreign private infrastructure investment is attracted also. Special channels for such funds may be provided to minimise administrative hurdles. Unfortunately our experience so far has been dismal. After five years of fast track policy only one power plant is constructed and even construction is not yet commenced (or recommissioned in the case of the suspended ENRON project as on January, 1997) in spite of more than 240 MOUs that have been signed. This underlines the need for streamlining procedures.

11.7.3.6 *Institutions*

To administer all these changes in the financial market, a new institution is required. The government has announced the establishment of such an institution, namely the Infrastructure Development Finance Company (IDFC) in the Union budget 1996-97. However, there has not been much progress in its development, mainly because of non-cooperative attitude of those opposed to liberalisation. It should be developed very fast, empowered to function autonomously, and allowed to offer various forms of financial instruments to boost the debt market infrastructure financing.

11.7.4 *Issues in Regulation*

As pointed out earlier, most infrastructure facilities have monopolistic elements which need to be regulated. One should emphasise that even government monopolies need regulation at least to prevent them from passing the burden of their inefficiency on the public. It is necessary to separate the two roles of government as an operator and a regulator. The responsibility of regulation should be vested with independent regulatory authorities and a level-playing field must be created in which both government and private operators are treated equally without any bias. With unbundling, this becomes particularly important.

11.7.4.1 *Legal Issues*

It is imperative to simplify legal and procedural formalities to encourage private investment in infrastructural projects.

At present, there exists no Act in India which defines the principles, procedures and rules to be followed in setting up and implementing an infrastructure project. Hence, the first and foremost requirement would be to set up such a legislation for project formats such as Build, Operate and Transfer (BOT). This legislation may be applicable to projects in all infrastructural sectors.

The BOT approach was developed at the end of the 1970s as a way for countries with severe budgetary restrains to acquire needed infrastructure. The salient characteristics of these projects are given below (Augenblick and Custer, 1990).

- Private sector sponsors, usually international construction contractors, heavy equipment suppliers, and plant and system operators, often together with local partners,
  - — making equity investments, typically 10 per cent to 30 per cent of the total project cost.
  - — private project company which will build the project, operate it for a period of time sufficient to pay back the project debt and equity investment, and then transfer it to the host government.
- Debt financing (typically 70% to 90% of the total project cost) is raised by the project company from commercial sources, usually backed by export credit guarantee agencies, and from bilateral and multilateral lenders.

The legislation should cover each of the above characteristics. As suggested in IIR (1996), the example of the BOT law of the Philippines may be followed. Some of the salient features of the provisions of this law are given below:

- Areas in which private participation would be allowed.
- Terms and conditions and standardisation of bidding documents and contracts.

- Extent of ownerships of projects.
- Competitive bidding.
- Format for operating the projects—BOT, BOLT, etc.
- Technology transfer.
- Grounds on which direct government guarantees could be available.
- Eligibility criteria defining the manner in which the bids could be evaluated and contracts awarded.
- Ensuring a rate of return—arrangements for collecting toll, fees, rent, etc. and formulae for calculating them reasonably.
- Grounds on which a project can be terminated by either of parties.
- Setting up of regulatory agencies.

In addition, existing legal structures should be strengthened to cope up with the problems expected as a result of private provision of infrastructure. For example, the scope of existing consumer protection legislation (including the consumer courts) should be expanded to include infrastructural services. Rules should be made much stronger for a declining quality of these services. When a consumer can sue and get compensation for an improper infrastructure service fast, consumer awareness will increase which will improve the quality of all services.

11.7.4.2 *Dispute Resolution*

A special legal system should be developed to resolve disputes in infrastructure projects very fast. Conventional legal procedures, which start with lower courts, take a very long time and the delays can be detrimental for the development of infrastructure owing to cost escalations (*e.g.*, the ENRON project). Special courts should be formed for resolving disputes related to infrastructure projects. Special overriding sections for settling disputes in infrastructure projects may be added to the relevant legislation (*e.g.*, The Industrial Disputes Act, 1947).

11.7.5 *Dominant Role of the State in Infrastructure Development*

While private sector participation is a welcome step in bridging the gap between the expected financial needs of infrastructure and the funds available to the government, it should be highlighted that State still has the dominant role in infrastructure development. For example, though the future share in infrastructure investment of the public sector is expected to decline from the current 80 per cent, it will still be more than 50 per cent in 2000-01.

There are several other avenues that require a catalytic role of the State in infrastructure development. As many infrastructure investments have low returns, private sector may be reluctant to take up certain projects even though the projects are socially vital. In these cases, government should provide additional incentives (such as the development of auxiliary facilities for road and rail track projects) which will make the project more attractive. Alternatively, government can provide subsidies to the private parties for taking up the projects (*e.g.*, shadow tolling of road projects).

Infrastructure investment is particularly risky during the construction period and in the initial years of the project. Hence, many private investments cannot be immediately expected in infrastructure, especially when the projects are at their beginning stage. It is then imperative for the government to take up significant equity positions in these projects to start with and use this to attract commercial equity funds as well as debt from different sources. However, once the project becomes commercially viable, the government should disinvest and reinvest in new projects.

12

URBAN TRANSPORT POLICY

Like the trend worldwide, India is undergoing rapid urbanisation. This means not only that more people than ever before will be living and working in cities, but also that more people and more goods will be making more trips in urban areas, often over longer distances. How Indian cities meet this burgeoning demand for urban travel has implications for the environment, the economic efficiency, and the liveability of these areas.

Urban vehicular growth closely follows the trend of urbanisation. Motor vehicles offer undeniable advantages such as speed and convenience; indeed during the early stages of the development of a city, motor vehicles are vital to economic growth. However, the costs of increasing dependence on cars in the world's cities are becoming all too apparent. These include expensive road building and maintenance; clogged, congested streets that undermine economic productivity; high levels of energy consumption along with its impact on economic and environmental costs; worsening air and noise pollution; traffic accidents; and social inequities that arise when poor find transportation services to be increasingly unaffordable.

Vehicle growth in urban areas has close relationship with the level of urbanisation. Some details of urbanisation has been discussed in Chapter 2, its linkages with vehicular growth in Indian cities in Chapter 4, and some problem areas pertaining to urban transport in the previous chapter. In this chapter, some policy issues pertaining to urban transport in India will be discussed in detail.

12.1 Urbanisation in India

India has witnessed a tremendous growth in urbanisation since independence (Table 12.1). Urban population has increased from 62.4

Note: This chapter is partly based on Ramanathan (1998b) and Ramanathan (1999a).

million in 1951 to 217.2 million in 1991, nearly 3.5 times. In 1991, urban population accounted for 25.7 per cent of total population. Urban population has approximately doubled in two decades (say 1961-1981 or 1971-1991). There were 296 Class I cities (forming just 8.2% of the total towns of all classes) accommodating 65.2 per cent of the urban population in 1991. Just 23 metropolitan cities (having a population of one million and above) had more than 50 per cent of the population of Class I cities.

TABLE 12.1: Growth of Urbanisation in India

Description	*1951*	*1961*	*1971*	*1981*	*1991*
No. of UAs/towns	2,843	2,365	2,590	3,378	3,768
Urban Population (millions)	62.4	78.9	109.1	159.5	217.2
% of Urban Population	17.3	18.0	19.9	23.3	25.7
Decennial growth rate of urban population (%)	41.4	26.4	38.2	46.1	36.2
% Urban population in					
—Class I	44.6	51.4	57.2	60.4	65.2
—Class II	10.0	11.2	10.9	11.6	10.9
—Class III	15.7	16.9	16.0	14.3	13.2
—Class IV	13.6	12.8	10.9	9.5	7.8
—Class V	13.0	6.9	4.5	3.6	2.6
—Class VI	3.1	0.8	0.4	0.5	0.3

Note: Class I towns (called cities) have a population of 1,00,000 and above; Class II: 50,000-99,999; Class III: 20,000 to 49,999; Class IV: 10,000 to 19,999; Class V: 5,000 to 9,999; and Class VI: less than 5,000.

Source: 1991 Census Data, Government of India, New Delhi.

Table 12.2 shows the trends in the evolution of metropolitan cities in India. India had only 5 metropolitan cities in 1951, which has increased

TABLE 12.2: Trends in the Growth of Metropolitan Cities in India

	No. of Metropolitan Cities	*Average Population in millions*	*Share (%) of Population of Metropolitan Cities in*	
			Total Population	*Urban Population*
1951	5	2.35	3.25	18.81
1961	7	2.59	4.12	22.93
1971	9	3.09	5.08	25.51
1981	12	3.51	6.16	26.41
1991	23	3.07	8.37	32.54

Source: Census of India, 1991.

to 23 in 1991. The number has nearly doubled during 1981-91. The proportion of urban population living in metropolitan cities grew rapidly, from about 19 per cent in 1951 to 33 per cent in 1991. This indicates the increasing urban population densities in the metropolitan areas.

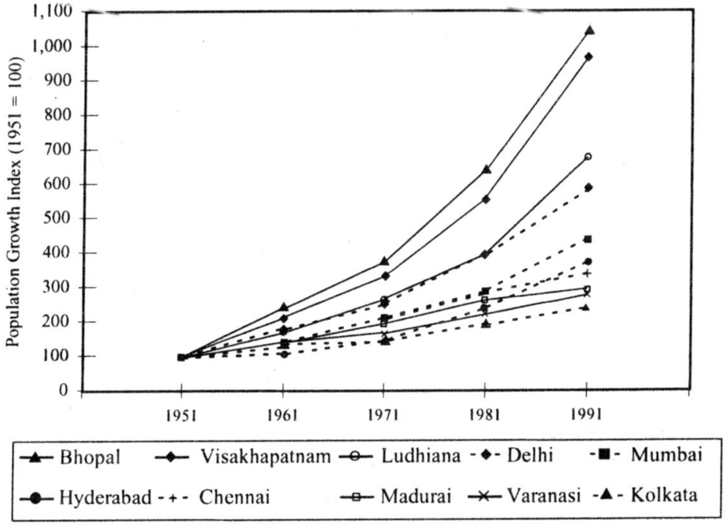

FIG. 12.1: Population Growth of Top and Bottom Five Metropolitan Cities in India
Source: Census of India, 1991, Government of India.

Most of the smaller metropolitan cities have been registering higher population growth (Fig. 12.1). Bhopal has been registering the highest growth — its population in 1991 was more than 10 times its population in 1951.

India had 93 cities with population above 0.2 million, and 73 cities with population above 0.3 million in the year 1991 (Census of India, 1991). A study by the Government of India has projected that there will be 83 cities in India by 2001 with a population of 0.25 million (MoUD, 1987).

12.2 Patterns of Growth of Urban Transport in India

In general, vehicle population in cities, mostly dominated by personalised vehicles, follows urbanisation. This pattern is not sustainable as personalised vehicles are inefficient users of energy, and inflict a number of externalities such as pollution and congestion. The problems of such a rapid urbanisation and associated energy issues have been discussed by Jain, Satsangi and Kothari (1994). They have highlighted the problems due to pollution, traffic congestion, waste generation and slums. They have been discussed in Chapter 3 and Chapter 11 of this book also.

Some details on vehicular population in selected Indian cities have been discussed in Chapter 2 (see Table 2.6). On the basis of these data, the existence of a logistic relationship between the number of vehicles and population in Indian cities has been empirically established in Chapter 7. It has been further highlighted in that chapter that the S-shaped logistic pattern of growth of vehicles in urban India has important implications for formulating proper policies for urban transport. It has been observed in the last section that a number of towns in India are urbanising rapidly. Many of them will enter rapid phase (as outlined in Fig. 7.1) in the near future, and hence a very high level of vehicle growth can thus be expected in the future.

Note that the logistic pattern can be altered by policy formulations. For example, if a city is developed to encourage walking and cycling by providing all the facilities with a smaller geographical area, the growth of motorised vehicles may be reduced. Many cities expand because people settle in the cheaper periphery regions of the city, and prefer travel for work. This can happen so long as travel is relatively inexpensive compared with land. However, if travel is made more expensive, the horizontal growth of the geography of cities will be arrested and consequently there will be lesser travel.

A more detailed data on vehicular growth in the four mega cities of India is shown in Table 12.3. The growth of three wheelers as important intermediate public transport modes for passengers is highlighted in this table. Both Mumbai and Chennai have recorded high growth of these vehicles. Chennai has recorded highest growth of two wheelers during the period. Mumbai has shown a favourable trend in passenger transportation by recording high growth in the number of buses, and a negative growth in the number of cars, jeeps and taxis.

12.3 Issues associated with the Growth of Urban Transport

The disproportionate growth of the personalised vehicles in Indian cities has many implications: severe road congestion, reduction in speed, increase in accidents, increased energy consumption, and emission of local and global pollutants.

12.3.1 *Uneven Growth of Private and Public Transport*

The composition of personalised vehicles in Indian cities is very high,

TABLE 12.3: Vehicles Data as on 31 March, 1994

	All India	*Mumbai*	*Delhi*	*Kolkata*	*Chennai*	*4 Megacities*	
						Total	*Share*
Two Wheelers	1,83,38,000 (8.90)	2,58,960 (2.28)	14,92,201 (6.93)	2,33,634 (6.21)	4,97,640 (8.78)	24,82,435 (6.69)	13.54%
3 Wheelers—Pass.	a	35,567 (13.11)	72,102 (4.60)	6,973 (6.65)	20,202 (23.79)	1,34,844 (9.05)	a
3 Wheelers—Goods	a	8,633 (−16.40)	b	16,874 (5.10)	1,912 (9.36)	27,419 (−3.77)	a
Cars, Jeeps and Taxis	36,17,000 (6.98)	2,53,047 (−5.44)	5,34,110 (9.34)	2,27,736 (3.48)	1,34,829 (5.24)	11,49,722 (3.76)	31.79
Buses	4,19,000 (8.18)	11,394 (12.67)	24,211 (8.69)	13,457 (0.75)	8,716 (3.70)	57,778 (6.52)	13.79
Trucks	16,50,000 (6.76)	33,110 (−1.73)	1,16,379 (4.55)	35,969 (0.90)	19,517 (6.03)	2,04,975 (2.91)	12.42%
Others[c]	32,03,000 (8.14)	51,785 (5.31)	72,102 (4.60)	33,961 (8.87)	28,441 (17.59)	1,86,289 (7.22)	5.82%
All Vehicles	2,72,27,000 (8.40)	6,08,296 (−1.08)	22,39,003 (7.29)	5,44,757 (4.67)	6,89,143 (8.20)	40,81,199 (5.65)	14.99%

Note: a—included in Others and separate All India information is not available;
b—included in trucks;
c—includes 3 Wheelers, tractors, trailors and other vehicles.

Note: Figures in parenthesis indicate annual growth rate, 1991-94.

Source: Based on data from Motor Transport Statistics of India, 1991-94, by Transport Research Wing, Ministry of Surface Transport, 1995.

and their growth has been much higher than that of public transport vehicles. In the four major metro cities, they form nearly 83 per cent (two-wheelers 52% and cars 31%) of the total number of vehicles. Public buses formed only 30 per cent of the total number of buses in 1991-92 (declined from about 46% in 1980-81). The State Transport Undertakings operating bus transport systems have recorded losses for the past few years (see Table 11.4). The share of public transport buses in the total number of vehicles reduced drastically to just 1.9 per cent in 1989-90 from 11.5 per cent in 1960-62. In contrast, personalised and the intermediate passenger transport vehicles (taxis and auto-rickshaws) have increased considerably in these metropolises and other lower order towns.

The share of mass transport in total passenger traffic was less than 55 per cent in major Indian cities during the year 1980 (NCU, 1988). Important exceptions are Mumbai, Kolkata and Chennai, where the suburban rail traffic plays a very important role in passenger traffic. Share of mass transport modes in total trips in Delhi, Mumbai, Kolkata, Chennai and Bangalore were 63 per cent, 67 per cent, 54 per cent, 55 per cent and 70 per cent respectively in the late eighties or early nineties. In Lucknow, cycling and walking accounted for 55 per cent of the total trips (Habitat, 1994; CSE, 1996).

12.3.2 *Insufficient Road Infrastructure*

The share of urban roads in total roads in India has declined significantly, from about 8 per cent in 1971 to just about 6 per cent in 1996. In contrast, the urban areas have always had more than 20 per cent of total population, and metropolitan cities alone (which constituted just 7.7 per cent of total number of Class I cities in 1991 or 0.65 per cent of the total number of all towns of all classes) account for more than 33 per cent of the total motor vehicles. This highlights the gross inadequacy of the supply of urban roads to meet to the growing user demands.

This inadequacy of urban road network has been compounded by the rapid increase in the number of vehicles, most of which will ply on the urban roads. The de-licensing of the auto industry in 1991 has fuelled an unparalleled growth in the passenger car segment. About 22 projects involving total investment of more than Rs. 20,000 crore have been committed in this sector so far. Of these, eight projects of Rs. 7,500 crore are completed and fourteen others are under various stages of implementation. Those completed have a collective capacity to manufacture around 3,00,000 cars. The annual sale of all vehicles, which was around 3 million in 1994-95, is expected to nearly double to 5.7 million in 2000-01. Most of them will occupy urban roads and add to the existing congestion, unless sufficient road networks are planned and made available.

While no time series data are available to identify the transportation changes with urbanisation, certain trends can be observed with the cross-sectional data on mobility and congestion indicators for selected cities (Table 12.4). With the exception of Chennai, a general reduction in the per capita road length is observed as the size of the city increases. With a few exceptions, there is a general decrease in the ratio of road length to area as the city size increases. There is also a general increase in the PCUs and an increase in number of PCUs per km of road length as the city grows. These indicate the improvements in road structure have not been in tune with the growth of vehicles. The situation was much worse in the nineties than in the eighties. PCU per 1000 population has increased by more than 2.5 times in Delhi, Mumbai and Kolkata. Delhi has recorded the highest increase. Per capita road length has decreased. More importantly, the number of vehicles per km of road has tremendously increased, with Delhi registering nearly five-fold increase.

12.3.3 *Congestion*

The most visible evidence of the deteriorating urban transport system in India is the rising number of traffic jams and the discomfort of suburban train travel. This may indirectly lead to a decline in the overall economic productivity of the cities.

The rapid growth of personalised modes of transport in Indian cities gives rise to serious congestions problems. A study has estimated that an increase in the share of bus travel from 57 per cent to 80 per cent in big Indian cities will lead to 54 per cent reduction in the number of vehicles on road (MoUD, 1987).

Insufficient road infrastructure also leads to more accidents, injuries and deaths. The congestion problem in many cities is compounded by the fact that there is no lane for slow moving vehicles and animals.

The share of Passenger Car Units (PCU)* of the personalised vehicles is quite out of proportion to their share of traffic fulfilment. Their average number of trips served in some of the principal cities is 21 per cent, while in terms of PCUs these vehicles have accounted for 87 per

* PCU is a measure of the equivalent space occupied by a vehicle while on road. The equivalences are: Bus = 3 PCU; Two Wheeler = 0.5 PCU; Three Wheeler = 0.75 PCU.

TABLE 12.4: Mobility and Congestion Indicators for Selected Cities

Cities	*PCU*[a] *('000)*	*PCU per 1000 Population*	*Road Length per Million People (km)*	*Road Length (km) per 100 sq.km*	*Transport Area as % to Total Area*	*PCU's per km of Road*	*Trip Length (km)*
Kolkata	205.9	224	91	148	6.4	245	5.8
Mumbai	318.6	387	173	325	NA	224	10.8
Delhi	508.8	888	278	357	NA	319	13.4
Chennai	91.9	214	389	292	17.0	55	7.6
Ahmedabad	106.7	419	356	974	5.6	118	7.3
Bangalore	225.9	773	411	687	17.0[c]	188	10.6
Kanpur	107.5	656	587	322	4.1	112	5.7
Pune	149.0	884	309	375	11.6	286	7.9
Jaipur	179.3[b]	1,767	243	120	12.1	726	NA
Thane	NA	NA	148	65	NA	NA	NA
Coimbatore	100.1	1,335	547	388	NA	244	9.8
1990-91 data for three metros							
Delhi	2,312	268	185	357	NA	1,450	NA
Mumbai	809	73	128	326	20[d]	567	NA
Kolkata	704	60	71	148	6.4	838	NA

Note: [a] PCU is a measure of the car equivalent of space occupied by a vehicle while on road. The equivalences are: Car = 1 PCU; Bus = 3 PCU; Two Wheeler = 0.5 PCU; Three Wheeler = 0.75 PCU.

[b] 1985 data.

[c] Habitat (1994) puts the value as 27 per cent for 1991.

[d] for 1991, as per Habitat (1994).

Source: Ramanathan (1999a).

cent. This is to be contrasted with the public transport vehicles (Buses). While they fulfil 79 per cent of the trips, their share of PCUs is only 13 per cent (Patankar, 1991). Thus the rapid growth of personalised modes of transport in Indian cities gives rise to serious congestion problems.

The average speed of vehicles has also reduced in many Indian cities. For example, in Mumbai, the average speed of vehicles was about 38 kmph in 1962, which has reduced to about 26 kmph in 1979, and further to about 15-20 kmph in 1993-94. The average speed in Kolkata reduced from 17 kmph in 1963 to about 14 kmph in 1994. Average speed in Delhi was only about 15 kmph in 1993-94.

12.3.4 *Energy and Environmental Issues*

Rapid growth of personalised is very unsustainable and results in avoidable energy consumption and pollution. Because of the rapid passenger transport growth in Delhi, its petrol consumption has been estimated to increase by more than 5.5 times between 1990-91 and 2000-01. Similar trends are expected in other metropolitan cities as well, including Mumbai and Kolkata (CSE, 1996).

Energy consumption has direct linkages with the emission of air pollutants. In the three metropolitan cities, the share of automobiles in total pollutant emissions is quite high. According to the World Resources Report (1996-97), motor vehicles were responsible for 90 per cent of the Carbon Monoxide emissions, 85 per cent of hydrocarbon emissions, 59 per cent of the emission of Nitrogen Oxides (NOx), 13 per cent of Sulphur dioxide (SO_2) emissions and 37 per cent of emissions of Suspended Particulate Matter (SPM) in Delhi during 1987. According to the same study, automobiles caused about 52 per cent of the total NOx emissions, 5 per cent SO_2 emissions and 24 per cent of SPM emissions in Mumbai in 1992. In the year 1993-94, the share of automobiles in total pollutant load was as high as 64 per cent in Delhi and 52 per cent in Mumbai. The share was 30 per cent in Kolkata in 1988-89. The contribution of automobiles to the atmospheric concentrations of air pollutants is very significant. Measurements indicate that while SO_2 levels in the metros are generally within the prescribed limits, the concentrations of nitrogen oxides and SPM are well above the standards (Table 12.5). Another study (Opinion survey, 1998) conducted by the Union Environment Ministry in Delhi puts the SPM concentration between 362-452 micrograms per cubic metre on an average day. The study puts a very bleak picture on the environmental conditions of Delhi, measured in terms of water quality of the Yamuna river, noise pollution and the total pollution load. For example, Delhi's average noise level is 75-85 decibels compared to the limits of 45-75 decibels. The study also shows that the total pollution load in Delhi is rising very rapidly, from 1450 tonnes per day (tpd) in 1991 to 2890 tpd in 1995.

TABLE 12.5: Average Annual Emissions, 1993

(*Values in microgram per cubic metre*)

City	*SO_2*	*NO_2*	*SPM*
Delhi	33	46	543
Mumbai[a]	23	205[b]	159[c]
Kolkata	62	39	394
National Ambient Air Quality Standards			
— Residential areas	60	60	140
— Industrial areas	80	80	360
— Sensitive areas	15	15	70
WHO standards	50	100	75

[a] At Mumbai Chatrapati Shivaji Terminus, in 1998.
[b] NOx levels.
[c] Respirable Suspended Particles (RSP).
Source: Ramanathan (1999a).

This trend should be checked. It is important to promote mass transport modes that are energy efficient and environmentally benign (Table 3.4). It is possible to convert the energy units mentioned in the table to more popular units, namely the quantity of petrol or diesel. For example, in India, buses consume, on an average, about 0.212 MJ of direct fuel energy (equivalent to about 6 ml of diesel) per passenger kilometre. Diesel and electric tractions of railways consume about 0.241 (about 7 ml of diesel) and 0.115 (about one thirtieth of a unit—kWh) MJ per passenger kilometre respectively. These are quite small compared to the energy consumption of personalised transport modes, which averages to about 0.532 MJ (equivalent to about 16 ml of petrol) per passenger kilometre. Thus, huge savings in direct fuel consumption can be effected if the traffic from personalised modes is diverted to mass transport modes. This diversion can also be environmentally benign. As fuel consumption can be directly related to the emission of carbon dioxide, significant reductions in transport related emission of global pollutants could be achieved.

It has been estimated that an increase in the share of bus travel from 57 per cent to 80 per cent in big Indian cites will lead to a saving of 1.1 million tonnes of oil, 36 per cent reduction in air pollution, 27 per cent reduction in CO_2 emissions (MoUD, 1987).

12.3.5 *Accidents and Casualties*

In 1993-94, there were 2.86 lakh accidents in Indian roads, resulting in 2.88 lakh injured persons and 60,595 casualties. The largest 12 metropolitan cities accounted for 44,653 accidents (16%), 36,888 injuries (13%) and 5,197 casualties (8.6%). There seems to be no direct relation between accident statistics and vehicular or population density. This may be attributed to the slow vehicular speed in urban areas.

According to an international study (*Reader's Digest*, October 1998), Indian drivers are ranked second among Asia's traffic offenders, just after China. Although India has only about the same number of vehicles as Thailand and Taiwan combined, it accounts for more than 10 per cent of the world's traffic fatalities each year.

12.4 Steps Ahead: Key Policy Suggestions

Several options are available for improving urban transport in India. We can learn from the experiences of cities around the world. First of all, it is necessary to plan well in advance. Use of any single option in isolation will not solve the problem, and an integrated use of all these options is essential. For example, a policy to reduce the number of private vehicles will have detrimental effects on the economic growth of a city unless an efficient public transport system is made available. The public transportation system can function efficiently only when it is integrated well with land use patterns. Similarly, larger investment in public transport modes without controlling the growth of personal vehicles will encourage avoidable and luxurious travels, and hence can lead to unsustainable transport performance—large transport costs, more congestion, pollution, etc. More importantly, the commitment of the implementing authority in properly implementing the options is a very crucial factor in deciding the success of these options.

For efficient management, both the demand and supply sides of transport should be considered. They are discussed below.

12.4.1 *Travel Demand Management (TDM) Measures*

12.4.1.1 *Integrated Planning of Public Transport and Urban Land-Use*

Growth of transport in a city and its land-use patterns are highly interlinked. Hence, it is possible to affect transport demand favourably by adjusting land use patterns judiciously. An integrated approach towards land-use and transportation can increase the accessibility of jobs, shops, and other facilities without increasing the need to travel for long distances (May and Roberts, 1995). Several cities across the world have successfully adopted such an integrated strategy (see Tables 12.6 and 12.7), and it is possible to learn from their experiences.

TABLE 12.6: Curitiba: An Example of Efficient Integration of Land-Use and Public Transport

Curitiba, the capital of Parana state in southeastern Brazil, can provide a good example of sustainability and exemplary urban planning. It is one of the fastest growing cities in a nation of urban booms. Its population growth was dramatic, from 300,000 in 1950 to 2.1 million in 1990. It also transformed from an agricultural centre to an industrial and commercial powerhouse during this period. Such developments are likely to cause several urban related problems, including congestion and environmental decay. But, Curitiba defined conventional wisdom and adapted to the transformation in a human-friendly way.

The most important unifying feature of Curitiba's success is its emphasis on an integrated approach to the public transportation system, land-use legislation and the hierarchy of the road network. The key concept was to channel the city's physical expansion away from the central city and along five pre-determined linear corridors. Each corridor is built around a central or structural road that has exclusive lanes for express buses, for local traffic, for high-speed car traffic flowing in and out of the city. Municipal government acquires land along and close to the newly developed corridors, prior to their construction, and organises construction of high-density housing programmes at these places. Zoning laws encourage high-density commercial development along these transport corridors, while land away from the corridors is zoned at low densities. On sites located along the corridors, buildings are permitted to have a total floor area of up to six times the plot size. The coefficient decreases as distance of the site from public transport increases. This has encouraged new commercial development outside the central city along the corridors and ensured public transport to high density residential and commercial areas. These developments in turn have greatly reduced traffic congestion and noise in the CBD area, which is meant mainly for pedestrians.

There is also a hierarchy of roads. Each road is assigned a function in relation to its location and importance. First, there are five structural roads or corridors. There are "priority" links connecting traffic to the structural roads. "Connector" streets have commercial activity along them with all forms of traffic. "Connector" streets link the structural corridors to the industrial city.

Along the corridors, a central lane was set aside for buses only. New bus lines were created and expanded as the city grew. A series of circular inter-district bus routes has been developed since 1979 to complement the express bus ways. Buses are colour coded: the express buses are red, inter-district buses are green, and conventional (feeder) buses are yellow. There is full integration among the three sets of buses for facilitating easy transfer. There are large bus terminals at the end of each of the corridors, where people can transfer to inter-district, feeder or inter-municipal buses. One single fare is valid for all buses within Curitiba. Smaller bus terminals are located approximately every two kilometres along the express routes.

The express bus system is designed to facilitate rapid boarding. Bus-stops have an innovative "boarding tubes" concept with raised platforms at the same height as the bus

(Contd.)

TABLE 12.6 *Contd.*

floors. The design cuts boarding and deboarding times. An express bus system with these boarding tubes are estimated to take three times as many passengers per hour as a conventional bus operating in a normal street. Tickets can be bought at the boarding tubes, thus eliminating the need for a crew on the bus to collect fares, which frees up space for more passengers. Another bus design, the bi-articulated bus with a capacity of 270 passengers, has five lateral doors for passenger entry or exit. Automatic fare collection, articulated buses, traffic lights that give priority to buses allows the optimisation of the system's operation and low operating costs.

The public transport system is operated by ten private companies and governed and regulated by a mixed capital company created by the municipal government. Companies are paid according to the length of the routes they serve rather than the number of passengers they carry, giving the city a strong inventive to provide service that increases ridership. The efficient public transport has attracted more than a quarter of Curitiba's automobile owners. This has obviously saved a lot of fuel energy.

In addition to tackling the transport problems with low-cost technologies, Curitiba has much to offer to solving the needs of the rapidly growing cities. For the innovative low-cost ideas adapted by Curitiba in waste management, sanitation, housing, historic preservation, social development, environmental education, etc., one should refer to more detailed articles such as Rabinovitch and Leitmann (1996).

The most important component behind the success of Curitiba can be attributed to strong leadership, which promoted flexible attitude of city officials and strong public participation. The key man behind the success has been Jaime Lerner, who served as mayor for three different five-year periods between 1970 and 1992.

Sources: Rabinovitch (1993), Rabinovitch and Leitmann (1996) and O'Meara (1998).

TABLE 12.7: Singapore's Land Transport Policy

Singapore is one of the few major cities in the world that is able to maintain a smooth traffic flow within the city area at any time of the day. The keys to Singapore's success in urban transport management lies with its good planning, coordinated multi-prone approach and strong political and institutional commitments.

Road space occupies 10 per cent of Singapore's land. Further road expansion had to be limited because of the limited space. Hence, a comprehensive approach was adopted based on the principle of increasing road network capacity while containing road traffic and optimising road use. Singapore's land transport policy is built on four main pillars.

1. Increasing road capacity, using a network of roads, expressways, tunnels, junction interchanges, flyovers and underpasses. Traffic junctions are fully computerised.
2. Integrated land-use planning to bring schools, factories, offices, shops and recreational and other facilities into or near housing estates to minimise the need to travel far or frequently for work and other activities.
3. Promoting public transport (buses and the urban rail or MRT) by providing enough infrastructure such as bus stops, MRT stations and bus interchanges. Special lanes are designated for exclusive use by buses during peak hours. Special cards can be used with both buses and MRT stations.
4. Managing vehicle ownership and use in order to control congestion. Earlier, the Government has tried to curb rising vehicle ownership through fiscal disincentives such as very high registration fees, road tax and parking charges. These measures had limited success. A Vehicle Quota System (VQS) was introduced in 1990 to

(*Contd.*)

TABLE 12.7 *Contd.*

control the growth of vehicles directly by setting a quota on the number of new vehicles allowed on the roads. The quota ensures that vehicular growth is commensurate with gains in the carrying capacity of the road network. Under the VQS, a vehicle can only be registered with a Certificate of Entitlement (CoE), which is obtained through monthly tenders. CoE is valid for ten years only, and needs to be renewed thereafter. An Area Licensing Scheme (ALS) has been in place to limit traffic entering the CBD, which requires vehicles entering the CBD to pay a license fee. The ALS scheme has recently been replaced by an Electronic Road Pricing (ERP) to allow charges to be fine-tuned depending upon the congestion level. A "Weekend Car" scheme allows more people to use private cars during off-peak hours on working days and during Sundays and public holidays.

Sources: Fwa (1997) and Shen (1993).

Integration of land-use with the development of public transport is vital for the relatively small, but highly growing urban centres of India. We have seen that there are several second level cities with a population more than one million, and that vehicle population in these cities is increasing at a high rate. We have further seen that the growth of road network is not in tune with the growth of vehicles in many Indian cities. Some of these second level cities (*e.g.*, Coimbatore) are the fastest growing in India, and they have the potential to become large metropolises in future. Hence it is essential that a long-term plan for all round development of these cities are prepared and implemented immediately.

Normally, cities grow in a concentric fashion. As the city grows, the city centre (Central Business District or CBD) will become more and more important, and new areas will be annexed along the periphery. This causes flow of traffic from periphery to the CBD, which will increase as the city grows causing congestion. In the absence of an efficient mass transport system, the traffic will be dominated by personalised vehicles, thereby compounding the problems of congestion.

Instead, if the development of the city is planned in such a way that the business and commercial activities are not concentrated at CBD but at locations along pre-decided structural axes, then these problems can be avoided. For example, if the city is developed in a circular fashion with inner and outer ring roads with many cross roads connecting them at regular intervals, and if business activities are established at specified locations along these ring roads, the traffic will not always flow towards the centre of the city, but also to the periphery on the ring roads. Similarly, for linear cities, the development can be planned along major parallel linear roads, with adequate cross roads connecting them at regular intervals. Business establishments may be planned along these major roads. This will cause an equitable distribution of traffic along the structural axes, reducing congestion problems. The choice of locations for commercial activities should be decided such that the mass transportation systems can reach these places quite efficiently, thereby avoiding the necessity for private vehicles.

Recently integrated transport, land-use and air-quality strategies for sustainable urban transport development (Rebelo, 1996) have received much attention of planners. Problems with air quality is especially severe in urban areas. Capturing the travel of private vehicle users by public transport can help to improve air-quality as well. Strategies for pollution control in transport such as efficiency improvements, alternative fuel technologies (especially electric vehicles) can be usefully integrated with public transport and land-use. Some of these options are discussed later in this chapter.

12.4.1.2 *Pricing and Taxes*

Countries world-wide adopt a policy of subsidising the costs of urban transport with the assumption that as increased mobility can stimulate economic growth and generate additional income. This subsidised transport has however its own adverse impacts. As a result of this subsidy policy, the direct cost that an individual spends for his travel is usually only a part of total cost of transportation. There are many costs that may not be adequately paid by the individual transport user, but are paid by some others or by the government. For example, increased transport usage requires increased investment by the government on transport infrastructure (such as roads), and in traffic regulation. But, these costs are not fully recovered by the government from transport users. These costs can be usually called as external costs or externalities. Some externalities may not be explicitly priced at all. Such non-market costs include costs due to accidents, environmental degradation, land-use impacts, social inequity, etc. (Litman, 1998; Button, 1990).

It is important to estimate the full costs of transportation because it helps to evaluate the effects of growing transportation demand on future plans and its sustainability. Several studies on full costs of transportation in cities world-wide have estimated that the actual costs a road user pays for his travel is only a small portion of the overall cost that he imposes on the government and society (Litman, 1998; Zegras, 1998; Delucchi, 1997). The unsustainable rapid growth of transport can be checked only when the transport user is made to pay the full costs of his transport. Taxes and fees are the conventional methods by which the cost can be recovered from the users. Road pricing can also be employed as another means of charging for road use. Car ownership may be restrained by increasing the costs of owning a car through registration fees and appropriate taxes. A vehicle quota system can also be used to restrict the growing number of vehicles in Indian cities. When road users are made to pay for the full expenses of their travel, uneconomical and avoidable travel are likely to be eliminated, and trips a traveller makes will tend to spread across longer periods of day. These improvements could lead to a reduction in congestion, an increase in the use of mass transportation systems, and may also affect land-use favourably.

Pricing: Pricing involves charging transport users so that part of the external costs of their travel is internalised. A variety of techniques can be used for the purpose—use of tolls, area licensing schemes, and electronic road pricing. Theoretically, an efficient road pricing scheme should cover all important roads of a city, and should employ differential pricing in accordance with the demand for road use (Newbury, 1990). For example, just like the telephone rates in India, higher prices should be charged for periods of maximum demand, namely the peak rush hours of the morning and evening. The goal is to encourage people to use public transport modes instead of private vehicles or to drive during off-peak periods. However, owing to technical, administrative and political complications, such theoretically efficient schemes are seldom implemented.

In India, road pricing as a means of generating revenue has received active consideration ever since private participation is encouraged for road construction. Now, the principle is being applied for state-owned roads as well. For example, the Maharashtra government is charging a toll on vehicles using the Vashi bridge to enter Mumbai. It is planning to charge a toll for using the Mumbai-Pune expressway. In addition, more than 50 flyovers are being constructed in various locations in Mumbai, and to generate sufficient resources, government has decided to levy a toll on motorists entering the city.

Taxes and fees: These can be other means of charging the full costs of transportation. However, there is already an array of taxes on vehicles and fuels (especially gasoline). Taxes are levied on vehicle manufacturers also. One can also think of levying an exclusive tax on car finance companies, as they are partly responsible for increasing the number of vehicles on road. These taxes are supposed to be used for the improvement of transport systems—construction and maintenance of roads, subsidising public transport, etc. However, in India, there seems to be no mechanism for earmarking the tax revenue generated from vehicles and fuels exclusively for road maintenance activities. As a result, improvements in transport infrastructure are not in line with large revenues generated in this sector. A good beginning in this direction has been made in the budget for 1999-2000, which introduced a cess of Re. 1 per litre of diesel and earmarked half of the revenue for the National Highway Development Fund.

Fuel tax can also be employed as a policy option to change travel behaviour. Economists have estimated the price elasticity of gasoline demand, which indicate the change in gasoline demand (for personalised travel) for a given change in fuel (gasoline) prices. Unfortunately, such elasticities are often low indicating relative inelastic behaviour. It has already been reported in Chapter 5 that the gasoline price elasticity for India ranges between –0.2 to –0.4, indicating that if gasoline prices in India are increased by 100 percentage, gasoline demand will decrease only by 20 to 40 percentage. Also, imposing duty on fuel uniformly throughout the country is very crude, as it makes no sense to penalise a rural motorist driving along empty country roads when the problem lies in cities and on congested roads. In this sense, road pricing, adjusted for place and time, is a better alternative as it can focus on the exact problem location.

In addition, pollution cess may be levied from polluting modes of transport to cover the costs of pollution abatement. As said earlier, private transport modes cause substantially larger pollution in India. Hence, a pollution tax may be imposed on their use, and a part of the revenue generated may be transferred to subsidise the environmentally benign mass transport systems.

Parking controls: It is possible to discourage private car usage by providing parking restrictions. If the price of parking is high, or parking is limited, then people tend to prefer car-pooling or mass transport modes. However, these restrictions require an efficient public transportation system as an alternative. By providing a parking facility at the periphery of the CBD and providing adequate public transport to move inside the CBD, a significant amount of congestion in the CBD area can be avoided. Vehicles desirous of entering into the CBD should be made to pay a hefty fee for the use of the road as well as for parking.

Entry barriers: Simply creating additional infrastructure such as the construction of roads or flyovers cannot solve the traffic problems of many of the cities. It is necessary to restrict the flow of traffic into the city. Unlike pricing and taxes, it is also possible to physically stop the entry of vehicles in most congested areas of a city. Several cities world-wide have tried several forms of restricting the entry of vehicles. Table 12.8 gives some forms of entry barriers practiced in different cities across the globe. It is important here to note that while the entry barriers adopted in some cities were successful, there were unexpected results in some cities. For example, in Mexico city, when the entry restrictions were limited according to number plates, many households bought a

TABLE 12.8: Strategies Adopted in Cities around the World for Restricting Car Entry into the CBD

City	*Entry Barrier*
Athens, Mexico city, Santiago	Car entry into city limited according to number plates
Curitiba	CBD area is mainly meant for pedestrians (see Table 12.6)
Portland	Conversion of a section of downtown road into an urban park, limit on downtown parking spaces, road construction projects scrapped in favour of new transit lines.
Singapore	Vehicle quota system, heavy fees for getting a certificate of entitlement for owning a car, downtown entry fee and heavy fuel levies (see Table 12.7)
Leichester, Vienna, Cologne, Strasbourg, Amsterdam, Turin	Cars are banned from entry into city centres
Several Dutch Cities	"*Woonerf*" concept for traffic calming. Cars are forced to navigate slowly around carefully placed streets and other landscapes. Cycling and walking has priority over automobiles.
Goteberg	The city centre is divided into five pie-shaped zones, all accessible by a ring road on the periphery. Automobiles are not allowed to cross the zone boundaries, while public transport, bicycles and mopeds may.
Geneva, Copenhagen	Car parking is prohibited at work places in the central city. Bicycle parking places are increased.
Munich	Creation of 85,000 square metre auto-free pedestrian zone, easily accessible by public transport.
Hanover	The number of streets on which cars are allowed has been reduced, thereby offering better facilities for pedestrians and cyclists.
Freiburg	Subsidised monthly rail passes.
Washington DC metro area, San Francisco, Honolulu	Carpoolers are provided special 'high occupancy vehicle' lanes.

Source: Lowe (1991), CSE (1996) and World Resources Report (1996).

second car or switched license plates to meet their mobility needs. In Athens, the number of households with two cars increased, and motorists who were not allowed to enter the city drove around the city to get to their destination, thus increasing the length of their trip while also increasing emissions. In addition, the second cars newly bought were often second hand ones, which tend to be more polluting. Similarly, restrictions on the entry of low-occupancy cars into the CBD area will encourage car pooling, but will have detrimental effect on the economic activities of the city if an efficient mass transportation system is not developed as an alternative. These experiences only mean that any Travel Demand Management (TDM) measure should not be used in isolation to solve traffic problems, and there should be an integrated policy, in which several TDM measures are parts.

Techniques such as the Area Licensing Scheme (ALS) practised in Singapore can be adapted to restrict the inflow of traffic in CBD areas of Indian cities. This scheme can be designed to facilitate easy implementation. This can be low cost and can be made labour oriented, too. Every car entering the CBD area should hand over a pre-bought coupon to the collector(s) at the entrance. The coupons should be available in the open market. To reduce the delay in purchasing the coupons at the entrance, they may be priced at a higher level when bought at the entrance. The coupons may also be considered as tradable permits, which can be traded in the market. There may be a few minutes delay at the entry point, but can avoid greater time delay during commuting in the CBD area More sophisticated systems may be installed in due course which can reduce the waiting time at the entry point.

12.4.1.3 *Other TDM Measures*

Several additional strategies are possible for controlling travel demand. If the working hours are staggered, the peak-hour rush will reduce. Telecommuting should be used as far as possible to substitute actual travel. They can be used whenever and wherever possible to control the traffic.

12.4.2 *Increasing and Improving Transportation Supply*

There is a vast scope for improving the insufficient and improperly maintained transportation infrastructure in Indian cities. Roads in Indian cities are plagued with deficient side walks, cross walks, bridges at railway crossings, etc. Roads are poorly surfaced and improperly maintained leading to safety hazards, congestion, increased fuel consumption, and pollution. Lives of vehicles plying on these poor quality roads reduce, leading to more expenditure on maintenance. It has been pointed out in the previous chapter that the cost of properly maintaining roads is only a fraction of the economic losses inflicted by bad roads. In addition, in spite of using several TDM measures to eliminate avoidable travel, growing cities need increased mobility over the next several years to meet the demands of their economic activities. Hence, strategies for increasing and improving transportation supply are essential for the growth of Indian cities. A sustainable transportation supply strategy for Indian cities should lay higher reliance in environmental friendly mass transport modes and lesser emphasis on private transport modes.

12.4.2.1 *Promoting Mass Transport*

Mass transport systems can move more people while occupying lesser road space. With the high occupancy rates of mass transport systems in India (they operate at super saturated capacity during peak periods), they are also very economical in terms of energy consumption and pollution for every passenger kilometres effected (see Table 3.4). At the Indian average occupancy of 1.6 per car and about 50 people per bus, a substantial saving (of more than 10 times in terms of PCU) is possible if a bus can substitute cars. Obviously, such a substitution can help tremendously in easing congestion in the roads.

However, forcing such a shift requires sustained strong efforts from the public transport authorities and the co-operation of the government and the commuters. Buses should be made punctual, comfortable, fast and reliable. For faster movement of vehicles, roads should have separate lanes for express buses (inter-state and inter-district), mofussil buses (inter-city), city buses (intra-city), trucks, cars and other personalised vehicles. Exclusive lanes for bicycles, and sufficient footpaths should also be provided. As far as possible, commuters should be able to travel on any of these buses with a single ticket. To make public transportation more attractive and punctual, buses should be given preference at signals and at traffic congestion.

Government is planning to set up mass transport infrastructure in many cities. A mass rapid transport system has been planned for Delhi.

There are plans to improve the transportation supply in many Indian cities. Metros are planned in Delhi and Mumbai, to be built with the help of international funding agencies (such as the Overseas Economic

Co-operation Fund of Japan for Delhi). The Mumbai Urban Transport Project (MUTP) II is being negotiated with international funding agencies. An elevated light rail transit system for Bangalore and a LRT/MRT project for Jaipur are under consideration for inclusion in the ninth five-year plan. Maharashtra State Road Development Corporation is building over 50 flyovers and two main elevated driveways in Mumbai. These will certainly help in meeting the growing needs of the economic activities of these cities by easing traffic snarls and open several arterial passages. However, there is a danger of uncontrolled, manifold increase in the number of vehicles in the city unless proper vehicle control measures are taken. The flyovers should be designed such that they have large exclusive bus lanes, and buses should get priority in congestion and signals. In addition, separate lanes may be planned for bicycles. The likely rapid vehicular growth should be arrested by using proper auto-restraining policies (see Table 12.8).

To maintain economic efficiency, a few companies (more than one) may be formed for operating the public transportation system to encourage competition. The companies should be made autonomous and allowed to price their services on economic principles. To win away sizeable commuter traffic from private cars, fast and luxury bus services should be provided at a reasonable price. Services of differentiated qualities may also be offered at a range of prices to suit the needs of different categories of commuters. Such efforts are being made by some bus operators in Indian cities. For example, luxury air-conditioned bus services have recently been introduced in Mumbai on selected routes. Of late, smart card system for automatic deduction of fare have also been introduced. These cards can be potentially used multi-application cards in the future—for travelling in buses, trains, taxis etc.

Integrated public transport system should be planned such that the commuters can buy a single ticket for travelling by different classes of buses and suburban rail, if there is one. This can also reduce the fare to the commuters due to telescopic pricing. The time wasted at the ticket counters can be minimised. Those who own a ticket should be preferred to enter the bus to avoid delays. Innovative bus designs, such as wide doors and closing doors, can improve the quality of bus service.

There is a tremendous scope for generating additional revenue by exploiting the commerce potential of mass transit points (bus stations and railway terminals). These are the places where people frequently visit and have vast scope for building shopping complexes. Multi-storeyed buildings can be constructed in which the first few floors can be used for mass transit purposes, while the remaining may be used for commercial purposes. This will also facilitate commuters as they can combine their work and shopping trips. The arrangements will increase the car population near the mass transit points, but they should be charged appropriate parking fees, which can be used to subsidise part of the mass transit operations.

12.4.2.2 *Promoting Walking and Cycling*

Cycling and walking as modes of transportation have been receiving lesser priority in Indian cities. Unlike poor African countries, owning bicycles is within the reach of an average household, especially in urban areas. In fact, India is emerging to be a major exporter of bicycles in world market. But, a cyclist in India is made to share road with high-speeding automobiles and hence cycling is unsafe. The automobile-friendly urban roads in Indian cities are not safe to pedestrians either. Heavy traffic is often caused as pedestrians step off pavements occupied by hawkers, and illegally extended shops. Sometimes, municipality decreases the footpaths. All these problems have resulted in increased accidents and fatalities.

As seen earlier, there is increase in automobiles in cities as its economic activity increases. Thus, more people tend to switch to automobiles from bicycles and walking as their income increases. However, if properly promoted and encouraged, bicycles and walking can be efficient alternatives to the problems of growing automobile use (Gardner, 1998). In fact, bicycles can be relatively easily incorporated if integrated transport—land use—air quality strategy is followed for the development of smaller but rapidly growing urban centres of India.

Most of the places in the CBD areas in cities (and any particular locality in the suburbs) can be reached by bicycles within a reasonable period of time. Constructing exclusive cycle lanes and according high priority to bicycles while on road may encourage the use of bicycles. Bicycles should be given preference for parking within the CBD area, near public transport stations and near suburban railway terminals. Exclusive signals for bicycles may be installed. A separate bicycle path may be constructed in railway level crossings (just like the bridges for pedestrians). Facilities may be created in local trains and public transport buses to house bicycles, so that people can use them in conjunction with the mass transport modes. Similar promotional arrangements can be considered for encouraging walking.

12.4.2.3 *Reducing Vehicle Pollution*

An integrated strategy for sustainable urban transport development should not only consider improving public transport for optimal land-use, and controlling the growth of private vehicles, but also consider urban air quality. Several options are possible. Use of unleaded petrol can be promoted which eliminates harmful lead emissions. Efficiencies of existing vehicles can be increased cleaner and low polluting fuels can be used. New low emission technologies can be promoted.

Engines may be designed such that they consume less fuel for moving the same distance. Technology changes such as conversion from two stroke to four stroke engines can effect significant savings in terms of both energy consumption and environmental emissions. Owing to these advantages, several two-wheeler manufacturers in India have started to switch to four stroke technologies. The progressively stricter pollution control norms also are ensuring the adoption of such environmentally benign technologies. As we have seen in Chapter 10, efficiency improvements in Indian vehicles can save as much as 26 per cent of energy consumption, and equivalent reductions are possible in environmental emissions.

Introduction of alternate transportation fuels can also reduce energy requirements and emissions. Compressed Natural Gas (CNG), bio-ethanol and methanol are the other possible fuels for transportation. Of these, the most relevant one for India is the CNG (Painuly and Parikh, 1993). CNG vehicles are more efficient and cleaner compared to their gasoline counterparts. In addition, pressures on cleaner environment especially in urban areas are expected to stimulate the introduction of electric vehicles in India. As we have analysed in Chapter 10, under normal diffusion levels of the new technologies, they may not provide much advantage in terms of energy consumption and emission reduction. However, introduction of alternate fuel vehicles can be especially beneficial in urban areas. They have the potential to reduce the emissions of carbon monoxide, nitrogen oxides, particulates etc. Also, the diffusion of these vehicles can be smooth if they are concentrated in urban areas, where the necessary infrastructure (such as CNG pumping stations, battery charging stations, etc.) can be provided relatively easily and efficiently. Adequate availability of these infrastructure should be ensured if these alternate technologies should make good inroads in urban Indian scenario.

12.4.2.4 *Proper Maintenance*

Older and improperly maintained vehicles produce disproportionately more pollution. It has been reported that a badly maintained older vehicle can emit 100 times the pollutants than a properly maintained new vehicle. In India, the problem of improper maintenance is rampant. A study has reported that, at a random check, 43.6 per cent of the total new vehicles failed to meet the existing emission standards. The proportion was higher (56.1%) for old vehicles. The study also reported that 57.2 per cent of the two-wheelers and 53.8 per cent of the three wheelers checked exceeded the emission limits (CSE, 1996). Authorities in some Indian cities are now thinking of banning older vehicles into city limits.

12.4.3 *Capacity Building Measures*

A sustainable transport development requires a significant change in the attitudes and life-styles of commuters. This change is possible only if the awareness on energy conservation and environmental preservation should be instilled on their minds. Various capacity building measures such as training, workshops and advertisements (through hoarding, televisions, etc.) can be employed in this regard. Free short-term courses should be organised at regular intervals by the different research and academic institutes in the cities to create the awareness on the need for maintaining the energy efficiencies of vehicles and for ensuring smooth traffic. These courses may be made compulsory for the drivers of vehicles (while issuing/renewing licenses), but others should also be encouraged to attend them.

12.4.3.1 *Private Co-operative Efforts: Transportation Management Associations*

It is possible to think of transportation management associations supported and managed by businesses located in a commercial district. They can pool their resources and provide efficient smaller-level public transport through co-operative efforts.

12.4.4 *Institutional Requirements*

It has been observed in India that development of urban transportation plans are beset with lack of co-ordination among multiple agencies. For example, in Mumbai, the suburban rail operations are managed by two zonal railways, and public bus transport is the responsibility of the State Transport Undertaking. Such a split in governing the Mumbai urban transport makes coordination difficult. Any plan on improving urban transport cannot be made in isolation, and both the bus and rail transport should form integral parts of such a plan. The problem is compounded by the fact that the Indian Railways, in its corporate plan in 1985, did not consider suburban as a priority item in their policy. The coordination problems are evident in the on-going efforts to initiate the new Mumbai Urban Transport Project (MUTP) II. The necessity to decouple urban rail transport from the Indian Railways was felt, and an autonomous corporation to unite both rail and road transport has been formed. However, the new corporation, the Mumbai Rail Vikas Corporation, is yet to acquire the status of a full time institution and resume its duties. Similarly, a Delhi Metro Rail Corporation Limited has been constituted to carry out the implementation of the mass rapid transport system in Delhi.

A possibility may be to set up a body under the Ministry of Surface Transport, which will work in co-ordination with the Ministry of Urban Development and the local governments of individual cities. The organisation and responsibility of this body may be in the line of the National Urban Transport Board suggested by the National Commission on Urbanisation (NCU, 1988). The cooperation of Indian Railways may be sought whenever necessary. Wherever co-ordination becomes difficult, because of the presence of rail and road transport, a new body at local level for each city may be formed to look after the urban transport plan in a comprehensive manner.

Government is planning to set up similar bodies. For example, setting up of the Directorates of Urban Transport in States, and setting up of a National Urban Transport Development Fund are being considered for inclusion in the ninth five-year plan. However, the activity is yet to gain momentum. We urge that the Directorates of Urban Transport be set up in different cities to oversee their developmental path.

Urban transport, as a part of a comprehensive urban development plan, requires huge funds. Privatisation is an important strategy for the government to develop this vital infrastructure sector. The issues related to privatisation have already been discussed in much detail in Chapter 11.

12.4.5 *Implementation*

Finally, a brief note on the implementation of sustainable urban transport plans is in order. There are reports that proper rules are not followed in issuing driving licenses in India, resulting in unfit drivers driving vehicles causing safety hazards to all transport users. We have also seen that pollution control rules are not implemented strictly (see discussion on maintenance above). It has to be noted that many of the options discussed in this chapter are likely to fail if implemented with a short-term point of view. Implementation of these options may change the day-to-day living habits of commuters, which is likely to create unrest among them in the shorter term leading to resistance to implementation. For example, from a political angle, persuading voters to pay for using roads that have long been free may result in loss of goodwill to the governing party. However, the resistance is likely to fade away in due course of time, once the benefits of the changes are realised. Hence, for the success of the options mentioned in this chapter, it is absolutely necessary to have a visionary authority with a political will to implement relevant measures single mindedly without regard to short-term losses to individuals but with the overall, long-term, national gain in mind.

APPENDICES

APPENDIX 1

COINTEGRATION ANALYSIS: THE METHODOLOGY

Cointegration is a relatively recent econometric tool used for estimating long-run relationships between two or more variables of interest using time-series data. This methodology in time-series econometrics was introduced in the mid 1980s, and has been regarded as the most important recent development in empirical modelling. For econometric analysis of time-series data, it is desired that the time-series variables are stationary. A time-series process is said to be stationary if the means and variances of the process are constant over time, while the value of the covariance depends only on the gap between the periods, and not the actual time at which this covariance is considered (Charemza and Deadman, 1992). If one or more of these conditions are not fulfilled, the process is non-stationary. Non-stationarity of time-series has generally been regarded as a problem in econometric analysis, as the statistical properties of regression using the series are shown to be dubious (Phillips, 1986).

A non-stationary series can be made stationary by detrending the series. A convenient way of detrending is by using first differences rather than levels of the variables. Sometimes, it is necessary to difference a series more than once in order to achieve stationarity. A non-stationary series which can be transformed to a stationary series by differencing d times is said to be integrated of order d, denoted $x_t \sim I(d)$ (Engle and Granger, 1987). Clearly, a stationary series is a $I(0)$ series.

Before proceeding with the econometric analysis, it is necessary to verify whether the variable under consideration is stationary, and if not, check for its order of integration. This can be accomplished by the so called *unit-root* test. The most widely used unit-root test is the Augmented Dicky-Fuller (ADF) test which involves running the following regression.

$$\Delta y_t = a_0 + a_1 y_{t-1} + \sum_{i=1}^{k} a_i \Delta y_{t-1} + \varepsilon_t \qquad (A1.1)$$

where y is the variable under consideration, Δ is the first difference operator, ε_t is the random error, and k is the number of lagged terms to allow for the existence of autocorrelation in ε_t. If the summation term in the above equation is omitted, the test is called simply as Dicky-Fuller (DF) test. The null hypothesis in the DF and ADF tests is that the undifferenced form of the series is non-stationary, *i.e.*, contains a unit-root. To reject the null hypothesis, the coefficient a_1 must be statistically significant. In other words, the *t*-statistic corresponding to a_1 should be smaller than the lower critical value reported in Charemza and Deadman (1992). Note that a number of authors have tabulated the critical values (*e.g.*, Fuller, 1976; Guilkey and Schmidt, 1989; MacKinnon, 1991). In general, the critical values reported in different publications do not agree because the values are not derived analytically, but are derived using simulation. For analyses in this book, critical values reported in Charemza and Deadman (1992) have been used because the tables are relatively recent, and their methodology takes into account the uncertainties associated with simulation modelling.

It may so happen that a particular combination of two or more non-stationary variables become stationary. In general, a particular combination of two or more $I(d)$ variables may become a $I(b)$ variable, $b \leq d$. In such a case, the non-stationary variables are said to be cointegrated. Such cointegrating relationships signify the existence of long-run equilibrium relationship(s) among the variables. Certain economic variables are generally expected to be linked by such long-run equilibrium relationships. Though the variables may drift away from equilibrium for a while, economic forces are expected to act so as to restore equilibrium.

Let the cointegrating long-run relationship among the variables is given by the following equation.

$$y_t = b_0 + b_1 x_{1t} + b_2 x_{2t} + \ldots + b_p x_{pt} + \upsilon_t \qquad \text{(A1.2)}$$

where y is the dependent variable and x_1, x_2, ..., x_m are independent variables. If only two variables appear in the above equation (*i.e.*, $p = 1$), then it is necessary that both (y and x_1) have to be of the same order of integration. If the number of variables is greater than two, that is if there is more than one explanatory variable, the order of integration of the dependent variable cannot be higher than the order of integration of any of the explanatory variables. Moreover, there must be either none or at least two explanatory variables integrated to an identical order higher than the order of the dependent variable. A more detailed discussion of the theory behind these requirements is available in Charemza and Deadman (1992).

The coefficients of the above model can be determined by ordinary least squares (OLS) regression. If the above equation specifies a cointegrating long-run relationship, then application of DF or ADF test on the estimated residuals v_t in equation (A1.2) should indicate that the residuals have a lower order b than the order d of $x_1, x_2, ..., x_m$ and y. In this case, the coefficients $b_1, b_2, ..., b_m$ represent the long-run elasticities of the dependent variable y with respect to the corresponding independent variables.

Once the cointegrating relationship is found, the final step of the cointegration analysis is the construction of an error-correction model (ECM). Cointegrating variables are expected to restore themselves to their long-run equilibrium whenever there is a drift, and the ECM is constructed to estimate this short-run behaviour. The ECM is estimated using the following equation.

$$\Delta y_t = c_0 + \sum_{i_1=0}^{n_1} c_{1i_1}\Delta x_{1(t-i_1)} + \sum_{i_2=0}^{n_2} c_{1i_2}\Delta x_{2(t-i_2)} + \cdots + \sum_{i_m=0}^{n_m} c_{1i_m}\Delta x_{m(t-i_m)} + \sum_{j=1}^{p} c_2\Delta y_{t-j} + c_3 v_{t-1} + u_t \quad \text{(A1.3)}$$

where $n_1, n_2, ..., n_m$ and p are the lagged terms of their corresponding variables, so chosen to make the residual u_t a white noise. The coefficients c_{1i} represent the short-run elasticities and c_3 represents the speed of adjustment toward the long-run equilibrium. If the coefficient c_3 is found to be negative and is statistically significant, then the long-run relationship is confirmed, and the variables involved are confirmed to be cointegrated. Kremers *et al.* (1992) have argued that this test for cointegration is more powerful than the ADF test on v_t described earlier.

APPENDIX 2

DATA ENVELOPMENT ANALYSIS

Data Envelopment Analysis (DEA) is a methodology based upon an interesting application of linear programming. It has been successfully employed for assessing the relative performance of a set of firms, usually called as the Decision-Making Units (DMU), which use a variety of identical inputs to produce a variety of identical outputs. The basic ideas behind DEA date back to Farrel (1957), but the recent series of discussions started with the articles by Charnes, Cooper and Rhodes (1978, 1979). Assume that there are *n* DMUs, and that the DMUs under consideration convert *I* inputs to *J* outputs. In particular, let the *m*th DMU produces outputs y_{jm} using x_{im} inputs. To measure the efficiency of this conversion process by a DMU, a fractional programme is proposed. The programme maximises the ratio of weighted outputs to weighted inputs for the DMU under consideration subject to the condition that the similar ratios for all DMUs be less than or equal to one. That is,

$$\max \frac{\sum_{j=1}^{J} \upsilon_{jm} y_{jm}}{\sum_{i=1}^{I} u_{im} x_{im}} \qquad \text{(Model A2.1)}$$

subject to

$$0 \leq \sum_{j=1}^{J} \upsilon_{jm} y_{jn} \Big/ \sum_{i=1}^{I} u_{im} x_{in} \leq 1 \qquad n = 1, 2, ..., N;$$

$$\upsilon_{jm}, u_{im} \leq \varepsilon ; \qquad i = 1, 2, ..., I; j = 1, 2, ..., J$$

where the subscript *i* stands for inputs, *j* stands for outputs and *n* stands for the DMUs. The variables υ_{jm} and u_{im} are the weights to be determined by the above mathematical programme. The term ε is an arbitrarily small positive number introduced in the model to ensure that all of the known inputs and outputs have positive weight values. The *m*th DMU is the base DMU in the above model. The optimal value of the objective function is the DEA efficiency score assigned to the *m*th DMU. If the efficiency score is 1, the *m*th DMU satisfies the necessary condition to be DEA efficient; otherwise, it is DEA inefficient. Note that the inefficiency is relative to the performance of other DMUs under consideration.

It is difficult to solve Model A2.1 because of its fractional objective function. However, if either the denominator or numerator of the ratio is forced to be unity, then the objective function will become linear, and a linear programming problem can be obtained. For example, by setting the denominator of the ratio equal to unity, one can obtain the following *output maximisation* linear programming problem. Note that by setting the numerator equal to unity, it is equally possible to produce *input minimisation* linear programming problem.

$$\max \sum_{j=1}^{J} \upsilon_{jm} y_{jm} \qquad \text{(Model A2.2)}$$

subject to

$$\sum_{i=1}^{I} u_{im} x_{im} = 1;$$

$$\sum_{j=1}^{J} \upsilon_{jm} y_{jn} - \sum_{i=1}^{I} u_{im} x_{in} \leq 0; \qquad n = 1, 2, ..., N$$

$$\upsilon_{jm}, u_{im} \geq \varepsilon; \qquad i = 1, 2, ..., I; j = 1, 2, ..., J$$

A complete DEA model involves solution of *N* such programmes (Model A2.2), each for a base DMU (m = 1, 2, ..., N), yielding N different set of weights (υ_{jm}, u_{im}). In each programme, the constraints are the same while the ratio to be maximised is changed.

Computation of efficiency score is usually done with the dual of Model A2.2. The dual constructs a piecewise linear approximation to the true frontier by minimising the quantities of the different inputs to meet the stated levels of the different outputs. The dual is given below.

$$\min \theta_m - \varepsilon \left(\sum_{i=1}^{I} s_i + \sum_{J=1}^{J} s_j \right) \qquad \text{(Model A2.3)}$$

subject to

$$\sum_{n=1}^{N} y_{jn} \lambda_n - s_j = y_{jm}; \qquad j = 1, 2, ..., J$$

$$\theta_m x_{im} - \sum_{n=1}^{N} x_{in} \lambda_n - s_i = 0; \quad i = 1, 2, ..., I$$

$$\lambda_n, s_j, s_i \geq 0$$

This dual rates a particular DMU (*m*th DMU here). This DMU is relatively efficient if and only if the optimal values of its efficiency ratio, θm, equals unity and the optimal values of all the slack variables s_i and s_j are zero for all *i* and *j*. Model A2.3 assumes constant returns to scale (CRS). However, variable returns to scale (VRS) can be incorporated in it by appending the constraint:

$$\sum_{n=1}^{N} \lambda_n = 1.$$

The literature on DEA contains many extensions to the basic models described above (see for example, Banker *et al.*, 1984). A more detailed discussion of the basic aspects of DEA is available in Ganley and Cubbon (1992) and Ramanathan (2003). Seiford and Thrall (1990), Charnes *et al.* (1994) and Seiford (1996) have provided detailed accounts of the important developments in the history of DEA. Golany and Roll (1989) have given broad guidelines for describing applications of DEA.

DEA has found a number of applications for productivity assessment in public sector. Ganley and Cubbin (1992) describe the applications of DEA to schools and prisons. An application of DEA to banks is reported by Yeh (1996). An application to the health sector is available in Bates *et al.* (1996). Fare *et al.* (1996) describe an application of DEA for environmental performance evaluation for the case of fossil-fuel-fired electric utilities. Further details of other applications are available in the bibliography compiled at the University of Warwick (Emrouznejad and Thanassoulis, 1996).

BIBLIOGRAPHY

Adolphson, Donald L., Gary C. Cornia and Lawrence C. Walters (1989), "Railroad Property Valuation using Data Envelopment Analysis", *Interfaces*, **19**(3), 18-26.

Annual Report (1995), *Annual Report: 1994-95*, New Delhi: Ministry of Surface Transport.

Augenblick, Mark and B. Scott Custer, Jr. (1990), *The Build, Operate and Transfer ("BOT") Approach to Infrastructure Projects in Developing Countries*, Working Paper WPS498, The World Bank, Washington D.C.

Baharumshah, Ahmad Zubaidi and Mohamed Ariff (1997), "Purchasing Power Parity in South-East Asian Countries Economies: A Cointegration Approach", *Asian Economic Journal*, **11**(2), 141-53.

Baltagi, B. and M. Griffin (1983), "Gasoline Demand in the OECD—An Application of Pooling and Testing Procedures", *European Economic Review*, **22**, 117-37.

Banker, R.D., Charnes, A. and Cooper, W.W. (1984), "Some Models for Estimating Technical and Scale Efficiencies in Data Envelopment Analysis", *Management Science*, **30** (9), 1078-92.

Bates, J.M., D.B. Baines and D.K. Whynes (1996), "Measuring the Efficiency of Prescribing by General Practitioners", *Journal of the Operational Research Society*, **47**, 1443-51.

Bentzen, Jan (1994), "An Empirical Analysis of Gasoline Demand in Denmark using Cointegration Techniques", *Energy Economics*, **16**(2), 139-43.

Blum, Ulrich C.H., Gertraud Foos and Marc J.I. Gaudry (1988), "Aggregate Time Series Gasoline Demand Models: Review of the Literature and New Evidence for West Germany, *Transportation Research- A*, **22A**(2), 75-88.

Button, Kenneth (1990), "Environmental Externalities and Transport Policy", *Oxford Review of Economic Policy*, **6**(2), 61-75.

Button, Kenneth J. (1993), *Transport Economics*, Edward Elgar Publishing Limited, England.

Chand, Mahesh (1994), "A Comparative Study of Public and Private Bus Operations", *Indian Journal of Transport Management*, **3**(2), 87-95.

Chandok, H.L. (1990), *India Database: The Economy—Annual Time Series Data* (two volumes), Living Media Books, New Delhi.

Charemza, Wojciech W. and Derek F. Deadman (1992), *New Direction in Econometric Practice: General to Specific Modelling, Cointegration and Vector Autoregression*, Edward Elgar Publishing Limited, Hants, England.

Charnes, A., Cooper, W.W. and Rhodes, E. (1978), "Measuring Efficiency of Decision-Making Units", *European Journal of Operational Research*, **2**, 429-44.

———— (1979), "Measuring Efficiency of Decision-Making Units", *European Journal of Operational Research*, **3**, 339.

Charnes, Abraham, William W. Cooper, Lewin, Arie Y. and Lawrence Seiford (1994), *Data Envelopment Analysis: Theory, Methodology and Application*, Kluwer, Boston.

Chen, Tser-yieth (1997), "Long-term Peak Electricity Forecasting in Taiwan: A Cointegration Analysis", *Pacific and Asian Journal of Energy*, **7**(1), 63-73.

CIRT (1995), *Performance Statistics of State Transport Undertakings—1993-94*, Central Institute of Road Transport, Pune, India.

CMIE (1994), *Basic Statistics Relating to Indian Economy*, Centre for Monitoring Indian Economy, Bombay.

———— (1995), *Infrastructure in India*, Centre for Monitoring Indian Economy Private Limited, August 1995, Bombay.

———— (1996), *India's Energy Sector*, Centre for Monitoring Indian Economy, Mumbai.

———— (1999), *Infrastructure*, Centre for Monitoring Indian Economy, Mumbai, December 1999.

———— (2000), *Energy*, Centre for Monitoring Indian Economy, Mumbai, March 2000.

CSE (1996), *Slow Murder: The Deadly Story of Vehicular Pollution in India*, Centre for Science and Environment, New Delhi.

———— (1998), "Small Towns—Big Mess", *Down to Earth*, **7**(13), November 30, 1998, 29-36.

Dahl, C. and T. Sterner (1990), *The Pricing of and the Demand for Gasoline: A Survey of Models*, Memorandum 132, Goteberg University, Sweden.

Delucchi, Mark A. (1997), "The Annualised Social Cost of Motor-vehicle Use in the U.S. based on 1990-1991 Data: Summary of Theory, Data, Methods and Results", in: David L. Greene, Donald W. Jones and Mark A. Delucchi (Eds.), *The Full Costs and Benefits of Transportation*, Springer, Berlin, pp. 27-68.

Dunkerley, J. and I. Hoch (1987), "Energy for Transport in Developing Countries", *The Energy Journal*, **8**(3), 57-72.

Eltony, M.N. and N.H. Al-Mutairi (1995), "Demand for Gasoline in Kuwait: An Empirical Analysis using Cointegration Techniques", *Energy Economics*, **17**(3), 249-53.

Emrouznejad, Ali and Emmanuel Thanassoulis (1996), *An Extensive Bibliography of Data Envelopment Analysis (DEA)* (in three volumes), Compiled at the University of Warwick, Coventry, England. (Internet address: http://www.warwick.ac.uk/~bsrlu)

Engle, Robert F. and Byung Sam Yoo (1987), "Forecasting and Testing in Co-integrated Systems", *Journal of Econometrics*, **35**, 143-59.

Engle, Robert F. and C.W.J. Granger (1987), "Co-integration and Error Correction: Representation, Estimation, and Testing", *Econometrica*, **55**(2), 251-76.

Fare, Rolf, Shawna Grosskopf and Daniel Tyteca (1996), "An Activity Analysis Model of the Environmental Performance of Firms—Application to Fossil-fuel-fired Electric Utilities", *Ecological Economics*, **18**, 161-75.

Farrel, M.J. (1957), "The Measurement of Productive Efficiency", *Journal of Royal Statistical Society (A)*, **120**, 253-81.

Fisher, J.C. and Pry, R.H. (1971), "A Simple Substitution Model of Technological Change", *Technological Forecasting and Social Change*, **3**, 75-88.

Fuller, Wayne A. (1976), *Introduction to Statistical Time Series*, John Wiley & Sons Inc., New York.

Fwa, T.F. (1997), *Impacts of Transport Sector Management on Energy Savings and Mitigation of Greenhouse Gas Emissions—A Case Study of Singapore's Experience*, Paper presented at the UNEP Workshop on Transport Sector, Nairobi.

Ganley, J.A. and J.S. Cubbin (1992), *Public Sector Efficiency Measurement: Applications of Data Envelopment Analysis*, North Holland, Amsterdam.

Garbacz, C. (1989), "Gasoline, Diesel and Motor-fuel Demand in Taiwan", *The Energy Journal*, **10**(2), 153-63.

Gardner, Gary (1998), "When Cities Take Bicycles Seriously", *World Watch*, September/October, pp. 16-22.

GOI (1987), *Estimation of Total Road Transport, Freight and Passenger Movement in India for the Year 2000 AD*, Report prepared for the Department of Surface Transport (Road Wing), Government of India, New Delhi.

Golany, B. and Y. Roll (1989), "An Application Procedure for DEA", *Omega*, **17**(3), 237-50.

Grubler, A. and Nakicenovic, N. (1991), *Evolution of Transport Systems: Past and Future*, RR-91-8, International Institute for Applied Systems Analysis, Laxenburg, Austria.

Grubler, A. (1993), "The Transportation Sector: Growing Demand and Emissions", *Pacific and Asian Journal of Energy*, **3**, December, 179-99.

Grubler, A., N. Nakicenovic and A. Schafer (1993), *Dynamics of Transport and Energy Systems: History of Development and a Scenario for the Future*, RP-93-19, International Institute for Applied Systems Analysis, Laxenburg, Austria.

Guilkey, D.K. and P. Schmidt (1989), "Extended Tabulations for Dickey-Fuller Tests", *Economics Letters*, **31**, 355-57.

Habitat (1994), *Improvement of Urban Public Transport in Developing Countries*, United Nations Centre for Human Settlements, Nairobi.

Hensher, David A. (1992), "Total Factor Productivity Growth and Endogenous Demand: Establishing a Benchmark Index for the Selection of Operational Performance Measures in Public Bus Firms", *Transportation Research*, **26B**(6), 435-48.

Hensher, David A. and Rhonda Daniels (1995), "Productivity Measurement in the Urban Bus Sector", *Transportation Policy*, **2**(3), 179-94.

Hjalmarsson, Lennart and James Odeck (1996), "Efficiency of Trucks in Road Construction and Maintenance: An Evaluation with Data Envelopment Analysis", *Computers and Operations Research*, **23**(4), 393-404.

IIP (1985), *State of Art Report on Vehicle Emissions*, Report prepared by The Indian Institute of Petroleum, Dehradun, for the Department of Environment, Government of India, New Delhi.

IIR (1996), *The India Infrastructure Report: Policy Imperatives for Growth and Welfare—Volumes I and II*, Expert Group on Commercialisation of Infrastructure Projects, Published for the Ministry of Finance, Government of India by the National Council of Applied Economic Research, New Delhi.

IR (1985), *Indian Railways: Corporate Plan (1985-2000)*, Ministry of Railways, Government of India, New Delhi.

Jain, Dileep K., P.S. Satsangi and D.P. Kothari (1994), "Urbanization and Energy-related Problems in Indian Cities", *Energy Sources*, **16**, 177-82.

Jones, Clifton T. (1997), "Long-run Price Responsiveness of Aggregate Industrial Energy Consumption by the G-7 Countries: Results from a Cointegration Analysis", *Advances in the Economics of Energy and Resources*, **10**, 97-109.

Karbuz, Sohbet, Faith Birol and Nadir Gurer (1997), "Electricity Demand in Turkey", *Pacific and Asian Journal of Energy*, **7**(1), 55-62.

Kikeri, Sunita, John Nellis and Mary Shirley (1992), *Privatization: The Lessons of Experience*, The World Bank, Washington, D.C.

Koutsoyiannis, A. (1977), *Theory of Econometrics*, Macmillan Education Limited, London.

Kremers, J.J.M., N.R. Ericsson and J.J. Dolado (1992), "The Power of Cointegration Tests", *Oxford Bulletin of Economics and Statistics*, **54**, 325-48.

Linden, Eugene (1996), "The Exploding Cities of the Developing World", *Foreign Affairs*, January/February, 52-65.

Litman, Todd (1998), *Transportation Cost Analysis: Techniques, Estimates and Implications*, Victoria Transport Policy Institute, Victoria, Canada.

Lowe, Marcia D. (1991), "Rethinking Urban Transport", in: Lester R. Brown (Ed.), *State of the World 1991: A Worldwatch Institute Report on Progress Toward a Sustainable Society*, W.W. Norton & Co., New York.

Mac Kenzie, J.A. (1994), *The Keys to the Car: Electric and Hydrogen Vehicles for the 21st Century*, World Resources Institute.

Mac Kinnon, James G. (1991), "Critical Values for Cointegration Tests", in: Engle, R.F. and C.W.J. Granger, eds., *Long-run Economic Relationships: Readings in Cointegration*, Oxford University Press, Oxford, 267-76.

Majumdar, Sumit K. (1997), "Modularity and Productivity: Assessing the Impact of Digital Technology in the U.S. Telecommunications Industry", *Technological Forecasting and Social Change*, **56**, 61-75.

Marchetti, Cesare (1987), "Infrastructures for Movement", *Technological Forecasting and Social Change*, **32**, 373-93.

Masih, Abul M.M. and Rumi Masih (1997a), "On the Temporal Causal Relationship between Energy Consumption, Real Income, and Prices: Some New Evidence from Asian-Energy Dependent NICS based on a Multivariate Cointegrated/Vector Error-correction Approach", *Journal of Policy Modelling*, **19**(4), 417-40.

———— (1997b), "Can Family Planning Programs 'cause' Significant Fertility Decline in Countries Characterized by Very Low Levels of

Socio-economic Development? New Evidence from Bangladesh based on Dynamic Multivariate and Cointegrated Time-series, 1965-1991", *Journal of Policy Modelling*, **19**(4), 441-68.

May, A.D. and M. Roberts (1995), "The Design of Integrated Transport Strategies", *Transport Policy*, **2**(2), 97-105.

McRae, Robert (1994), "Gasoline Demand in Developing Asian Countries", *The Energy Journal*, **15**(1), 143-55.

MEDEE (1991), *Sectoral Energy Demand in India*, Planning Commission, Government of India, New Delhi.

Michelis, Laurie and Ogunlade Davidson (1996), "GHG Mitigation in the Transport Sector", *Energy Policy*, **24**(10-11), 969-84.

Miller, G. Tyler (1993), *Environmental Science: Sustaining the Earth*, 3rd edition, Wadsworth, Belmont.

MoUD (1987), *Report of the Study Group on Alternative Systems of Urban Transport*, Ministry of Urban Development, Government of India, New Delhi.

Mustafa, Mohammad and Mathur Rahman (1995), "Cointegration between US Short-term and Long-term Interest Rates (both nominal and real)", *Applied Financial Economics*, **5**, 323-27.

Nakicenovic, N. (1979), *Software Package for the Logistic Substitution Model*, RR-79-12, International Institute for Applied Systems Analysis, Laxenburg, Austria.

NCU (1988), *Report of the National Commission on Urbanization*, New Delhi: Ministry of Urban Development, Government of India.

Newbury, David M. (1990), "Pricing and Congestion: Economic Principles Relevant to Pricing Roads", *Oxford Review of Economic Policy*, **6**(2), 23-38.

NTPC (1980), *Report of the National Transport Policy Committee*, Planning Commission, New Delhi.

O'Meara, Molly (1998), "How Mid-sized Cities can Avoid Strangulation", *World Watch*, September/October, pp. 8-15.

OECD (1993), *Cars and Climate Change*, Organisation for Economic Co-operation and Development, Paris.

——— (1991), *Estimation of Greenhouse Gas Emissions and Sinks*, Paris: Organization of Economic Cooperation and Development.

Okano, Yukihide (1990), "Privatization of Railways in Japan", in: Jacques Pelkmans and Norbert Wagner (Ed.), *Privatization and Deregulation in ASEAN and EC: Making Markets More Effective*, Institute of South Asian Studies, Singapore, pp.144-56.

Okken, P.A. (1991), "A Case for Alternative Transport Fuels", *Energy Policy*, **19**(4), 400-05.

Opinion Survey (1998), "Pollution in Delhi Threatening to Get Out of Hand: Ministry", *Monthly Public Opinion Survey*, March 1998, 33-34.

Oum, Tae H., Michael W. Tretheway and W.G. Waters, II (1992), "Concepts, Methods and Purposes of Productivity Measurement in Transportation", *Transportation Research*, **26A**(6), 494-505.

Painuly, J.P. and Jyoti Parikh (1993), "Policy Analysis of Oil Substitution by Natural Gas in India: Transport and Industry Sectors", *Energy Policy*, **20**(1), 43-52.

Pangotra, Prem and G. Raghuram (1995), *Resource Mobilization Strategies for Financing of Transport Infrastructure and Services*, Working Paper No.1245, Indian Institute of Management, Ahmedabad.

Parikh, Jyoti K. (1980), *Modelling Energy Demand for Policy Analysis*, Planning Commission, Government of India, New Delhi.

——— (1994), "Joint Implementation Survey: Supporting North-South Cooperation", *Climate Change Bulletin*, Issue 4.

Parikh, Jyoti K. and Subir Gokarn (1993), "Climate Change and India's Energy Policy Options: New Perspectives on Sectoral CO_2 Emissions and Incremental Costs", *Global Environmental Change*, **3**(3), 276-91.

Parikh, Jyoti K., Manoj K. Panda and N.S. Murthy (1994), *Consumption Pattern Differences and Environmental Implications: A Case Study of India*, Discussion Paper No. 116, Indira Gandhi Institute of Development Research, Mumbai, October.

Parikh, Jyoti K. and Ramanathan, R. (1997), "Trend in Transport Sector in India", *Energy Scenario*, **1**(1), 15-20.

Parikh, Kirit S. and Ramanathan, R. (1997), "Recent Reforms in Infrastructure with Special Reference to Indian Railways: An Analysis", in: Hiten Bhaya (Ed.), *Indian Planning: Search for Change*, Asian Institute of Transport Development, New Delhi, pp. 165-92.

Parikh, J., and J.P. Painuly (1991), *Compressed Natural Gas (CNG) in Transport Sector: Techno-economic Assessment for India*, Discussion Paper No. 49, Indira Gandhi Institute of Development Research, Mumbai.

Patankar, P.G. (1991), *Urban Transport in India in Distress*, Central Institute of Road Transport, Pune, India.

Patankar, P.G. (1991), *Road Passenger Transport in India*, Pune, India: Central Institute of Road Transport.

Peterson, P. and von Weizsacker, E. (1993), "Mobility in the Greenhouse", *Industry and Environment* (Transport and Environment), **16**(1-2), 7-10.

Phillips, P.C.B. (1986), "Understanding Spurious Regressions in Econometrics", *Journal of Econometrics*, **33**, 311-40.

PLAN (1992), *Eighth Five Year Plan: Volumes I and II*, New Delhi: Planning Commission, Government of India.

Rabinovitch, Jonas and Josef Leitman (1996), "Urban Planning in Curitiba", *Scientific American*, March, 26-33.

Rabinovitch, Jonas (1993), "Urban Public Transport Management in Curitiba, Brazil", Special Issue on Transport and the Environment, *Industry and Environment*, **16**(1-2), 18-20.

Raghuram, G. and G. Padmanabhan (1992), "Analysis of Wagon Utilization for the Indian Railways", *Rail Transport*, **1**(2), April-June.

Ramanathan, R. (1996), "Indian Transport Sector: Energy and Environmental Implications", *Energy Sources*, **18**(7), 791-805.

——— (1997) "Transport: A Crucial Infrastructure", in: Kirit S. Parikh, ed., *India Development Report—1997*, Oxford University Press, New Delhi, 219-38.

——— (1998a), "Development of Indian Passenger Transport", *Energy—The International Journal*, **23**(5), 429-30.

——— (1998b), "Urban Transport in India: Some Issues and Suggestions", Proceedings of the *First Asia Pacific Conference on Transportation and the Environment*, National University of Singapore, pp. 60-68.

——— (1999a), "Urban Transport", in: Kirit S. Parikh (ed.), *India Development Report 1999-2000*, Oxford University Press, New Delhi, Chapter 6, pp. 98-112.

——— (1999b), "Using Data Envelopment Analysis for Assessing the Productivity of the State Transport Undertakings ", *Indian Journal of Transport Management*, **23**(5), 301-12.

——— (1999c), "Short and Long-Run Elasticities of Gasoline Demand in India: An Empirical Analysis Using Cointegration Techniques", *Energy Economics*, **21**(4), 321-30.

——— (2000a), "Link between Population and Number of Vehicles: Evidence from Indian Cities", *Cities—The International Journal of Urban Policy and Planning*, **17**(4), 263-69.

——— (2000b), "A Holistic Approach to Compare Energy Efficiencies of Different Transport Modes", *Energy Policy*, **28**(11), 743-47.

Ramanathan, R. (2001), "The Long-Run Behaviour of Transport Performance in India: A Cointegration Approach", *Transportation Research—Part A: Policy and Practice*, **35**(4), 309-20.

———— (2003), *An Introduction to Data Envelopment Analysis: A Tool for Performance Measurement*, Sage Publications, New Delhi.

Ramanathan, R. and Jyoti K. Parikh (1996), "Indian Transportation Sector: An Analysis in the Context of Sustainable Development", in: *Structural Transformation Processes towards Sustainable Development in India and Switzerland: Synthesis and Case Studies*, INFRAS, Zurich, Switzerland, Chapter B.IV, pp. 255-88.

———— (1997), "Transport Sector in India: Energy and Environmental Aspects", Paper presented at the *UNEP Workshop on Controlling GHG Emissions from the Transport Sector*, March 14-15, 1997, Nairobi, Kenya.

———— (1999), "Transport Sector in India: An Analysis in the Context of Sustainable Development", *Transport Policy*, **6**(1), 35-45.

Ramanathan, R., and S. Geetha (1998), "Gasoline Consumption in India: An Econometric Analysis", Proceedings of the *First Asia Pacific Conference on Transportation and the Environment*, held in Singapore during 13-15 May, 1998, pp. 312-19.

Rao, Raghavendra D. and Jyoti K. Parikh (1996), "Forecast and Analysis of Demand for Petroleum Products in India", *Energy Policy*, **24**(6), 583-92.

Razavi, Hossein (1996), "Financing Oil and Gas Projects in Developing Countries", *Finance and Development*, June 1996, pp. 2-5.

Rebelo, Jorge M. (1996), *Essentials for Sustainable Urban Transport in Brazil's Large Metropolitan Areas*, The World Bank Policy Research Working Paper 1633, Washington D.C.

Report (1996a), "Report of the Working Group on Urban Transport: Part I", *Indian Journal of Transport Management*, (August 1996): 525-38.

Report (1996b), "Report of the Working Group on Urban Transport: Part II.", *Indian Journal of Transport Management*, (September 1996): 575-87.

RITES (1993), *Study on Productivity Optimization on Indian Railways*, Railway Fare and Freight Committee, Rail India Technical and Economic Services, New Delhi (Vol. I and II).

Samimi, Rodney (1995), "Road Transport Energy Demand in Australia: A Cointegration Approach", *Energy Economics*, **17**(4), 329-39.

Saxena (1992), *Four Decades of Indian Railways*, Academic Publishers, New Delhi.

Schafer, A. (1998), "The Global Demand for Motorized Mobility", *Transportation Research*, **32**(5), 455-77.

Seiford, Lawrence M. (1996), "Data Envelopment Analysis: The Evolution of the State of the Art (1978-1995)", *The Journal of Productivity Analysis*, **7**, 99-137.

Seiford, Lawrence M. and Robert M. Thrall (1990), "Recent Developments in DEA: The Mathematical Programming Approach to Frontier Analysis", *Journal of Econometrics*, **46**, 7-38.

Shen, Tong Ming (1993), "Singapore's Land Transport Policy and the Environment", Special Issue on Transport and the Environment, *Industry and Environment*, **16**(1-2), 26-27.

Taha, H.A. (1997), *Operations Research—An Introduction*, Prentice-Hall Inc., New Jersey.

TEDDY (1990/91), *TERI Energy Data Directory and Year Book*, Tata Energy Research Institute, New Delhi.

UN (1988), *Energy Balances and Electricity Profiles—1986*, New York: United Nations.

UN (1994), *Energy Balances and Electricity Profiles—1992*, New York: United Nations.

Viton, Philip A. (1997), "Technical Efficiency in Multi-mode Bus Transit: A Production Frontier Analysis", *Transportation Research*, **31B**(1), 23-39.

Wang, Q. and DeLuchi, M.A. (1992), "Impacts of Electric Vehicles on Primary Energy Consumption and Petroleum Displacement", *Energy—The International Journal*, **17**(4), 351-56.

Wasserfallen, Walter and Heinz Guntensperger (1988), "Gasoline Consumption and the Stock of Motor Vehicles: An Empirical Analysis for the Swiss Economy", *Energy Economics*, **10**, 276-82.

Williams, R.H. (1993), *Fuel Cells, Their Fuels and the US Automobile*, Paper prepared for the First Annual World Car 2001 Conference, University of California at Riverside, Riverside, California.

World Resources Report (1996), *World Resources: A Guide to the Global Environment—The Urban Environment*, Oxford University Press, New York.

Yeh, Quey-Jen (1996), "The Application of Data Envelopment Analysis in Conjunction with Financial Ratios for Bank Performance Evaluation", *Journal of the Operational Research Society*, **47**, 980-88.

Zegras, Christopher (1998), "The Costs of Transportation in Santiago de Chile: Analysis and Policy Implications", *Transport Policy*, **5**, 9-21.

INDEX